Unearthing an Old Roman Theatre at Verona, Italy.

(From an original photograph.)

American Theatres of Today

Illustrated with

PLANS, SECTIONS AND PHOTOGRAPHS OF
EXTERIOR AND INTERIOR DETAILS
of
MODERN MOTION PICTURE AND LEGITIMATE
THEATRES THROUGHOUT THE UNITED STATES

By

R. W. SEXTON AND B. F. BETTS, ASSOCIATE EDITORS
"THE AMERICAN ARCHITECT"

With a foreword by

S. L. ROTHAFEL, "ROXY"

NEW YORK
ARCHITECTURAL BOOK PUBLISHING CO., INC.
PAUL WENZEL AND MAURICE KRAKOW
THIRTY-ONE EAST TWELFTH ST.

Library of Congress Cataloging in Publication Data

Sexton, Randolph Williams, 1884–
   American theatres of today.

   Reprint of the ed. published by Architectural Book Pub. Co.,
New York; with new foreword.
   Includes index.
   1. Theaters—Construction.   2. Moving-picture theaters—United
States.   I. Betts, Benjamin Franklin, 1888–   joint author. II. Title.
NA6830.S4   1977   725'.822'0973   77-24013
ISBN 0-911572-15-5

Vestal Press Reprint
Edition © 1977 By
The Vestal Press
Vestal, New York, U.S.A.

PRINTED IN THE UNITED STATES OF AMERICA.

FOREWORD

During the many years of dreaming and planning of the great theatre which I hoped sometime to operate, I insistently retained certain principles, which I regarded as simple and elemental. Even in a theatre of over six thousand seats, there must be a feeling of intimacy, a clear and full view of the stage must be afforded from every seat in the house, and decorations must be in good taste. The modern theatre stands today as a result of the enthusiasm and sincerity with which these, and other problems which the design of the theatre presents, have been recognized, attacked and mastered by architects, engineers, designers and decorators.

In the past few years we have seen in this country an era of theatre construction of unprecedented proportions, with the result that nearly every community, no matter how small, now points with pride to its new theatre. I am of the opinion that behind all this there has been the sincere desire of the theatre owner and operator to do a better and finer thing by giving to his public and to the community an example of beauty and comfort. Without question, this spirit has led these owners far beyond the requirements of commercial necessity. Such support has given architects much latitude and enabled them to apply their designs and skill with greater freedom.

It is my hope that the continuation of this spirit of cooperation will result, in the years to come, in theatre structures which will gain in recognition as examples of everything that is fine and beautiful in architecture and decoration.

Foreword to the Vestal Press Reprint Edition

It is with a note of gratitude that these few lines are written to serve as a "foreword-piece" to this printing of AMERICAN THEATRES TODAY by R. W. Sexton. Gratitude to Vestal Press, and to Mr. Harvey Roehl, for taking such an interest in the work and for seeing the need of having these volumes issued in a reprint edition. Also, a feeling of joy for the splendid results and the high standards maintained throughout the project.

Mr. Robert Freeman, of Providence, R.I., in his Master's Thesis (Columbia University) notes that:

"Together with the skyscraper, movie theatres are perhaps the most distinctly American contribution to architectural history."

Certainly to the many aficionados of theatre architecture these works of R. W. Sexton have attained a place of highest regard (and of diligent search) as the finest source for photographs and background of American movie theatres; the architects involved and of technical articles to broaden our understanding. It is all here and now, once again, readily available to all.

All of this is especially opportune at this particular time when there is a renewed interest in the saving and the restoration of so many of these buildings for a new life of usefulness in the community. Modern architecture has recently taken an increased interest in designing for "effect" and sometimes for "fun". Here are super-effectual buildings with craftsmanship and design that cannot be duplicated today. These volumes are a splendid record of what was done and should be a source of encouragement to all to make every effort to save these buildings when at all possible. Unfortunately, this work will also serve as a splendid record of those buildings already lost.

B. Andrew Corsini
Editor: MARQUEE
(Official Journal of the Theatre Historical Society)
P.O. Box 101
Notre Dame, Indiana 46556

May 1977

A Dedication

and a Tribute

No one is more responsible for the re-birth of interest in the great movie palaces of the early years of the Twentieth Century than Ben M. Hall. His magnificent book "The Best Remaining Seats" served to awaken today's generation to the fantastic heritage of utter opulence in building design unmatched by anything since the advent of sound movies which sealed their doom, and matched previously only by palaces and castles of reigning Kings, Queens, Maharajahs, and other assorted potentates.

Literature in the field has been sparse, and even Ben had difficulty locating copies of the two volumes printed here. As early as 1958 they were hard to find, such that they drew big prices; in that year one antiquarian bookseller asked $50.00 for Volume I alone!

The copies that have been used to prepare this reprint were donated from his personal files to the Library of the Theatre Historical Society after his tragic death, and here and there we've left a few pencilled notations just as Ben made them.

This writer had the privilege of knowing Ben personally, and often read with fond amazement at his ability with the written word. Would that we could do a fraction as well.

All these buildings cannot be saved, of course. But it's with a sense of gratitude that we note a few, here and there, that are being rescued from oblivion through the work of interested Citizens in their communities — so that our children for many generations may be aware of a brief but glorious part of our Architectural history.

So it's with thanks to the late Ben M. Hall that we dedicate this reprint. We know he would have approved!

Harvey N. Roehl
The Vestal Press
May 1977

Theatre Contents

AMERICAN THEATRES *of* TODAY

THE motion picture has been responsible for a tremendous increase in theatres in this and other countries during the last quarter century. It is difficult to imagine that only twenty-five years ago it was considered a luxury to attend the theatre which only the wealthy could afford with any degree of regularity. The motion picture theatre, however, is a democratic institution. Opportunity is afforded the inhabitants of the smallest towns to see on the "silver screen," for ten, twenty and thirty cents, the very same pictures which patrons in the metropolitan districts pay as high as two dollars to witness. The small town theatres in which these picture plays were at one time presented were often not theatres at all, according to our ideas of what a theatre should be. But they served the purpose, nevertheless, for the screen was so much the center of attention that it mattered little what the design of the theatre itself might be. Now, however, due to the psychological effect of the better type of photoplays and their efforts to cultivate good taste, the audiences, which began by adoring the "movie," have actually been educated beyond it. A revolution therefore in the status of the motion picture theatre is already taking place. The "movies,"—at one time, not so long ago, offering an entire program,—are being relegated to a position of almost minor importance in a program of what might be described as a new form of theatrical entertainment. The average audience in a motion picture theatre today expects a large and capable orchestra to play classical selections and "jazz" tunes by turns, and to hear good soloists, or a chorus, with elaborate stage settings, while it seems to have difficulty in keeping awake through an uninteresting picture at the end of the evening's program. This necessitates extensive changes in the design of the small and even in that of the larger theatres. The modern motion picture theatre must prepare for this new form of theatrical entertainment. A stage in embryo, with a "silver screen," will not now suffice. Equipment for the most elaborate scenic displays must be installed; the stage must be of sufficient size for complete sets, and a clear view of the entire stage, and of the orchestra as well,—not only of the screen—must be had from every seat in the house. Acoustic properties must be considered, where before only sight lines counted. The design of the modern motion picture theatre is actually subject to all the intricacies of the legitimate house and more. The theatre of the future will feature the spoken drama with the movies—the spoken movies are already a reality—and in its design it must permit of satisfactory presentation of both these forms of entertainment. And the theatre itself in which this elaborate performance is staged must keep pace. Many of the numbers are presented with lights turned on all over the house. Colored light complements the music which the orchestra plays. The house is dark during only a portion of the duration of the entertainment and its decorations are largely influential in diffusing the romantic spirit of the theatre in the minds of the audience. The theatres illustrated and described in the following pages are typical of modern tendencies throughout the country. Both types of theatres are shown — legitimate theatres and motion picture houses; small theatres on main street and palatial cinemas of the metropolitan districts; houses that seat four hundred, and others that have a capacity of over six thousand. Yet all American and all expressing the romantic spirit of the theatre!

1

DESIGNING THE MODERN THEATRE

The Plan

IT IS impossible to lay down any rules governing the plan of theatres. Each theatre presents its own individual problem. Strict and rigid building codes and safety ordinances, enforced in the majority of cities, control to a very great extent the more important features of the plan of a theatre. The population from which its patrons are to be drawn and the money available for its construction are also important considerations. Then, too, there is the site to be considered—the size and shape of the lot, and its possibilities as regards the plan of a theatre. The plan is in reality a problem in satisfactory arrangement of seats, practically and economically. In large metropolitan districts, where land cost is high and population large, it is necessary to arrange for maximum seating capacity in order to reduce the cost per seat, as theatre construction is generally figured. The arrangement of the seats is primarily a matter of sight lines and is treated in a special article later on devoted to that subject. It may be said that a well-planned theatre is one in which a clear and unobstructed view of the stage is enjoyed from every seat in the house. It is interesting to note in this connection that sight lines in certain portions of the auditorium sometimes allow people to see *between* the heads of those in front, but this fact should not too generally govern the arrangement of

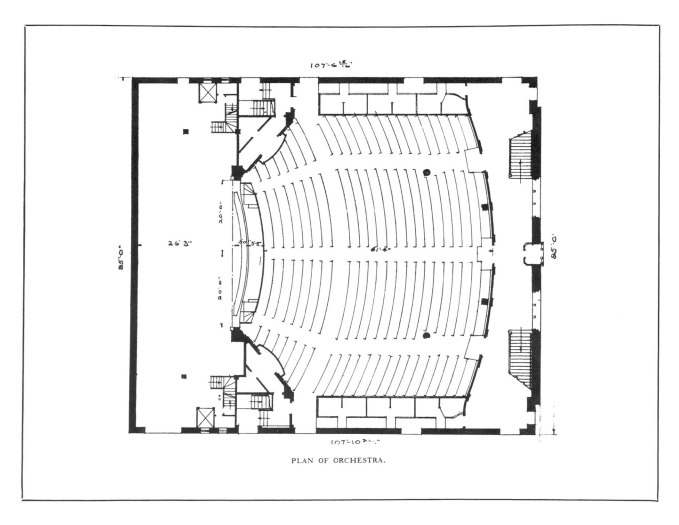

PLAN OF ORCHESTRA.

PALACE THEATRE, JACKSONVILLE, FLA.

ROY A. BENJAMIN, ARCHITECT.

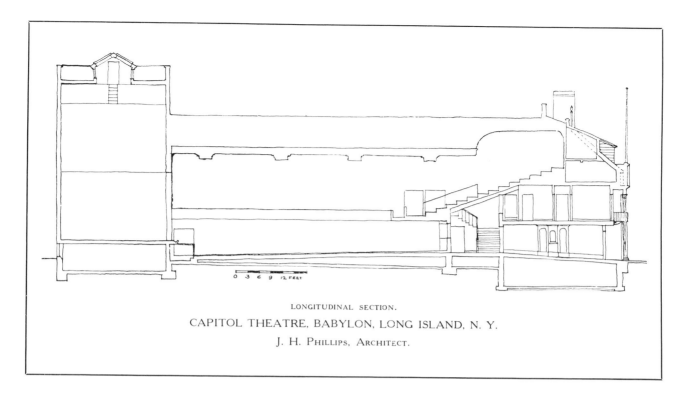

LONGITUDINAL SECTION.

CAPITOL THEATRE, BABYLON, LONG ISLAND, N. Y.

J. H. Phillips, Architect.

seats, as it is generally taken for granted that to see *over* the heads is more satisfactory.

One of the features of modern theatre equipment which has an effect on the plan is the installation of an organ in addition to the space allotted to the musicians who compose the orchestra. In the larger houses, arrangements are made for raising and lowering the orchestra platform so that when a musical number is featured the orchestra is raised to a prominent level and disappears again when the picture or some other feature is put on.

In order to draw a parallel between various theatres, it may be said that there are five different types of theatre plans: the one floor house; the bleacher type; the stadium; the single balcony, and the balcony-mezzanine. It may readily be seen that these variations in types of plans are based to a great extent on increased seating capacity. They also allow of an improvement of sight lines. Where a limited number of seats are to be provided for at a minimum cost, the one floor house is most desirable. In the less congested districts, where larger

sites are available, but only a limited number of seats required, the stadium plan is preferred. The slope of the orchestra floor from the stage to the rear wall of the theatre in any case is regulated by building codes. The stadium plan, however, allows a pitch to the rear part of the auditorium, for the rear one-third is arranged with steps, somewhat in the form of a balcony, which would be too steep to come under the building codes which regulate the pitch of aisles when the orchestra floor is continuous from the proscenium arch to the projection booth, as is the case in the one floor type theatre. If, of course, the site is unusually small, or if, due to its location or to the high cost of land, the maximum number of seats are required, balconies and mezzanines are necessitated.

Balconies are controlled, too, in many details by law. In New York, for example, a row of fourteen seats is permitted in both balcony and orchestra, or not more than six seats between any seat and an aisle. The space between seats, back to back, is two feet eight inches under the New York law allowing people to pass through without necessitating those who are already seated

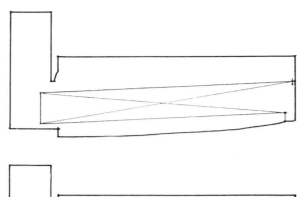

One Floor Type

The theatre in its simplest form, consisting of an orchestra floor only. When the lot area and good sight lines permit of the required number of seats on one floor, this type is an economical form.

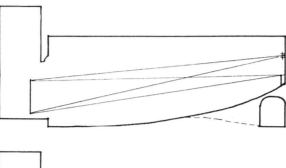

Bleacher Type

A variation of the one floor type, used where the depth of the auditorium requires the use of a steep gradient at the rear to secure correct sight lines.

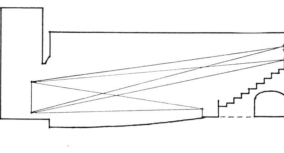

Stadium Type

A variation of the bleacher type. The seats back of the cross-over aisle are raised so that patrons using the cross-over aisle do not interfere with the line of sight. This portion of the house is steep and requires steps as in the balcony.

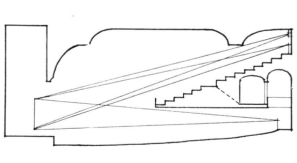

Single Balcony Type

The introduction of a balcony to secure greater seating capacity without necessarily increasing the lot area. The additional cost per seat is slight considering the results obtained.

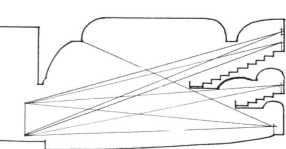

Balcony-Mezzanine Type

Where the desired seating capacity of the balcony brings the balcony rail too near the proscenium arch, seats lost by reducing the length of the main balcony are obtained in a mezzanine balcony. Sight lines of rear orchestra seats are greatly improved by reducing the balcony projection.

LONGITUDINAL SECTIONS OF VARIOUS TYPES OF THEATRES.

to arise. Steps are seldom allowed in the orchestra floor, but the pitch of the balcony, regulated by building codes, is so steep that steps are necessary. The tendency of architects is to gain as many seats as possible in the balcony, thus projecting the balcony too far forward and practically limiting the sight lines of those in the seats in the rear of the orchestra to a view of the screen. This also tends to make the area beneath the balcony uncomfortable and difficult to properly ventilate. Acoustic properties in this portion of the house, too, are seriously interfered with under these conditions. Balconies should be kept back as far as possible to allow the occupant of every seat to see not only the screen but a part of the orchestra, and at least the full proscenium arch. This is especially true in the modern theatre where feature numbers are presented as well as a picture play.

The modern theatre makes a particular appeal through its lobby. A large lobby is not merely to create a good first impression, but in the more congested districts, especially, crowds are frequently kept waiting, and it is necessary to consider their comfort. This applies with equal force to the plan of the foyer, to allow of comfortable standing room. Psychology enters into the placing of the ticket booth at the center of the entrance near the street. It must never be necessary to pass through doors or by any other obstructions to purchase a ticket. The larger theatres have additional ticket booths installed inside the lobby, but invariably a ticket booth is located at the street entrance also. Consideration must be given in laying out the plan to the location of rest and smoking rooms. In the larger theatres these rooms are of such importance and so elaborately designed and furnished that they give more the air of a club or hotel than of a theatre. These details all have to do with the comfort of the patrons, which is throughout of first importance in the plan of the modern theatre.

ENTRANCE LOBBY, ANNEX THEATRE, DETROIT, MICH.
JOHN EBERSON, ARCHITECT.

5

FOYER, ROYALE THEATRE, NEW YORK.
HERBERT J. KRAPP, ARCHITECT.

ENTRANCE LOBBY, LAFAYETTE THEATRE,
SUFFERN, N. Y.
EUGENE DE ROSA, ARCHITECT.

In theatres of the balcony type, the logical location of the rest and smoking rooms is under the balcony, with entrances from a mezzanine promenade. The main staircase, which is very generally treated as a feature of the foyer or lobby, according to where it is placed, leads to this mezzanine promenade, and access to the balcony is obtained by ramp passageways or stairs. In the larger theatres, where space allows, it is advisable to include rehearsal and screen rooms. During solo numbers by the organ, it thus becomes possible for the orchestra to rehearse its score for the next week's performance, eliminating overtime and thereby cutting down expenses. In the screen room future runs of photoplays are demonstrated and selected and accompanying musical scores arranged. Due to the varied character of the entertainment featured by the modern theatre, allowances must be made for dressing rooms, quick change rooms, property rooms, and apparatus for stage setting. All these details are treated on following pages, as they have more to do with the equipment of the theatre than with its design.

A reading of the plans and sections reproduced on following pages will show that there are three important reference lines in the development of the drawings for any theatre. All dimensions on the plan, back of or in front of the stage, are given in their relation to the "curtain line" (line of asbestos curtain). Dimensions to the right and left of the stage are figured from the center line of the proscenium arch, which is also the center line of the auditorium, and is drawn at right angles to the curtain line. Vertical dimensions are figured in their relation to the elevation of the stage floor, which is taken as zero. The plan is developed only after these three lines have been located.

The Design of the Exterior

The purpose which a building is intended to serve should be the dominating and controlling factor in the development of its architectural and decorative design. In other words, the character or style of the design of a building, both inside and out, should be actually an expression of its purpose. Individuality in architectural design can only thus become a vital thing. In this country, due to the prevailing tendency to designate each and every architectural conception as belonging to a certain 'period' or 'style,' we overlook too often the real purpose of the building in an effort to pattern the design after the manner of some past period of European art. The Greecian orders stand in this country today for bank architecture; actually, security and stability, which they suggest as typifying banking service, might be even better expressed in forms more appropriate to the surroundings and in greater conformity to the spirit of the times. Gothic motives have become synonymous with American collegiate architecture, although the methods of education practiced today and the subjects taught are vastly at variance with those of the fourteenth century. It was long the custom of architects in this country to introduce an occasional mask to give the necessary atmosphere or character to a building used as a theatre.

In some instances, it is not easy to point to any one outstanding and definite purpose which a building is intended to serve, and the problem in architectural design thus presented assumes greater proportions. The

EXTERIOR DETAIL, ROXY THEATRE, NEW YORK, N. Y.

WALTER W. AHLSCHLAGER, ARCHITECT.

(Copyright, 1927, Tebbs & Knell, Inc.)

TWIN THEATRES, CHICAGO, ILL.
C. Howard Crane & Kenneth Franzheim, Architects.

design of a theater presents no such difficulty. There is only one possible use to
which a theatre may be put. Its purpose
is always and ever to offer entertainment to

ZIEGFELD THEATRE, NEW YORK, N. Y.
Joseph Urban and Thomas Lamb, Associated Architects.

the public; to allow those who come within
its walls to live for an hour or two in the
land of make-believe and romance. This
purpose should, then, be the controlling
influence in its architectural and decorative
design. There is a psychological aspect to
the design of a theatre. This has its effect
especially on its exterior design. The problem is to create a facade that shall first have
an attractive theatrical appearance, in pleasing contrast to the general stiff and cold
character of its commercial surroundings,—
one that invites the attention of the public
and tends to lure them to its doors with
pleasurable expectation. This demands that
it be evident in the design of its facade that
this building is a theatre. The spirit of
romance should enter its design as it does
in the design of the interior.

The entrance should be the center of
attraction. It should give a suggestion of
what is within. This may be accomplished
by making it of such size that a view of the
interior of the lobby may actually be obtained from the street. If the design of the
entrance is of such a character that it lures
the prospective customer to only look within, it has accomplished its purpose. The
final capturing of the customer is then in the
hands of the designer of the interior, assisted
by the logical placing of the box-office.

ELECTRIC THEATRE, ST. JOSEPH, MO.
BOLLER BROTHERS, ARCHITECTS.

LOEW'S CONEY ISLAND THEATRE, NEW YORK, N. Y.

REILLY & HALL, ARCHITECTS, SAMUEL L. MALKIND ASSOCIATE.

Consideration is given to these two phases of the design on following pages.

The design of the ticket-booth, from a psychological point of view, is also important, then. The whole appeal of the exterior design is to sell the passerby a ticket. The entrance lures him, but the booth must actually sell him. Its design must be such as to hold the interest which the entrance has aroused.

One of the most important functions of

the exterior facade of a theatre, and one which further expresses its purpose, is to announce what theatre it is and the name of the performance that is being presented. Electric signs are perhaps most appropriate for this use. Such signs should, however, be studied carefully as a part of the architectural composition, for they are as vitally a part of the architecture of the theatre in attaining its purpose as are the entrance

MANSFIELD THEATRE, NEW YORK, N. Y.
HERBERT J. KRAPP, ARCHITECT.

BILTMORE THEATRE, NEW YORK, N. Y.
HERBERT J. KRAPP, ARCHITECT.

ROOSEVELT THEATRE, CHICAGO, ILL.

C. Howard Crane & Kenneth Franzheim, Architects.

MUSIC BOX THEATRE, NEW YORK, N. Y.

C. Howard Crane & Kenneth Franzheim, Architects.

doors and the ticket booth. A more careful study of these signs as architectural elements would tend to eliminate the unsightly signs which often obscure fine theatre fronts in which no allowances were made for such manner of display.

PARAMOUNT THEATRE, NEW YORK.

C. W. & George L. Rapp, Architects.

MODJESKA THEATRE, NEW YORK, N. Y.

Herbert J. Krapp, Architect.

TEXAS THEATRE, SAN ANTONIO, TEXAS

Boller Brothers, Architects.

ROYALE THEATRE, NEW YORK, N. Y.

Herbert J. Krapp, Architect.

DETAIL OF BOXES.
MUSIC BOX THEATRE, NEW YORK, N. Y.
C. HOWARD CRANE & KENNETH FRANZHEIM, ARCHITECTS.

DETAIL OF BOXES.
ROYALE THEATRE, NEW YORK, N. Y.
HERBERT J. KRAPP, ARCHITECT.

DETAIL OF BOX
MARTIN BECK THEATRE, NEW YORK.
G. ALBERT LANSBURGH, ARCHITECT.

DETAIL OF BOX
APOLLO THEATRE, CHICAGO, ILL.
HOLABIRD & ROCHE, ARCHITECTS.

The Design of the Interior

While the purpose of the theatre in its entirety is very decidedly to entertain those who pay admittance to enter therein, it must not be overlooked that this applies with special force to the performance which is presented on the stage. For there is a marked distinction between the theatre and the stage. The entertainment takes place on the stage. The theatre affords opportunity for its patrons to enjoy that entertainment to the utmost. It is there that its purpose is seen. Its design, therefore, must stimulate the imagination of those who enter that the spirit of romance in them may be immediately quickened. In order to best serve its purpose, it must make them comfortable; no one can enjoy a performance if he is not made comfortable; it must put the audience in a happy frame of mind and hold their interest during any intermissions. The theatre itself can seldom bear any direct relation to the scenes depicted on the stage. With the frequent changing of scenes, this would be well-nigh impossible, although many of us may recall the special decorations installed in a New York theatre a season or two ago when the entire interior of the theatre in which "The Miracle" was being presented was transformed into the interior of a cathedral. The effect was truly magnificent and one was immediately embibed with the spirit of the play.

It is rather the spirit of the theatre, or what the theatre stands for, that the design of the interior of the theatre must suggest, in most cases, not the spirit of the play presented. The stage settings may properly be described as theatrical. In its applica-

TAMPA THEATRE, TAMPA, FLA.

JOHN EBERSON, ARCHITECT.

(Courtesy The American Architect.)

tion to the stage theatrical means an illusion, an effect, something unreal, yet something that at once suggests the real. These are all terms which have no relation to architecture or to the design of the theatre proper. In order to embody the spirit of the theatre, its design should be romantic, even fantastic. Yet it must be based on the fundamental principles which govern architectural design.

The motion picture has revolutionized the design of the theatre as well as the nature of the performance and certain details of its construction. The "movies" have democratized the theatre. It seems only a few years ago that to attend the theatre was considered a luxury. The great mass of people seldom could afford to go to the theatre. Today, rich and poor alike attend the theatre regularly—sometimes with every change of bill. All people pay practically the same price; people of all classes sit side by side and enjoy the same performance. And all are made equally comfortable. An unusual condition has thus been brought about. The masses, revelling in luxury and costly beauty, go to the theatre, partly, at least, to be thrilled by the gorgeousness of their surroundings which they cannot afford in their home life. And they are disappointed if they do not find the thrill they have come for. Their favorite "movie house" is the one which

GRAND FOYER, TAMPA THEATRE, TAMPA, FLA.
JOHN EBERSON, ARCHITECT.
(Courtesy The American Architect.)

FOYER, CAPITOL THEATRE, PORT CHESTER, N. Y.　　FOYER, BELASCO THEATRE, LOS ANGELES, CAL.

Thomas W. Lamb, Architect.　　Morgan, Walls & Clements, Architects.

LADIES' PARLOR, ANNEX THEATRE, DETROIT, MICH.

John Eberson, Architect

(Courtesy The American Architect.)

gives them the biggest thrill. The management must necessarily take this fact into consideration, for the biggest part of their audience must come from the masses.

The design of the average modern motion picture theatre is elaborate in the extreme; it is a mass of ornament, rich in color, and gorgeous in decoration. It makes its appeal to the masses to whom it caters because in their eyes it is wonderful, beautiful and luxurious. Many architects, in designing interiors of theatres, emphasize this phase of the design over the romantic spirit which it should ever express. However, the present tendency towards elaborateness and ornateness may be only a stepping stone in the revolutionary process through which the theatre is passing; and, as the masses become more educated in what beauty really is, the theatre will not need to depend on such methods to lure its patrons, but will rather appeal to them by the very spirit which it embodies.

The proscenium arch may be considered as the center of interest in the architectural design. It serves as a frame for the stage settings. It can readily be seen that a too elaborate frame will be apt to attract from the picture within it. And yet it must be taken into account that many of the pictures which the scenes depict are gorgeous in themselves and a too severe frame would be entirely out of place. The scale of the proscenium arch is important, for consideration must be given to its relation to the stage sets, the actors and the furnishings, as well as to its relationship to the components of the architectural design of the theatre.

The type of theatre influences its interior design. Projecting balconies and mezzanines cut up the wall spaces, besides necessitating greater height to the ceiling over the orchestra. Similarly, it reduces considerably the height of the wall surfaces under the balcony. This all tends to emphasize the fact that each theatre presents

ENTRANCE LOBBY, BOULEVARD THEATRE, JACKSON HEIGHTS, N. Y.
(Ticket Booth and Frames by Libman-Spanjer Corp.)

Ticket Booth
CENTRAL THEATRE, JERSEY CITY, N. J.
(By Libman-Spanjer Corp.)

Ticket Booth
CLAIRIDGE THEATRE, MONTCLAIR, N. J.
(By Libman-Spanjer Corp.)

ENTRANCE, CARLTON THEATRE, BROOKLYN, N. Y.
(Ticket Booth and Frames by Libman-Spanjer Corp.)

its own problem in interior design as it does in its plan.

The greatest problem which the design of the interior of a theatre presents is to suggest coziness and intimacy. Theatre-goers, generally, at least, go to the theatre to see and enjoy the peformance, not to see the audience. To do this properly, they must be made to feel on intimate terms with the actors. The large theatre must be so treated that it even appears cozy and intimate. This requires great skill in the scale of architectural and decorative features. Details in too small scale will tend to make the interior seem larger than it actually is, while a treatment in too large scale will ruin any attempt at intimacy.

In theatres of the more congested districts special attention must be paid to the design of the lobby and foyer. Crowds are frequently kept waiting. The big problem is to so design this part of the house that instead of a pushing, complaining mob the crowd becomes a throng of joyous, contented people. This is accomplished by giving such interest to the design that the minds of the people are kept off the fact that they are waiting. Their interest in the details of the design may even tend to enliven their desire to gain admittance to other parts of the house. A staircase of comfortable proportions, suggestive of opportunities to lead one away from the crowd, should be conveniently placed and attractive in appearance, as it entices some to follow it upstairs and thus tends to further distribute those that are waiting.

In order to further consider the comfort of its patrons, the modern theatre includes rest and smoking rooms which are often as attractively designed and furnished as the rooms of the most pretentious private houses. These rooms should be intimate in design, not in any way suggestive of the theatre, but rather of a purely personal character. They afford opportunities for further distribution of the waiting crowds

and allow the occupant to entirely forget for the time being any annoyance he may have felt in not being able to immediately obtain a seat.

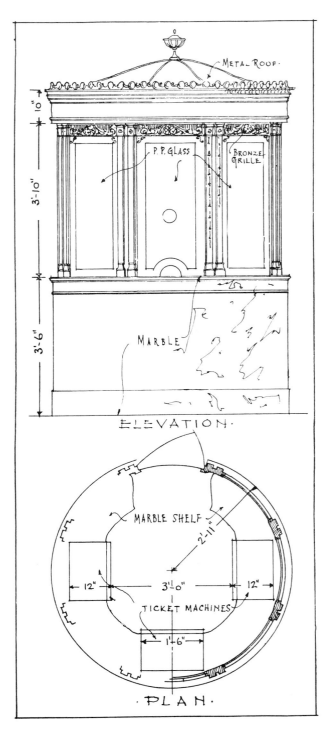

TICKET BOOTH.

LOEW'S THEATRE, HOUSTON, TEXAS.

ALFRED C. FINN, ARCHITECT.

ENTRANCE, EMBASSY THEATRE, ORANGE, N. J.
(TICKET BOOTH AND FRAMES BY LIBMAN-SPANJER CORP.)

ENTRANCE, SANFORD THEATRE, IRVINGTON, N. Y.
(TICKET BOOTH AND FRAMES BY LIBMAN-SPANJER CORP.)

DETAIL OF BOX, BILTMORE THEATRE, NEW YORK, N. Y.

HERBERT J. KRAPP, ARCHITECT.

DETAIL OF BOX, ANNEX THEATRE, DETROIT, MICH.

JOHN EBERSON, ARCHITECT.

THE LOBBY OF THE EMBASSY THEATRE, NEW YORK, N. Y.

THOMAS J. LAMB, ARCHITECT.

(Courtesy The American Architect.)

20

Services of Production and Comfort

A theatre is a project that incorporates the most modern and comprehensive engineering knowledge and skill to make it function properly. Although the design of a theatre draws upon all the resources of structural, mechanical and electrical engineering, it requires an architect to coordinate these and so plan and clothe the structure that it may contribute to the work of the stage.

It is not so very many years since the first "moving picture" houses were built as a radical change from the "legitimate." They differed principally, perhaps, in the reduction of the stage to a shallow platform as a setting for the screen, the addition of a moving picture machine booth, and a ticket seller's booth at the street entrance. Theatre owners later began to question whether the ready acceptance and general popularity of motion pictures would continue. This led to the building of motion picture theatres with stages that would permit them to be readily converted into "legitimate" theatres if the necessity arose. With a stage available, it was logical that some form of entertainment should be added to the film showing. From its beginning the silent drama demanded an element to satisfy the ear. One may trace in logical sequence the piano of the "nickleodian," the general adoption of the pipe organ and the addition of a concert orchestra.

These developments have had an important bearing upon the design of structures built for the showing of motion pictures. Due to the phenomenal growth in the number of theatres, most cities have adopted "theatre codes" as public safety measures. As a result, architects cannot proceed very far with the planning of a theatre without having a very complete knowledge of the requirements of the local ordinances and National Board of Fire Underwriters' theatre code. It is further necessary that they have a reasonably clear idea of the type of entertainment that will be presented in the theatre under consideration.

Extravagance is, perhaps, today the keynote of the motion picture theatre. This is not only true as respects the entertainment and the decoration of all parts of the theatre with which the audience has contact, but in planning as well. A few years ago theatres were built with minimum seat spacing; minimum exit facilities and stairways; and aisles, passages and lobby areas that would just conform to the building codes. This practice is gradually changing and there is a marked tendency toward extravagance in the provision of more exits, stairways, standing area, etc., than the code requires. This is due, in part at least, to the fact that theatre owners have found that it is often advantageous to provide fewer seats in order to relieve quickly and more easily the congestion incurred by incoming and outgoing patrons between or during performances. It is also recognized that it is better business to fill all the seats rather than only a portion of the seating capacity.

Even sight line clearances have tended toward extravagance. Before the motion picture came into being, it was usually considered satisfactory if every seat in the theatre had a view of a part of the stage, even if some of the patrons were obliged to look either side of persons seated immediately in front or around a column supporting the balcony. The advent of the picture screen as the scene of action demanded a clear view of the entire screen area at least. For years, sight lines were laid out with minimum clearances between the assumed eye locations and any elements that might obstruct a view of the picture. These clearances did not always take into consideration that some people are taller than others, that some sit erect and others "slump" down in their seats, and that seats often occur in a direct line with the view point of some seats rather than in a staggered position. Where the laying out of sight lines was not thoroughly understood, or carefully made, chance no doubt played an important role. The coming of the "movies" brought with it the demand for balconies supported without columns to obstruct the view of orchestra patrons. The increased use of musical and other features as a part of the entertainment has necessitated providing every seat with a clear view of the entire stage and orchestra pit as well as the screen. This immediately resulted in the use of extravagant sight line clearances in so far as a view of the screen is concerned.

Theatres are costly to build and operate, and become regrettable failures when cost, income and location are not accurately balanced. The first important step in designing a theatre is to analyze the location, the present and probable future character of patronage, and to forecast the probable future trend in the development of the immediate vicinity, as well as the area upon which the theatre will depend for its patronage. A careful location analysis is indicative of the expenditure warranted, probable admission price and the number of seats that must be obtained to provide a reasonable return on the investment.

It is sometimes found that the cost of the site, the type of theatre required and the admission that can be charged, require the operation of other projects or the providing of areas in conjunction with the theatre that can be profitably rented. These are usually stores, offices, hotels, and apartment houses. The city code may complicate this. For instance, Boston permits building over the auditorium and stage; Chicago, Washington and Philadelphia allow building over the auditorium; but New York City permits no building over the stage or auditorium.

This analysis further determines whether or not a balcony is justified. It also indicates the scale of the services of production and comfort that must be provided. These vary with every theatre, and must usually be developed through cooperation with the owner and director. A sympathetic understanding of the problem that confronts both architect and owner is of utmost importance from the beginning, for unlike other buildings, theatres are not readily converted to other uses, should the venture prove unprofitable.

The services of a theatre, though often overlapping, may be roughly divided into two groups. Lighting systems, heating and ventilating systems and plumbing systems, often referred to as such, are more logically approached from the standpoint of design, as to the service they must render. It is, therefore, logical to consider the design of theatres from the standpoint of, first, service of production and second, service of comfort.

The service of production is rendered through the stage and the projection booth. The service of comfort begins with the planning of the theatre from the lobby to auditorium, the supplying to the auditorium of a sufficient quantity of air at a comfortable temperature, and the selection and arrangement of comfortable seats. Illumination and sight lines may be classed as services that overlap both production and comfort.

Another service that should be at least mentioned is the service of public safety. The planning and construction of theatres and similar structures to reduce or eliminate the hazard of accident, fire and panic, require the most careful consideration. Building codes are of necessity designed as general precautionary measures and as minimum standards to meet usual conditions. Bare compliance with the codes having jurisdiction does not always provide adequate or complete protection. This is particularly true where the theatre contains more than 1800 seats. Moving picture theatre operation requires ample corridor and passage space, stair widths and exit facilities far in

LOUNGE IN GUILD THEATRE, NEW YORK.

C. Howard Crane & Kenneth Franzheim, Architects.

LOUNGE IN HARRIS THEATRE, CHICAGO, ILL.

C. Howard Crane & Kenneth Franzheim, Architects.

excess of usual minimum code requirements. In a large theatre recently built in New York City, the width of the stairways from the upper levels to the street level are approximately one and three-quarters times the width required by the code. Corridor and passage space devoted entirely to the handling of patrons is about four times greater than that legally required. The seating capacity of this theatre required a minimum of twenty exits. Thirty-three exits, or one and two-thirds the requirements, were provided. It is not only good business but a moral responsibility to provide every possible safeguard to the protection of the theatre public.

The Stage

The selection of the type of stage to be used is largely determined by the kind of entertainment to be presented. For the showing of pictures only, there is no necessity for a large stage. In this case the stage becomes but a shallow platform from five to ten feet in depth with the screen set near or against the back wall. The ceiling of the platform type may be located a few feet above the proscenium opening and any valance or side curtains required may be fixed with the exception of the proscenium curtain, which can be a draw curtain operated on an overhead track by means of hand ropes. An orchestra pit may or may not be required. When an organ only is used the console may be located in front of the platform at the center or to one side. This requires less space than an orchestra pit. However, since the first row of seats should not be located nearer to the screen than 25 feet, a saving of space by eliminating the orchestra pit may or may not be an advantage.

FOYER, EL CAPITAN THEATRE, HOLLYWOOD CAL.
G. Albert Lansburgh, Architect.

In some theatres the platform stage has been adopted with the stage loft and proscenium so built that it can be converted into a regular stage at some future time if desired. In this case the auditorium seats are extended beyond the true proscenium opening into the space that would normally be used as the stage. These seats would be removed in the event of conversion into a "legitimate" type theatre.

The second type of stage is one in which the depth of 15 to 18 feet removes it from the platform type. It is in reality a small stage but limited as to the stage settings that can be used. Owing to the additional depth of the stage the screen can be set at least 4 feet from the back wall to provide a passage way. The stage, if extended beyond the curtain line of the proscenium, is suffi-

ciently large to provide settings for solo numbers that do not require elaborate scenic effects. A variation of this, like the platform type, is to extend the orchestra seats down to the proscenium opening and step the stage down to form an orchestra pit.

The third type of stage has a depth of 25 to 35 or more feet and should be fully equipped to handle practically any type of stage setting. The following notes on stage equipment and sizes refer to stages of this class. These notes also apply to smaller stages except for such equipment as would be useless owing to their limited size.

The use of the orchestra pit elevator is favored where a concert orchestra is featured. The entire floor of the orchestra pit is raised and lowered from the basement to stage floor level under the control of the

ORCHESTRA PIT ELEVATOR RAISED TO STAGE LEVEL.

ORIENTAL THEATRE, CHICAGO, ILL.

GEORGE L. & C. W. RAPP, ARCHITECTS.

(Installation by Peter Clark.)

25

musical leader. An intermediate level below the sight lines of the audience is used when the orchestra accompanies the screen showing. The organ console may be on this or a separate elevator. The separate elevator gives greater flexibility for varying the program by organ solo numbers. The operation of these elevators is automatic and they are electrically controlled.

The proscenium opening forms a frame for the entertainment shown on the stage and its size is largely a matter of securing a pleasing proportion in the auditorium. The frame around the opening, as a matter of fact, is usually higher than the actual opening. This is accomplished by recessing the wall above the true stage opening to the proscenium arch. A grand valance is hung in the recess to conceal the wall. The width of the proscenium opening should be as wide as possible, usually from 35 feet to 45 feet, 40 feet being an average. A number of theatres recently built in some of the large cities have stage openings from 55 to 60 feet in width. The height of the opening above the stage floor should be at least 25 or 30 feet.

On either side of the proscenium opening on the stage face are the curtain slots for the asbestos curtain that act as guides and smoke shields. These are made of steel plates or steel channels, and may extend from the stage floor to within a few feet of the rigging loft or gridiron. Local regulations in many cases permit the slots to stop 18 inches above the top of the proscenium opening.

The gridiron is located at twice the height of the proscenium opening plus 4 or 5 feet. For a 30 foot opening the gridiron is about 65 feet above the stage level. The rigging loft should be designed for a live load of 70 pounds per square foot. The gridiron usually consists of 3 inch channels spaced about 3 inches apart extending across the stage and supported on channel beams. These channels are in turn supported on pairs of heavier channels, set about 10 inches back to back. The gridiron supports the blocks or sheaves over which the ropes supporting curtains, scenery, border lights, etc., pass. The slots between the channels permit the ropes or cables to pass between them. The numerous openings thus provided in the gridiron allow for a flexible arrangement of hoisting ropes. The gridiron extends from the back wall about 2 feet either side of the stage to within about 2 feet of the front wall. Above the gridiron every stage loft should be provided with an automatic vent operated by a rope that extends to the stage floor. This rope is fitted with fusible links at the opening and can be cut or released at the stage floor in case of emergency.

The traditional fly gallery, located approximately at the height of the proscenium opening at one or both sides of the stage, with its pin rail from which back drops, borders, wings, curtains, etc., could be raised or lowered by means of the ropes over the gridiron sheaves, is rapidly being replaced by the counter balanced system operated from the stage level. The scene handling equipment should be located on the same side of the stage as the switchboard. The asbestos and act curtains are now usually raised by motor and are counterweighted to descend by gravity. The counterweights run in T bar guides. The asbestos curtain rigging is usually required to be kept separate from all other rigging. Other equipment that may be required are loading platforms, scene racks, spot light racks or galleries, and trunk hoists. The balance of the stage equipment is largely electrical.

The stage floor is built of edge grain Georgian Pine flooring, 1¾ inches thick to withstand the repeated use of stage screws. The floor construction is usually of wood, although in a few cities, a fireproof arch is required below the wood top floor. In past years, it was customary to make the entire

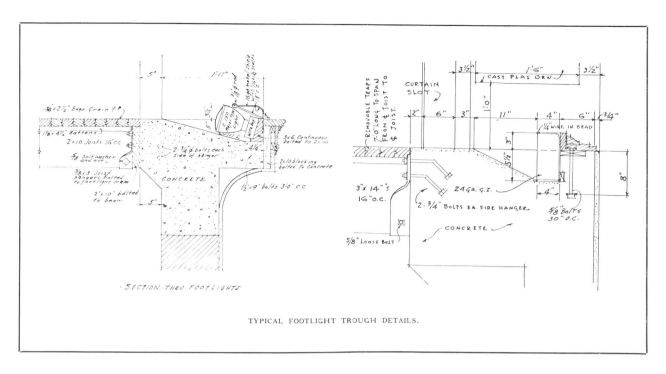

TYPICAL FOOTLIGHT TROUGH DETAILS.

DISAPPEARING TYPE FOOTLIGHTS.

PARAMOUNT THEATRE, NEW YORK.

GEORGE L. & C. W. RAPP, ARCHITECTS.

(Installation by Peter Clark.)

27

ELECTRIC OPERATOR FOR ASBESTOS CURTAIN.
(Installation by Peter Clark.)

stage floor of removable trap units, divided into small size panels that could be conveniently handled. In recent years less attention has been given this item. An advantageous arrangement adopted by one of the large theatre operating circuits is a standard panel in the center of the stage, 10 feet wide up and down stage and 16 feet long across the stage, fitted with traps.

Where only a screen platform is used one

or two dressing rooms should be provided for the use of soloists. If a stage is provided additional dressing rooms for the artists are essential. One dressing room, called a "quick change" room, is often located at the stage floor level. The others may be placed on one or more levels reached by means of a stairway from the stage floor. Toilets and shower baths should be arranged convenient to the dressing rooms. A lavatory should be placed in each dressing room as well as a "make-up" table and mirror. Musicians' rooms, chorus rooms, toilets, locker rooms and storage rooms are often desirable adjuncts to the stage. Space in large theatres is also provided for a stage hands' room, electric shop, carpenter shop and paint shop. Scene docks or paint galleries are rarely provided in modern theatres since practically all of this work is done in outside shops or the artists carry their own stage settings.

The Organ

The pipe organ is now considered essential equipment for all motion picture theatres. The organ chambers are usually located in the auditorium adjacent to the proscenium or above the center of proscenium. A small organ may require but one chamber. A large organ requires several chambers and occasionally an echo organ is located at some remote point in the auditorium. A recent theatre installation has six organ chambers, there being three superimposed on each side of the auditorium. The chamber should be as soundproof as possible to enclose the tone so that complete modulation control is secured through the Venetian swell shutters. The chambers are preferably located about 12 feet above the stage floor. The size of the chambers depend upon the size of the organ. For an average size organ the chambers should be at least 12 feet high. The width of the swell shutter openings should be about 85% of the length of the chamber and the height about 8 feet, with the bottom of the opening located 4 feet above the organ chamber floor. The grill work covering the shutter openings must have a free opening area of at least 70% of the size of the opening. The walls of the organ chamber should be built of either hollow tile plastered both sides, metal lath and plaster with deadening quilt in between, or concrete plastered. The inside walls should be painted. The organ blower is located in the basement and removed as far as possible from the auditorium. The air supply is preferably taken from the inside so that it is of the same temperature and humidity as the air in the auditorium in which the organ speaks. Air filters are often provided to avoid drawing dust into the organ mechanism. The organ equipment should be determined before the plans are too far advanced so that the space and arrangement essential for correct installation may be developed in conjunction with the organ maker.

The Projection Room

A projection room or booth is an essential part of the service of production in practically every theatre whether built strictly for the presentation of motion pictures or not. The location, layout and equipment of this room is of the utmost importance for in a sense it is the very heart of the motion picture presentation. Practically all of the "action" that usually takes place back stage in a legitimate theatre is transferred to the projection room of a motion picture theatre. The success of the theatre, as respects the showing of films is dependent upon a properly located and planned projection room.

In the main-floor theatre, without balconies, and in theatres with balconies and relatively shallow auditoriums, the projection room must usually be placed in the rear of the house at the back wall of the auditorium. Where the auditorium is very deep and a single balcony or balcony and mezzanine are used, it may be advantageous or even necessary to locate the projection room near the front and at the center of the balcony. The Roxy Theatre, New York City, is an example of this type. The center portion of the balcony is cut back far enough to provide the required head room in the projection booth. This arrangement avoids the necessity of an excessively long throw from machine to screen and an excessive projection angle. Two considerations are involved in the vertical location of the projection room. First, the light beam, through the projection ports, from the motion picture machine lens, must have a clear, unobstructed "throw" to the screen. Where this is not carefully checked, it is often found after the job is completed that some make-shift arrangement must be used as a last resort to avoid a deep girder, hanging chandeliers or persons standing in the path of the light beam. The second consideration is to avoid an excessive projection angle. The projection angle is the

AUTOMATIC HYDRAULIC CHECK FOR ASBESTOS CURTAIN.

(Installation by Peter Clark.)

angle formed by a line drawn from the center of the projector lens to the center of the screen and at horizontal line. This angle should be as flat as possible for satisfactory results and should preferably not exceed 20 degrees. An excessive angle of projection is responsible for distortion and improper focusing of a portion of the picture. While any reasonable condition can usually be overcome by adjustment of the screen

and the use of a special projector lens, it is expensive, questionable as to results and unnecessary if the projection room is correctly located. The height of the projector lens must be such that the light beam will have ample clearance above the heads of persons standing on the seat platforms in front of the booth.

The projection room must be of fireproof construction throughout. The floor must

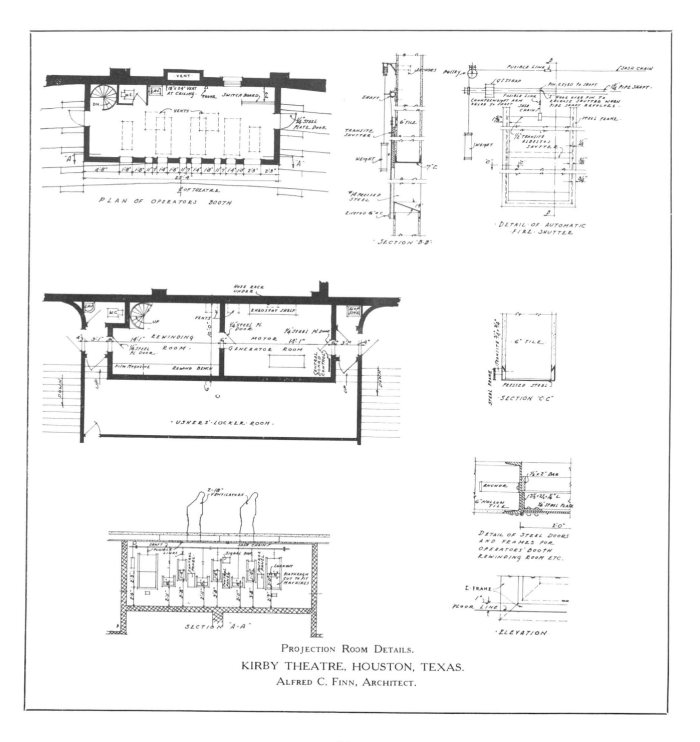

PROJECTION ROOM DETAILS.
KIRBY THEATRE, HOUSTON, TEXAS.
ALFRED C. FINN, ARCHITECT.

be substantially constructed to support the projection machines and avoid vibration. The projection and observation ports must have gravity shutters that close automatically in case of fire and that are absolutely tight when closed. The booth must be provided with adequate exit facilities for the operators in case of an emergency. All doors should be of the automatic self-closing type. Adequate ventilation is mandatory.

It is essential that the port holes be of correct size and location. Four types of ports should be provided,—observation, projector, stereopticon and spot light. Observation ports for operators are usually about 15″ square with the center of the opening 5′ 0″ above the floor. Projector ports are 12″ square, and the stereopticon port about 8″ wide by 15″ high. The centers of these openings should be approximately 4′ 0″ above the floor of the projection room. The exact height of all openings in the front of the booth depends upon the angle of projection and the layout should be carefully studied. The spot light requires a port at least 18″ high and 24″ wide. Its center is located about 4′ 6″ above the floor. In a horizontal direction projector ports are located about 4′ 0″ on center. Since the

machines used in the projection room are standardized as to size, the incorrect location of the ports produces unsatisfactory results and a condition difficult to correct. Ordinarily a booth requires ports for at least one spot light, one stereopticon, two motion picture machines and three for observation. Where the equipment consists of two spot lights, a stereopticon and three projectors, a room at least 10 feet by 25 feet is required. Ample working space is essential to the operation of the machines by the operators who must often work quickly and unhampered. Adjacent to the projector room there should be provided a toilet and work room. The work room or rewind room should contain a substantial work bench and metal cabinet. A separate room should be provided for a motor generator set where DC current is not available and must be converted from AC current.

The Screen

While the screen is equipment that is not actually a part of the construction of the theatre, it has some bearing on the design and its size bears a relation to the size of the auditorium. A picture projected on a screen 12 feet wide is approximately life size. Obviously a larger picture in a small

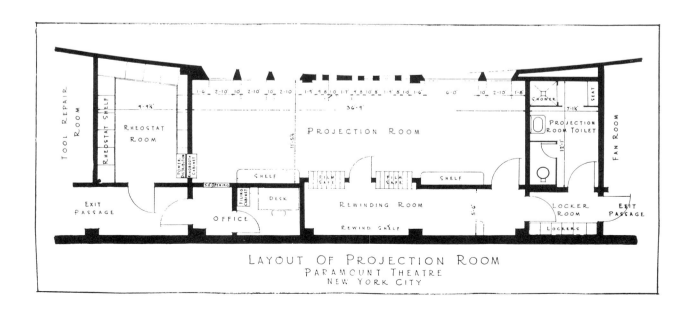

LAYOUT OF PROJECTION ROOM
PARAMOUNT THEATRE
NEW YORK CITY

auditorium is as objectionable as a smaller picture in a large auditorium. It has become a custom to select a screen and projection equipment that will produce results approximately as follows:

Approximate Size of the Picture		Auditorium Seating Capacity
Width	Height	
14′ x	11′	
16′ x	12′	
17′ x	12′ 8″	2000
18′ x	13′ 6″	2500
19′ x	14′ 4″	3000
20′ x	15′	3500 and up

Since an unobstructed view of the entire picture must be assured every seat in the auditorium, the size of the picture screen has some bearing upon the sight lines. The screen is usually located not less than 25 feet from the back of the first row of seats on the orchestra floor, measured on the center line. The bottom of the picture is placed about 2 feet above the stage floor. This dimension varies with each individual theatre since it must often be adjusted to improve the sight lines. Other factors enter into the selection of the screen, but these concern its construction and projection machine equipment, to correct distortion, focus, and shape of picture, due to projection angle and distance.

Sight Lines

Every seat in a motion picture theatre must provide an unobstructed view of the stage and the entire screen. Where such is not the case, the project is sure to be unpopular or a total failure. The question of sight lines is therefore of utmost importance in theatre design and cannot be left to chance or later adjustment. There is no mystery in the sight line problem for it is a matter of projection and the use of good judgment and common sense. Longitudinal sections are of utmost importance in checking the sight lines, although in a few instances the lines of sight may require checking on the plan. The longitudinal

section taken on the center line of the stage and auditorium is rarely sufficient. Numerous other sections should be taken to make sure that no chandeliers, girders, railings, cornices, boxes or other projections prevent a complete view of the entire picture screen. The minimum area to be included within the range of vision should provide for a view of the entire stage width at the curtain line and vertically from the front of the stage, just in front of the footlights, to a point about 20 feet above the stage level measured on the screen. Since the general tendency in theatre operation is to provide large orchestras as part of the attraction, the entire orchestra pit should be included within the lines of sight from the balcony. In large theatres a view of at least 14 feet and often more is provided in front of the foot lights.

In plan it has been found that lines of sight greater than 35 to 40 degrees with the central axis of the stage and auditorium result in the picture on the screen appearing distorted to those seated beyond the limits of this angle. While this can be corrected in a measure by the use of a curved screen, an angle greater than 35 degrees should be avoided.

The eyes of a person standing back of the last row on the orchestra floor may be assumed as being 5′ 0″ to 5′ 6″ above the floor at that point. The eyes of a person seated in any row are assumed to be 4′ 0″ above the floor and the tops of the spectator's head immediately in front of this row is taken as 4′ 6″ above the floor. In general seating, rows are usually made 2′ 8″ back to back. It is at once apparent that every row of seats must be located at different elevations to secure an uninterrupted line of sight. The only difficulty usually encountered is that of keeping the elevations of the rows within the gradients and steppings permitted by the building code, and practical considerations.

While it is true that patrons may see

between the heads of persons seated in rows ahead, too much dependence should not be placed upon this, especially after the first

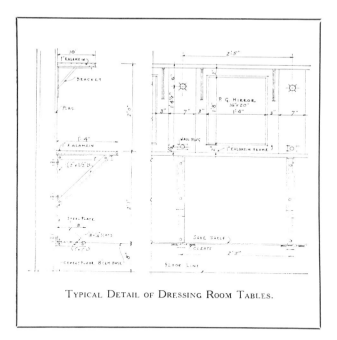

TYPICAL DETAIL OF DRESSING ROOM TABLES.

25 or 30 rows. Steps are rarely if ever permitted on the orchestra floor. The orchestra floor may be level for the first five to seven rows of seats. Beyond this the floor should be sloped. The gradient permitted the orchestra floor is sometimes limited by the building code. In New York City the grade of the orchestra floor is limited by the aisle gradient of 1 inch rise to 12 inch run

required by the theatre code. A much steeper slope is allowed in balconies and steps are permitted to each row of seats. A rise of about 7 to 7½ inches per step is the maximum that should be used.

Lighting

The lighting of the theatre may be grouped, as to its requirements, as stage, auditorium, and general. The last includes the lobby, mezzanine if there is one, passages, stairways and rooms provided for the convenience of patrons. The principle lighting of any theatre is not a matter of rule but one requiring careful consideration and development with the director.

The stage is ordinarily equipped with footlights, proscenium lights, border lights, bridge floods, stage pockets for plugging in spot lights, musicians' lights and switch board. The foot lights are commonly arranged for three colors, each color separately controlled. These may be colored bulbs or clear bulbs with color screens, and may be arranged in single or double rows. There are three general types—semi-flush, portable, and disappearing.

While the footlights will probably never be entirely eliminated, there is a noticeable tendency to supplant or supplement their use with balcony spot lights. These spot

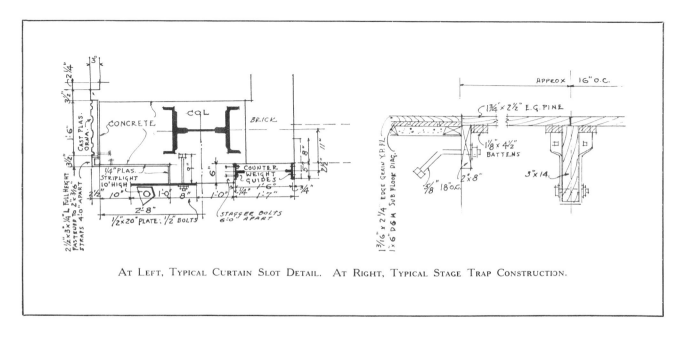

AT LEFT, TYPICAL CURTAIN SLOT DETAIL. AT RIGHT, TYPICAL STAGE TRAP CONSTRUCTION.

Stage pockets are located about 5 feet back from either side of the proscenium opening beginning about 6 feet back of the curtain line and spaced at intervals of about 7 feet. A stage 30 feet deep should be provided with four pockets on either side. In addition a similar pocket should be provided near the rear wall at the center of the stage and several in the footlight trough. The musicians' lights consist of a series of floor and wall receptacles to which are plugged in the cords from the lighting units on the music stands. Bridge floods are spot lights on bridges, platforms or steel pipe battens used to throw beams of light from overhead on the stage to supplement or replace the borderlights.

The main switch board and dimmer bank, controlling all lights connected with the stage and auditorium, is located on the stage preferably to the right of the proscenium. A theatre switchboard is a fairly large piece of apparatus and adequate space should always be provided for it. This space includes not only the length, height and depth of the board and its mechanism, but working space both in front and in back. Where dimmers are incorporated in the stage switchboard, provision must be made for air circulation to carry off the heat generated. Space requirements vary depending upon the size and type of switchboard used. In general a floor space of 4 feet by 8 feet should be adequate for the switchboard apparatus.

The auditorium lighting includes general illumination, act announcers, aisle lights, step lights and exit sign lights. General illumination is secured by one of three methods,—direct lighting, strip reflectors or "cove" lights, or a combination of direct and cove. The latter is perhaps the more common method. In designing the lighting system, it is necessary to determine whether one or more colors will be required. All light circuits of the stage and auditorium should be controlled through the dimmer bank to secure variation in intensity and

lights are used to floodlight the stage and orchestra pit from the facia of the balcony railing. The balcony spot lights may, therefore, be properly grouped with the stage lighting equipment.

The proscenium lights may include a right and left strip either side of the opening on the stage side, a fixed valance borderlight in front of the curtain line, a concert borderlight back of the curtain line and the stage borderlights. Borderlights may be arranged for one, two, three, or four colors and, with the exception of the side strips and valance borderlight, are adjustable as to location. Border lights commonly consist of a reflecting trough containing bulb receptacles suspended from a pipe batten hung on cables from the gridiron sheaves.

possibly gradual color changes that become a part of the theatrical lighting effect.

The projection room should be well lighted preferably by indirect fixtures to provide proper illumination for the machine operators. The electrical equipment for this room also includes motion picture machine outlets, stereopticon and spot light outlets, rheostat, switchboard, control panels and may require a motor generator set. The operator's booth should be equipped with signal lights and telephone. Conduit for wires between the booth and orchestra leader's stand should also be provided for the possible wiring for speed meters. Lobby and corridor lighting requires two considerations—proper illumination and decor-

ative effect. The lighting of dressing rooms, retiring rooms, toilets, locker rooms and similar areas, is utilitarian in character. Other general lighting includes exterior signs, display boards and carriage calls. Outlets should be located in the ticket booths for electric ticket machines, heaters and fans. Where organ chambers are located against exposed walls or apt to be subject to variation in temperature, it is advisable to install heater outlets in these areas.

For public safety many cities have a theatre electric code that governs the electrical installation to a very large extent. The National Board of Fire Underwriters also have a code for theatre work. The

COUNTERWEIGHT SYSTEM OF STAGE SCENE HANDLING EQUIPMENT.
STAGE SWITCHBOARD AND DIMMER BANK LOCATED ON BALCONY ABOVE STAGE FLOOR.
HARRIS THEATRE, CHICAGO, ILL.
C. HOWARD CRANE & KENNETH FRANZHEIM, ARCHITECTS.
(Installation by Peter Clark.)

35

requirements of all boards and departments having jurisdiction should be fully known before an attempt is made to layout the electrical system.

Heating, Ventilating and Cooling

The proper control of air conditions in a theatre is not a matter of simple or ordinary design. It is a problem that should be intrusted only to competent engineers experienced in this type of work. Air conditioning in a theatre introduces a multiplicity of problems particularly to provide for seasonal changes. For example, while the animal or body heat from the audience and the heat from numerous electric light bulbs may be an asset in cold weather, they produce a highly objectionable condition in warm weather. A stage with too little radiation results in the front portion of the orchestra being under heated and induces noticeably strong air currents through the auditorium. The general procedure has been to have the auditorium moderately warm when the audience entered and then to gradually balance the bodily heat from the audience and heat from the lights by reducing the heat supplied from the boilers. The motion picture theatre, however, with an almost constantly changing audience, introduced new problems for solution. The proper heating of the auditorium has always proved an annoying problem. The size and shape of the room, the large opening to the stage and the large number of people seated close together, present a heating problem that requires the most careful consideration. The heating of dressing rooms, retiring rooms, toilet rooms and similar areas present no unusual heating problem. The lobby, however, where doors are continually opened and closed, requires entirely different and separate attention. To prevent cold air from being blown into the auditorium, the air in the lobby must be very quickly heated.

In contrast to the provision of a comfortably warm temperature in cold weather,

FOYER, STADIUM THEATRE, WOONSOCKET, R. I.
Frank B. Perry, Formerly Perry & Whipple, Architect.

36

there is the matter of providing a comfortably cool temperature in warm weather. A proper change of air or ventilation is further essential to the comfort of the patrons. This service of comfort, largely governed by the condition of the air in the auditorium, is dependent upon air movement, humidity and temperature.

A gravity two-pipe system or a vacuum return line system has been found to be the most satisfactory type of heating. Boiler locations are often practically fixed by the city theatre code. The New York City code prohibits placing the boilers under the auditorium or under the stage. This frequently requires placing the boilers under the sidewalk. Boston prohibits the installation of boilers under sidewalks or public thoroughfares and Chicago permits them to be installed as desired. The demands upon the boilers are heavy and ample capacity should be provided. The type of boiler selected depends very largely upon the size of the theatre. The heating mains should be so divided that the sections of the building having different heating demands are served independently.

As before stated, the stage must have a sufficient quantity of radiation. Wall radiators are usually placed at different levels on the back wall of the stage from a point near the floor to a point about two-thirds the height of the stage loft and pipe coils in the stage vent, and over the top of the proscenium. Direct radiation, placed in recesses near entrance and exit doors of the auditorium to warm the air at these points, is sufficient in this portion of the building. Banks of direct radiation in recesses near the lobby doors will usually be found the best solution of the lobby heating problem. A fresh air supply, separate or connected with the auditorium air supply, is sometimes used in the lobby to assure a circulation of air over these radiators.

Auditorium heating has been well described as a de-heating problem rather than one of heating, for it is practically entirely a matter of ventilation. One of two systems is commonly used. In one type, air is introduced at the floor line and taken out at the ceiling. The other system operates on the opposite principle, that is, the air is brought in through the ceiling and removed at the floor. The downward system has many logical arguments in its favor and is claimed to result in a greater uniformity of temperature. The amount of air that should be supplied the auditorium per person is a debatable question. It is well established, however, that the supply should not be less than 15 nor need be more than 30 cubic feet per minute per person. A difficulty encountered in designing the ventilating system is to secure uniform temperature in all parts of the auditorium. Where the system is not properly designed, the temperature will be found to vary from a low point in the front of the orchestra near the stage to a high point in the rear of the balcony. The fundamentals of proper ventilation in theatres are the proper distribution of a correct quantity of fresh air delivered at comfortable velocity, correct humidity and correct temperature.

Cooling systems are being extensively used in conjunction with theatre ventilation. Where these are used and the system is correctly designed and installed, the air conditions may be maintained uniformly comfortable at all seasons of the year. A modern and efficient air conditioning system consists of a refrigeration machine connected with a dehumidifier, motor driven fan, air supply ducts and return air ducts. Fresh air mixed with the return air from the auditorium is drawn, by means of a centrifugal fan, through the dehumidifier where it is cooled, cleansed and dehumidified. From this it is delivered to the ceiling of the auditorium and balcony soffit by ducts, and returned through air ducts connected with openings in the floors of the auditorium and balcony under the seats. The same system may be used summer and winter, except that in winter the refrigeration machine is not used.

Air conditioning has three distinct functions,—air movement, temperature control and control of relative humidity. The combination of these three functions presents a complicated problem and complete air conditioning cannot be secured unless all three are controlled. If such a system is to function properly, it must be automatically controlled.

The service of comfort is one of very great importance to the theatre owner for, if they can avoid it, people will not patronize theatres that are other than comfortable. This is true in spite of the possibility of better film and entertainment presentations. As a result it is false economy to attempt to secure results with inadequate equipment. Every theatre is an individual problem and the heating, ventilating and cooling equipment must be solved as such. No more definite rules can be given for their design than in the case of the design and plan of the theatre as a whole.

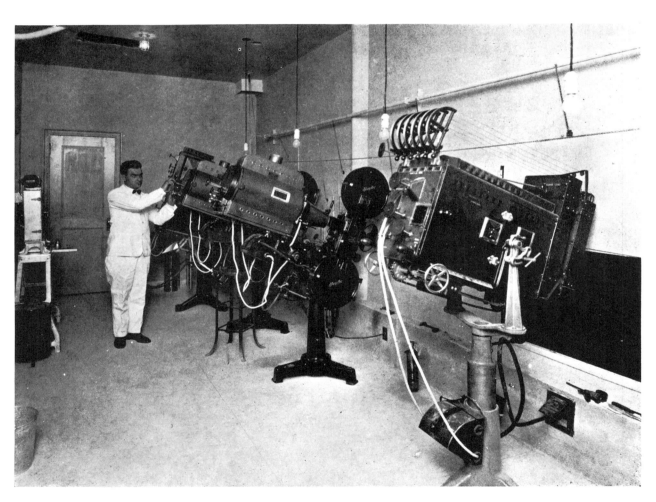

PROJECTION ROOM, CAPITOL THEATRE, PORT CHESTER, N. Y.
THOMAS W. LAMB, ARCHITECT.

CAPITOL THEATRE, PORT CHESTER, N. Y.
Thomas W. Lamb, Architect.

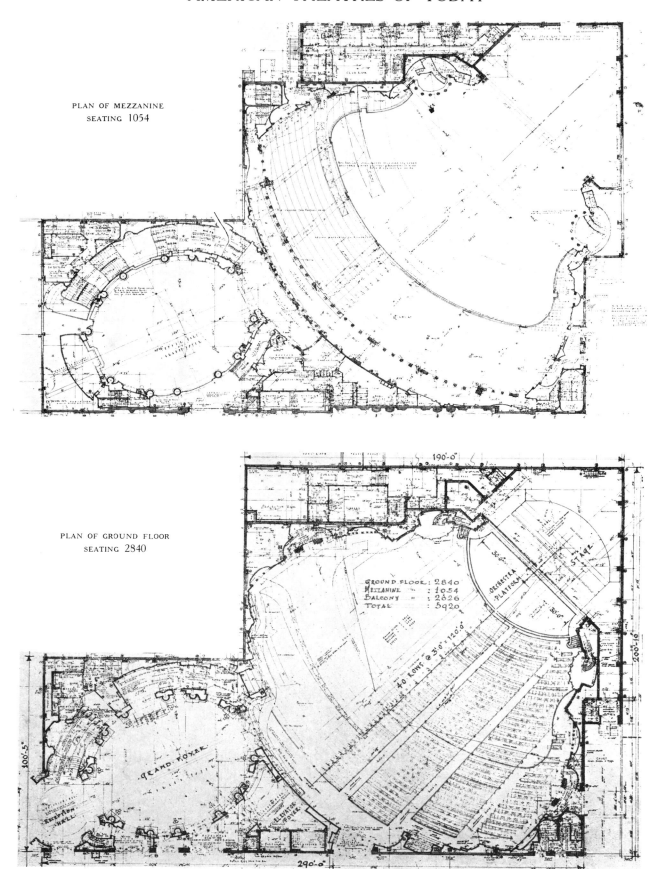

PLAN OF MEZZANINE
SEATING 1054

PLAN OF GROUND FLOOR
SEATING 2840

GROUND FLOOR : 2840
MEZZANINE " : 1054
BALCONY " : 2026
TOTAL : 5920

ROXY THEATRE, NEW YORK
WALTER W. AHLSCHLAGER, ARCHITECT.

ROXY THEATRE, NEW YORK

WALTER W. AHLSCHLAGER, ARCHITECT.

(Copyright, 1927, Tebbs & Knell, Inc.)

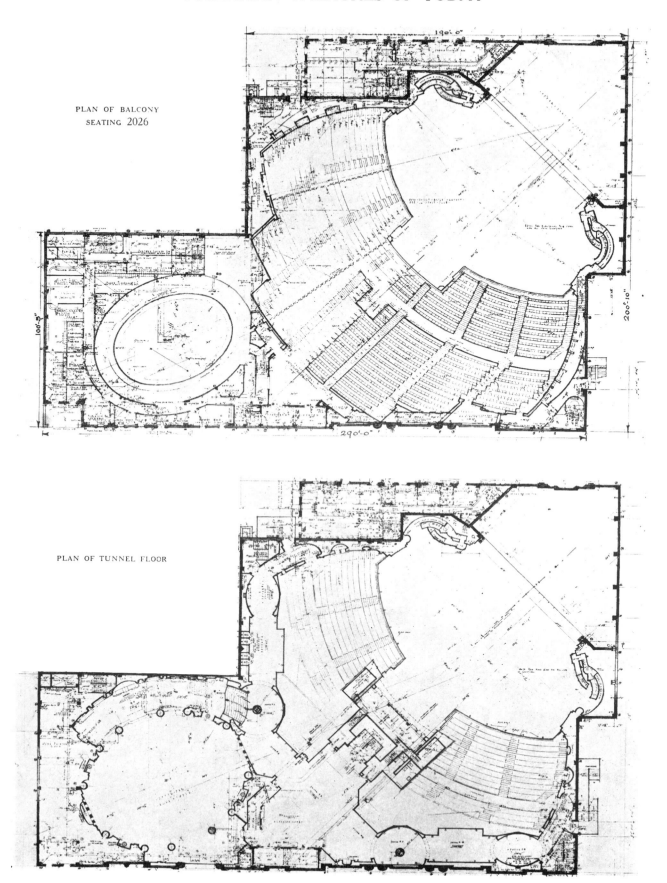

PLAN OF BALCONY
SEATING 2026

PLAN OF TUNNEL FLOOR

ROXY THEATRE, NEW YORK
WALTER W. AHLSCHLAGER, ARCHITECT.

ROXY THEATRE, NEW YORK
WALTER W. AHLSCHLAGER, ARCHITECT.
(Copyright, 1927, Tebbs & Knell, Inc.)

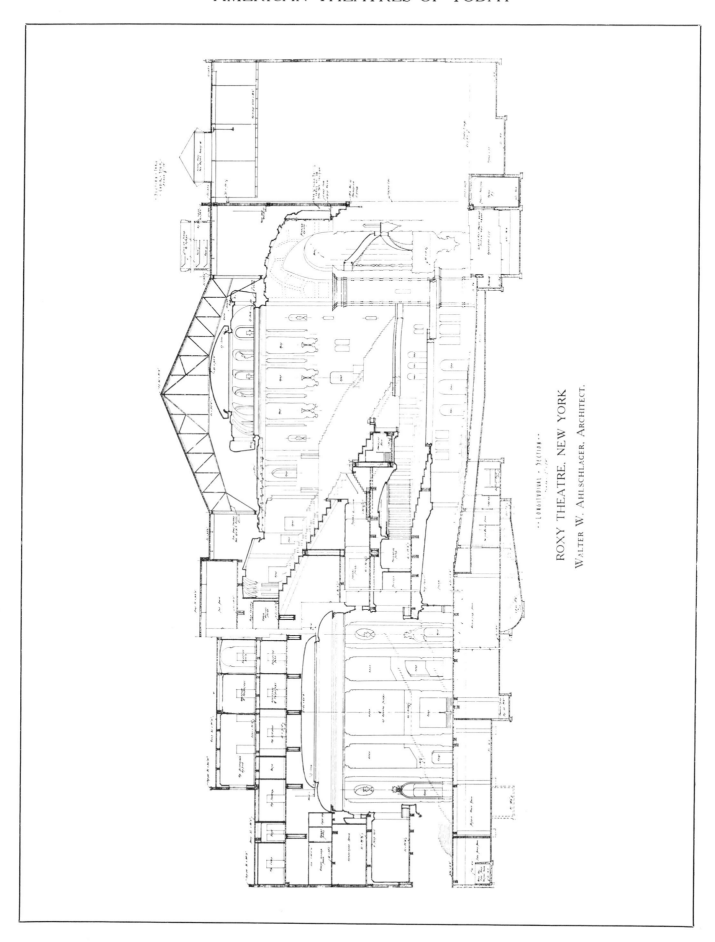

ROXY THEATRE, NEW YORK

WALTER W. AHLSCHLAGER, ARCHITECT.

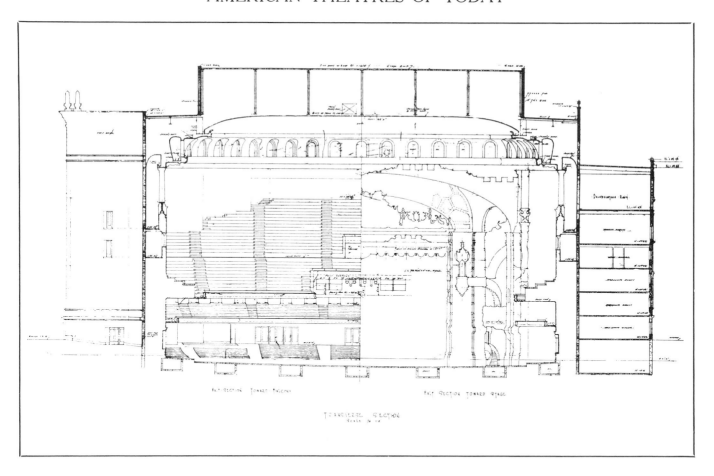

ROXY THEATRE, NEW YORK

WALTER W. AHLSCHLAGER, ARCHITECT.

(Copyright, 1927, Tebbs & Knell, Inc.)

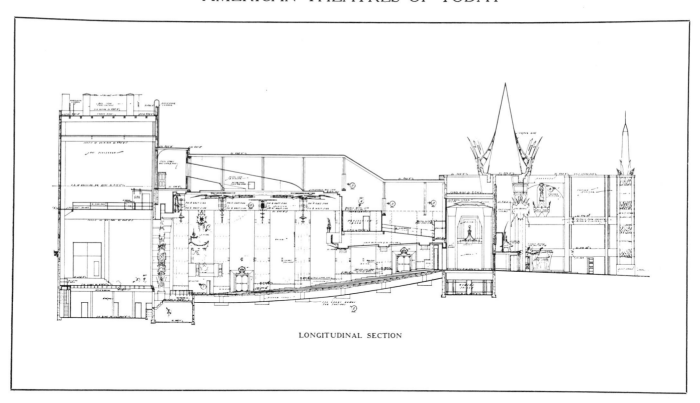

LONGITUDINAL SECTION

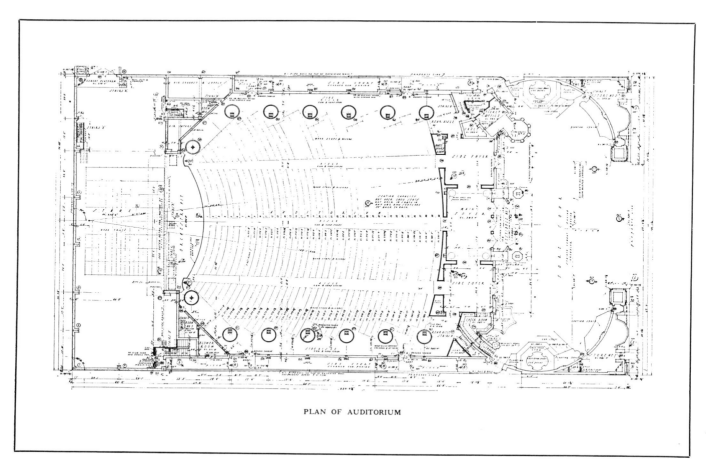

PLAN OF AUDITORIUM

GRAUMAN'S CHINESE THEATRE, HOLLYWOOD, CAL.
MEYER & HOLLER, ARCHITECTS.

GRAUMAN'S CHINESE THEATRE, HOLLYWOOD, CAL.

MEYER & HOLLER, ARCHITECTS.

(Courtesy The American Architect.)

GRAUMAN'S CHINESE THEATRE, HOLLYWOOD, CAL.

MEYER & HOLLER, ARCHITECTS.

(Courtesy The American Architect.)

GRAUMAN'S CHINESE THEATRE, HOLLYWOOD, CAL.

MEYER & HOLLER, ARCHITECTS.

(Courtesy The American Architect.)

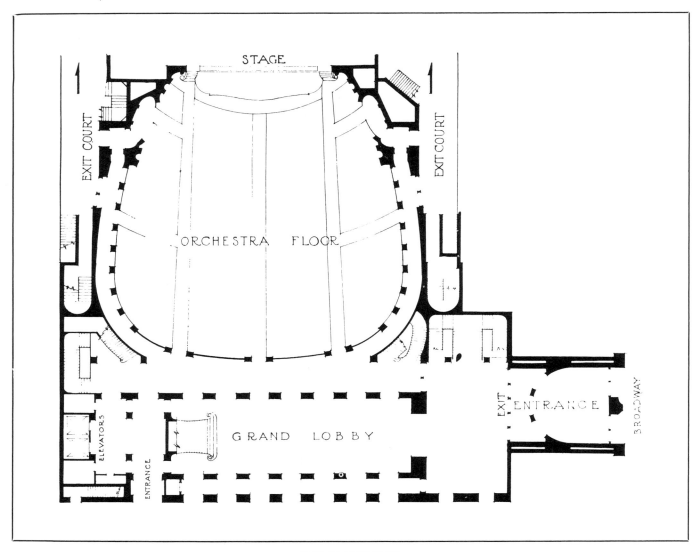

PLAN OF FIRST FLOOR

PARAMOUNT THEATRE, NEW YORK, N. Y.

C. W. & Geo. L. Rapp, Architects.

PARAMOUNT THEATRE, NEW YORK.
C. W. & George L. Rapp, Architects.

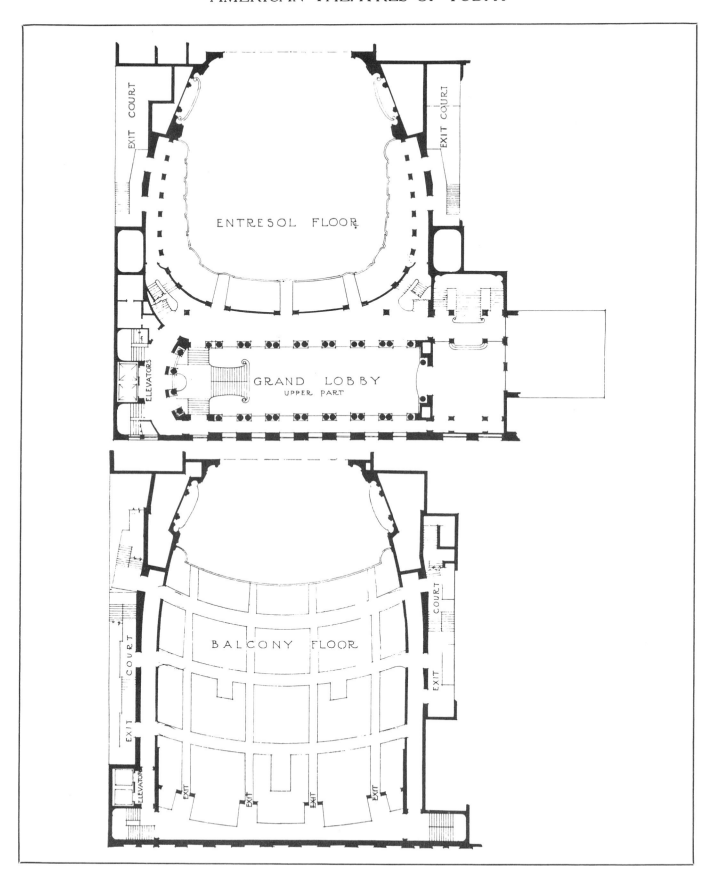

PARAMOUNT THEATRE, NEW YORK, N. Y.

C. W. & GEO. L. RAPP, ARCHITECTS.

PARAMOUNT THEATRE, NEW YORK.
C. W. & George L. Rapp, Architects.

PARAMOUNT THEATRE, NEW YORK.
C. W. & George L. Rapp, Architects.

PARAMOUNT THEATRE, NEW YORK.
C. W. & George L. Rapp, Architects.

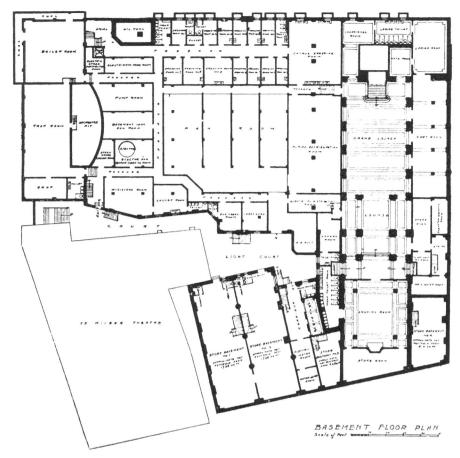

BASEMENT FLOOR PLAN
Scale of Feet

METROPOLITAN THEATRE, BOSTON, MASS.

BLACKALL, CLAPP & WHITTEMORE; C. HOWARD CRANE, KENNETH FRANZHEIM,
GEORGE NELSON MESERVE, ASSOCIATED ARCHITECTS.

(Courtesy The American Architect.)

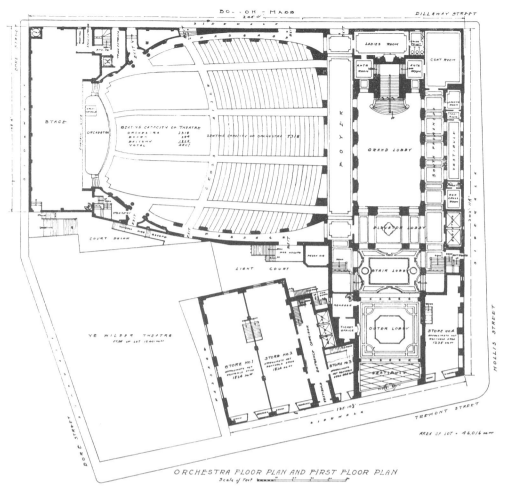

ORCHESTRA FLOOR PLAN AND FIRST FLOOR PLAN
Scale of Feet

METROPOLITAN THEATRE, BOSTON, MASS.

BLACKALL, CLAPP & WHITTEMORE; C. HOWARD CRANE, KENNETH FRANZHEIM,
GEORGE NELSON MESERVE, ASSOCIATED ARCHITECTS.

(Courtesy The American Architect.)

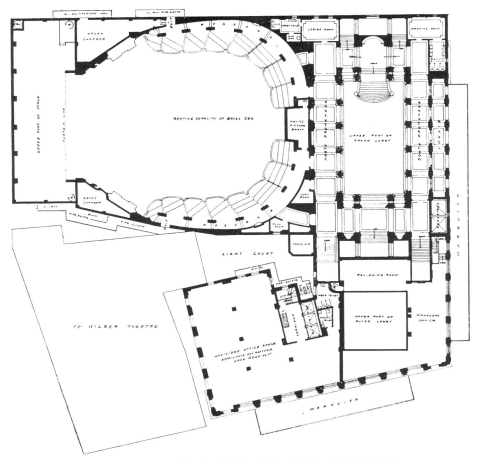

FIRST MEZZANINE FLOOR PLAN AND SECOND FLOOR PLAN
Scale of Feet

METROPOLITAN THEATRE, BOSTON, MASS.

BLACKALL, CLAPP & WHITTEMORE; C. HOWARD CRANE, KENNETH FRANZHEIM,
GEORGE NELSON MESERVE, ASSOCIATED ARCHITECTS.

(Courtesy The American Architect.)

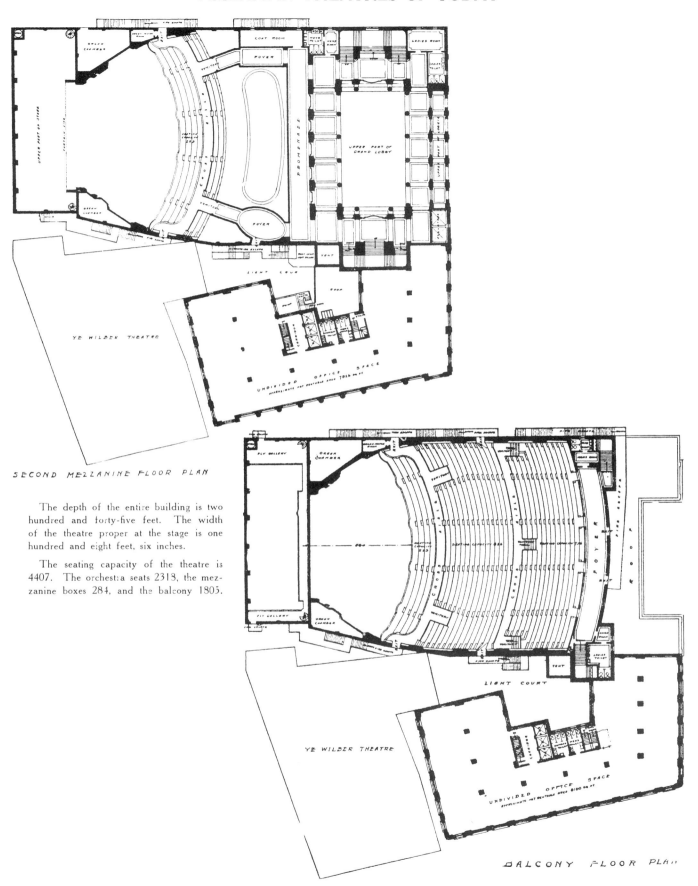

SECOND MEZZANINE FLOOR PLAN

The depth of the entire building is two hundred and forty-five feet. The width of the theatre proper at the stage is one hundred and eight feet, six inches.

The seating capacity of the theatre is 4407. The orchestra seats 2318, the mezzanine boxes 284, and the balcony 1805.

BALCONY FLOOR PLAN

METROPOLITAN THEATRE, BOSTON, MASS.

BLACKALL, CLAPP & WHITTEMORE; C. HOWARD CRANE, KENNETH FRANZHEIM, GEORGE NELSON MESERVE, ASSOCIATED ARCHITECTS.

(Courtesy The American Architect.)

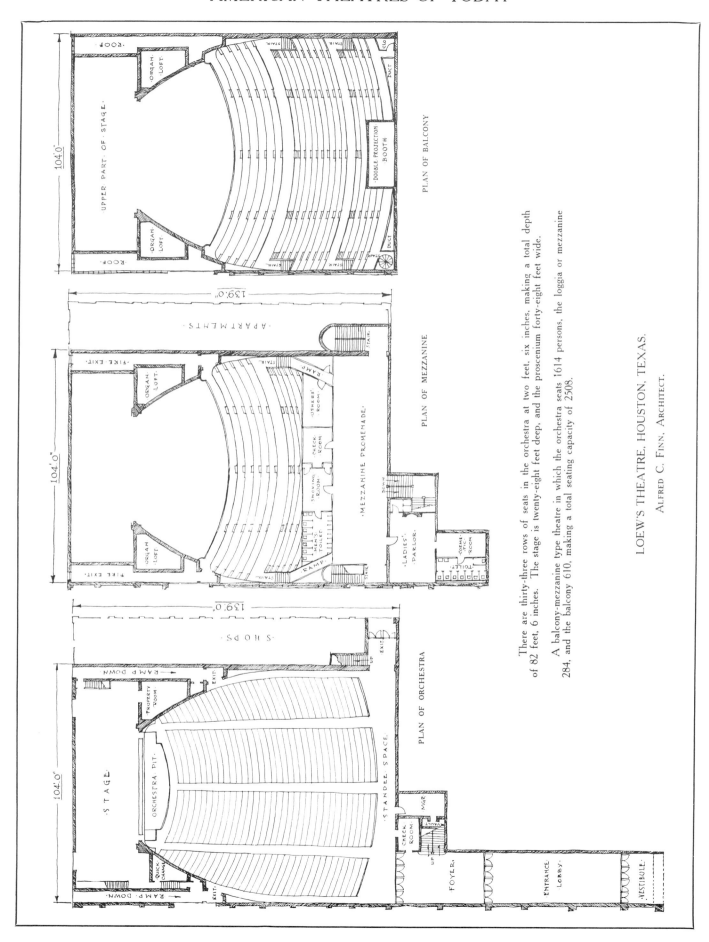

PLAN OF BALCONY

PLAN OF MEZZANINE

PLAN OF ORCHESTRA

There are thirty-three rows of seats in the orchestra at two feet, six inches, making a total depth of 82 feet, 6 inches. The stage is twenty-eight feet deep, and the proscenium forty-eight feet wide.

A balcony-mezzanine type theatre in which the orchestra seats 1614 persons, the loggia or mezzanine 284, and the balcony 610, making a total seating capacity of 2508.

LOEW'S THEATRE, HOUSTON, TEXAS.
ALFRED C. FINN, ARCHITECT.

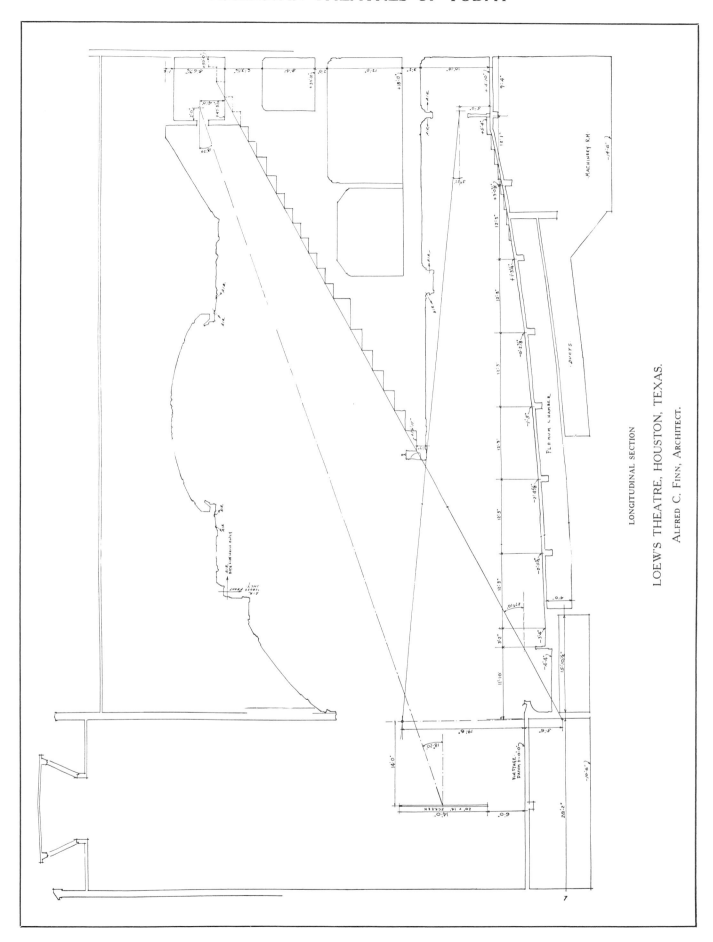

LONGITUDINAL SECTION

LOEW'S THEATRE, HOUSTON, TEXAS.

ALFRED C. FINN, ARCHITECT.

EASTMAN THEATRE AND SCHOOL OF MUSIC, ROCHESTER, N. Y.

GORDON & KAELBER, ARCHITECTS—McKIM, MEAD & WHITE, ASSOCIATED ARCHITECTS. R. E. HALL, CONSULTING ENGINEER.

(Courtesy The American Architect.)

GENERAL VIEW LOOKING TOWARDS THE STAGE, KILBURN HALL

EASTMAN THEATRE AND SCHOOL OF MUSIC, ROCHESTER, N. Y.
GORDON & KAELBER, ARCHITECTS—MCKIM, MEAD & WHITE, ASSOCIATED ARCHITECTS. R. E. HALL, CONSULTING ENGINEER.
(Courtesy The American Architect.)

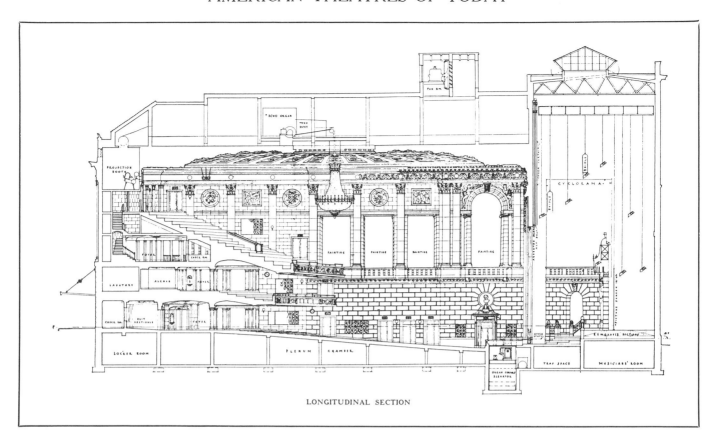

LONGITUDINAL SECTION

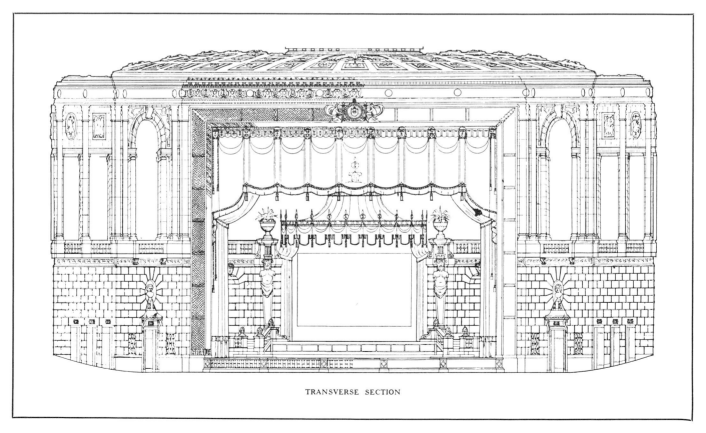

TRANSVERSE SECTION

EASTMAN THEATRE, ROCHESTER, N. Y.

GORDON & KAELBER, ARCHITECTS—McKIM, MEAD & WHITE, ASSOCIATED ARCHITECTS. R. E. HALL, CONSULTING ENGINEER.

(Courtesy The American Architect.)

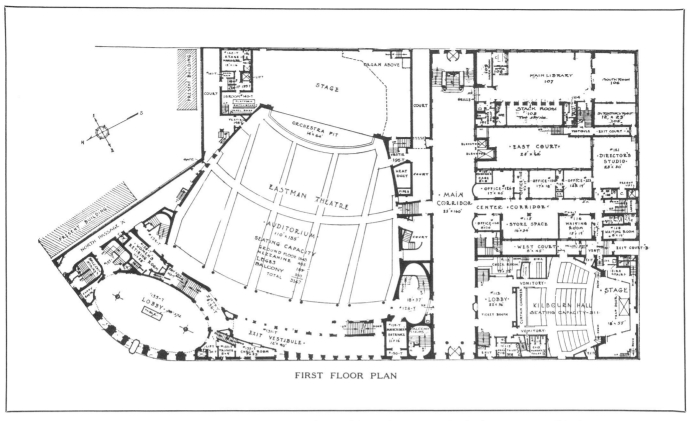

FIRST FLOOR PLAN

The seating capacity of the theatre is 3347. The orchestra seats 1843, the mezzanine 405, the loges 189, and the balcony 910. The auditorium measures 110 feet by 135 feet.

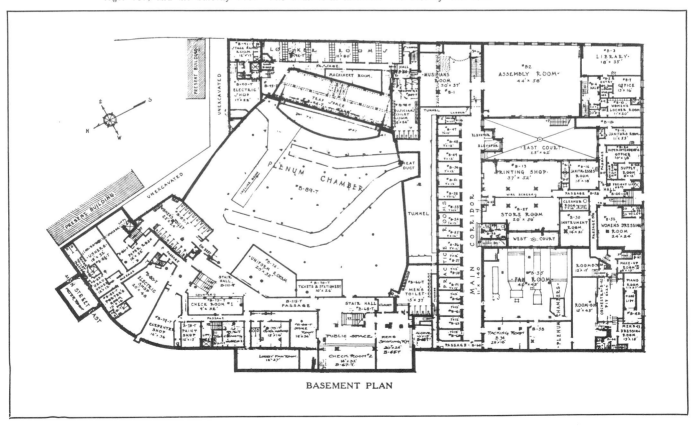

BASEMENT PLAN

EASTMAN THEATRE, ROCHESTER, N. Y.

GORDON & KAELBER, ARCHITECTS—MCKIM, MEAD & WHITE, ASSOCIATED ARCHITECTS. R. E. HALL, CONSULTING ENGINEER.

(Courtesy The American Architect.)

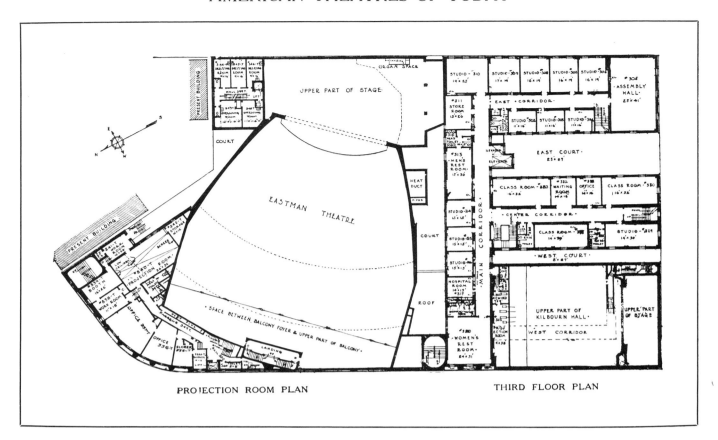

PROJECTION ROOM PLAN   THIRD FLOOR PLAN

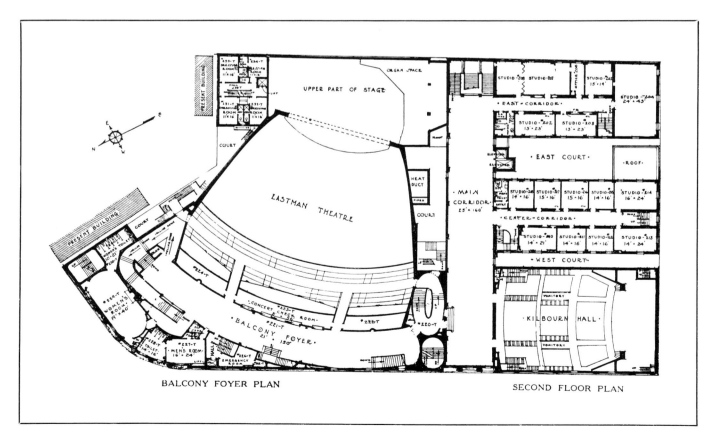

BALCONY FOYER PLAN   SECOND FLOOR PLAN

EASTMAN THEATRE AND SCHOOL OF MUSIC, ROCHESTER, N. Y.

Gordon & Kaelber, Architects—McKim, Mead & White, Associated Architects.   R. E. Hall, Consulting Engineer.

(Courtesy The American Architect.)

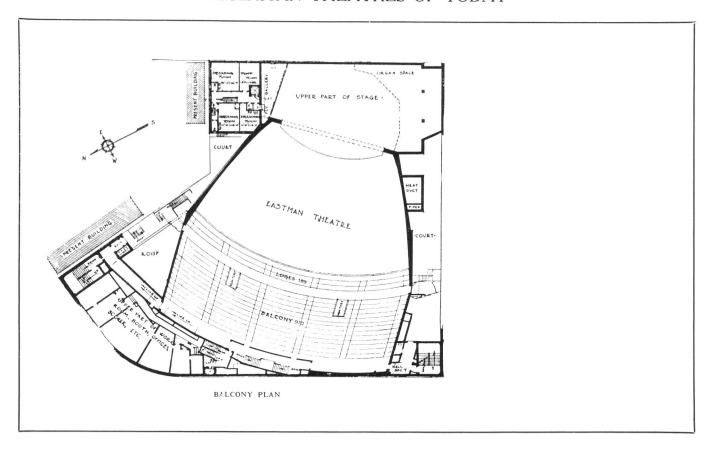

BALCONY PLAN

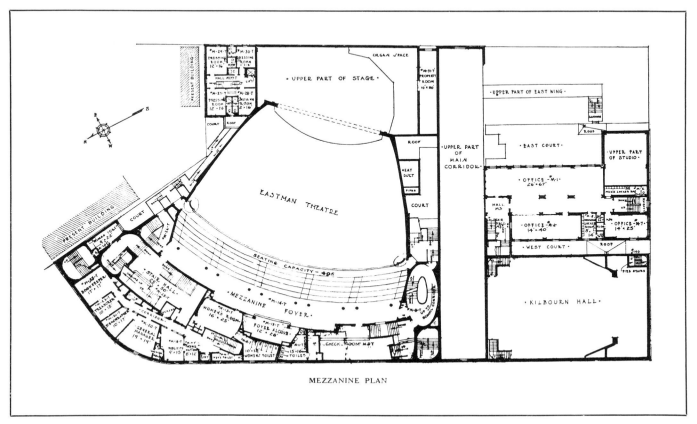

MEZZANINE PLAN

EASTMAN THEATRE AND SCHOOL OF MUSIC, ROCHESTER, N. Y.

Gordon & Kaelber, Architects—McKim, Mead & White, Associated Architects. R. E. Hall, Consulting Engineer.

(Courtesy The American Architect.)

ALABAMA THEATRE, BIRMINGHAM, ALA.

GRAVEN & MAYGER, ARCHITECTS.

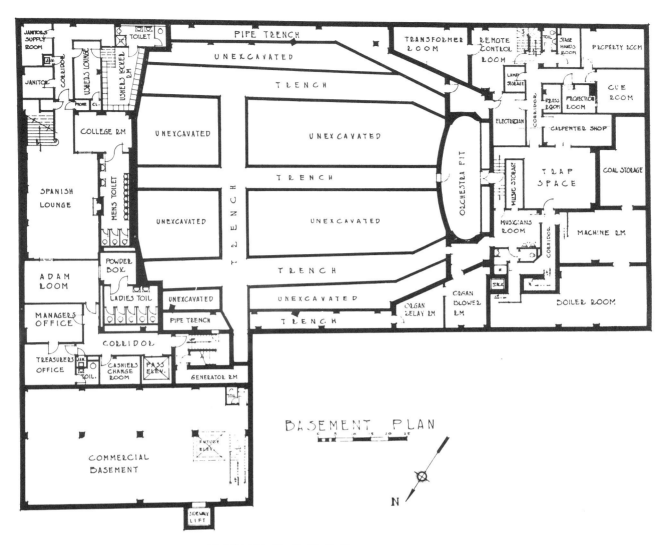

BASEMENT PLAN

ALABAMA THEATRE, BIRMINGHAM, ALA.
Graven & Mayger, Architects.

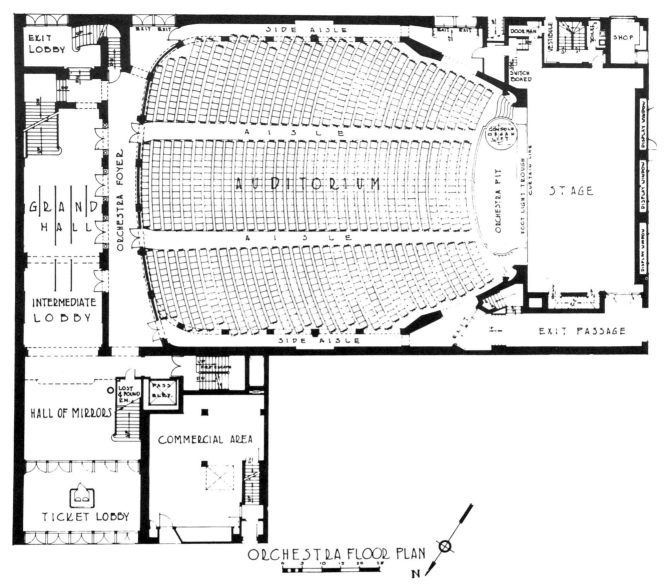

ORCHESTRA FLOOR PLAN

N

ALABAMA THEATRE, BIRMINGHAM, ALA.

Craven & Mayger, Architects.

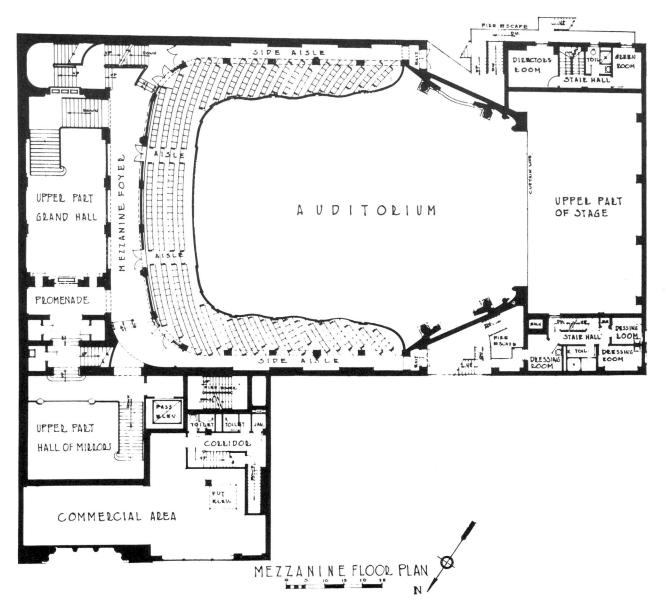

MEZZANINE FLOOR PLAN

ALABAMA THEATRE, BIRMINGHAM, ALA.
GRAVEN & MAYGER, ARCHITECTS.

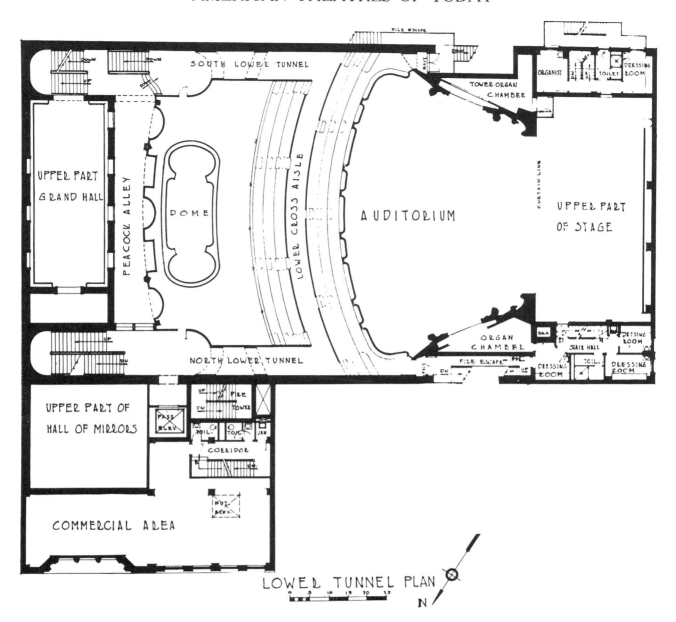

LOWER TUNNEL PLAN

N

ALABAMA THEATRE, BIRMINGHAM, ALA.

GRAVEN & MAYGER, ARCHITECTS.

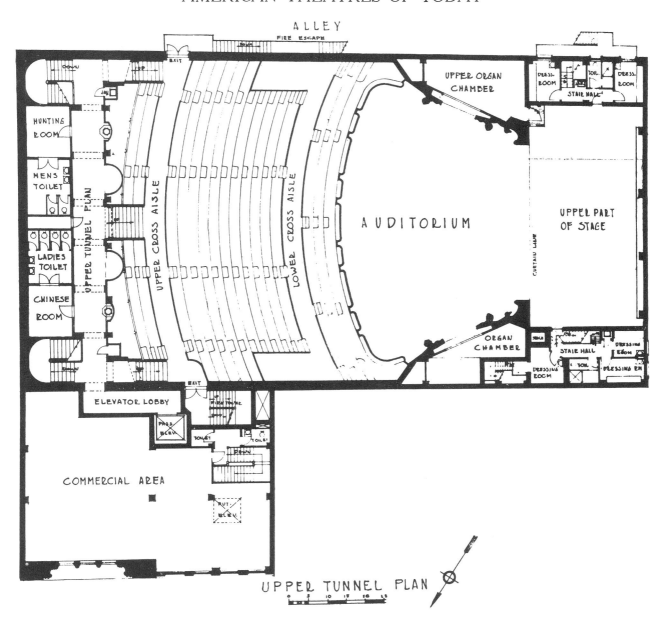

ALABAMA THEATRE, BIRMINGHAM, ALA.
GRAVEN & MAYGER, ARCHITECTS.

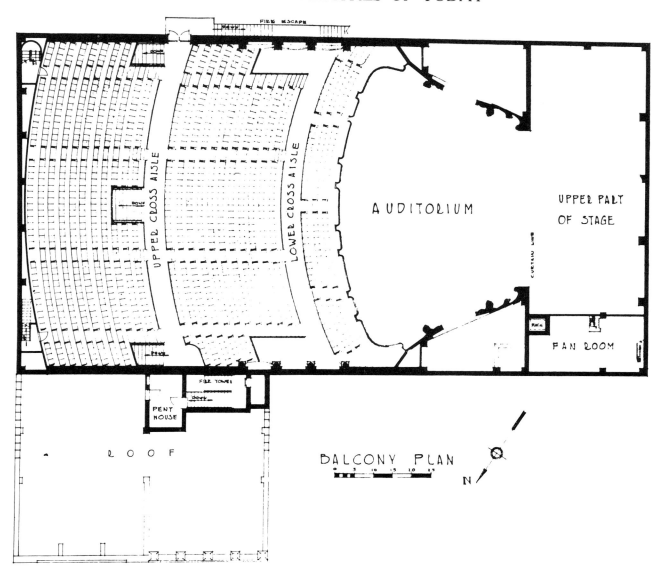

ALABAMA THEATRE, BIRMINGHAM, ALA.

CRAVEN & MAYGER, ARCHITECTS.

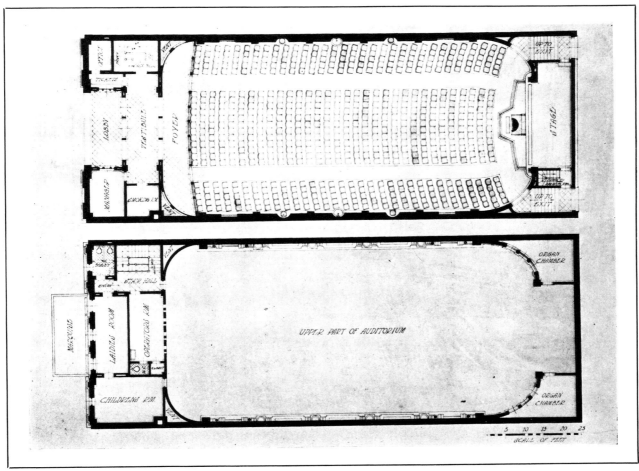

CAPITOL THEATRE, RICHMOND, VA.
CARNEAL & JOHNSTON, ARCHITECTS.

(Courtesy The American Architect.)

FLORIDA THEATRE, JACKSONVILLE, FLA.
R. E. HALL & CO., INC., ARCHITECTS AND ENGINEERS.

FLORIDA THEATRE, JACKSONVILLE, FLA.
R. E. HALL & CO., INC., ARCHITECTS AND ENGINEERS.

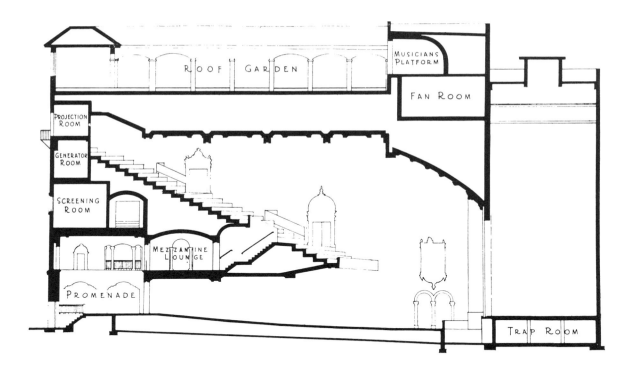

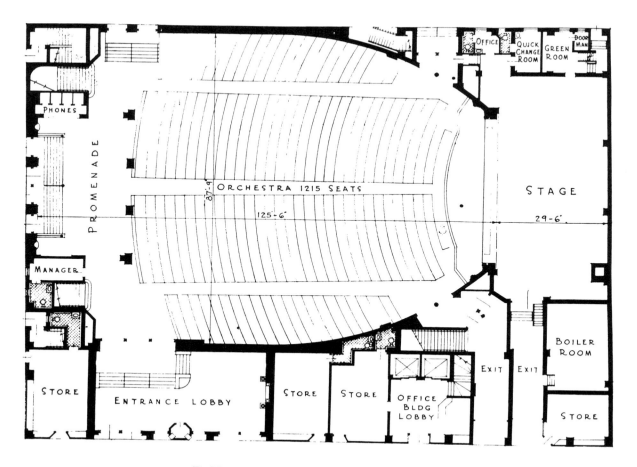

FLORIDA THEATRE, JACKSONVILLE, FLA.

R. E. HALL & CO., INC., ARCHITECTS AND ENGINEERS.

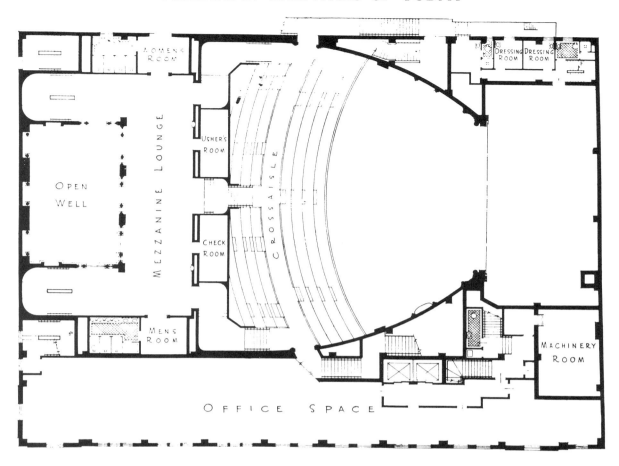

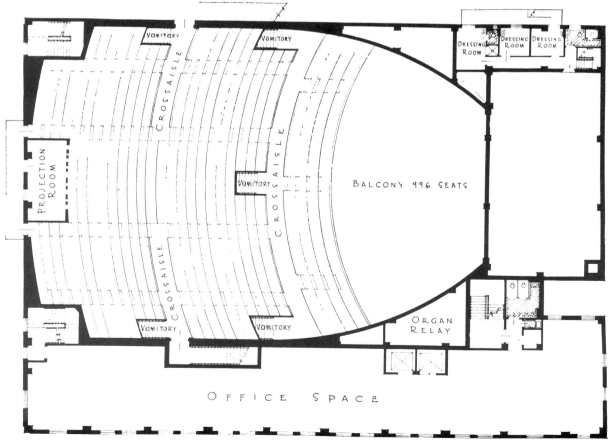

FLORIDA THEATRE, JACKSONVILLE, FLA.

R. E. HALL & CO., INC., ARCHITECTS AND ENGINEERS.

BELASCO THEATRE, HOLLYWOOD, CAL.
MORGAN, WALLS & CLEMENTS, ARCHITECTS.

BELASCO THEATRE, HOLLYWOOD, CAL.
Morgan, Walls & Clements, Architects.

81

BELASCO THEATRE, HOLLYWOOD, CAL.
Morgan, Walls & Clements, Architects.

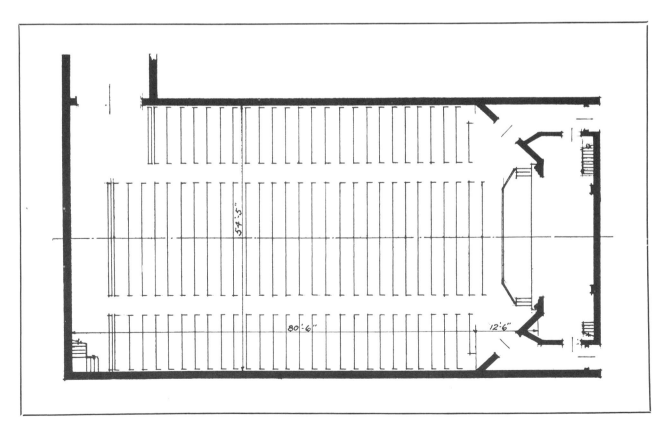

CAPITOL THEATRE, PLANT CITY, FLA.
ROY A. BENJAMIN, ARCHITECT.

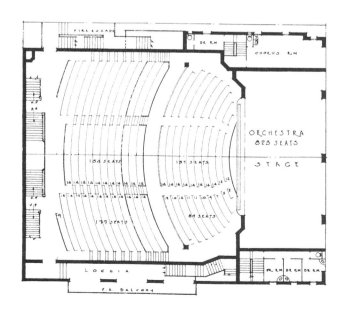
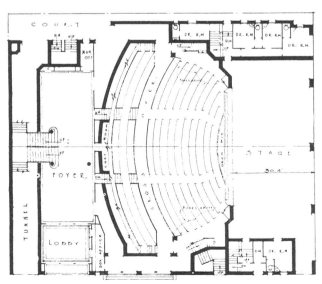

FORTY-SIXTH STREET THEATRE, NEW YORK, N. Y.
HERBERT J. KRAPP, ARCHITECT.

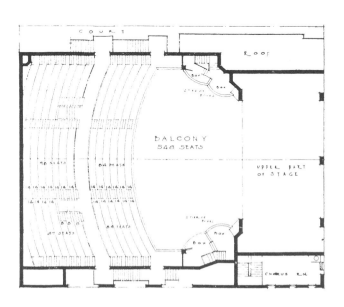

This theatre was designed for the presentation of the legitimate drama. It is of the balcony type, with a seating capacity of 1371, the orchestra seating 823 and the balcony seating 548 persons.

FORTY-SIXTH STREET THEATRE, NEW YORK, N. Y.

HERBERT J. KRAPP, ARCHITECT.

BELLEVUE THEATRE, MONTCLAIR, N. J.
J. H. Phillips, Architect.

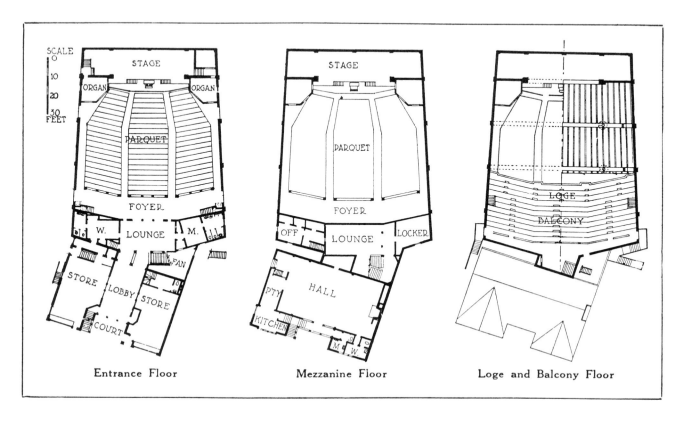

Entrance Floor   Mezzanine Floor   Loge and Balcony Floor

BELLEVUE THEATRE, MONTCLAIR, N. J.

J. H. PHILLIPS, ARCHITECT.

INWOOD THEATRE, NEW YORK, N. Y.
Eugene De Rosa, Architect.

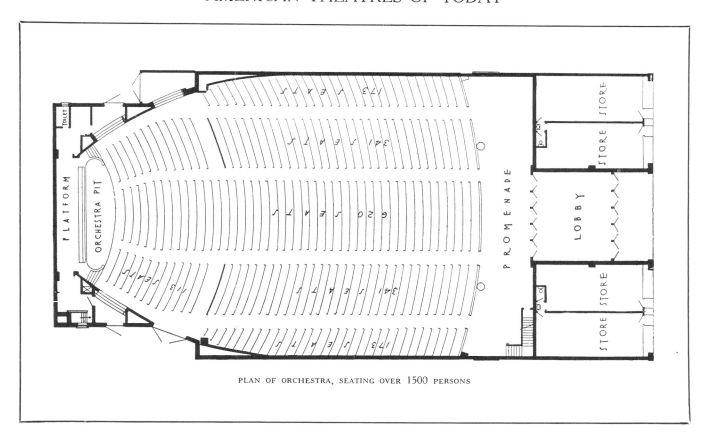

PLAN OF ORCHESTRA, SEATING OVER 1500 PERSONS

INWOOD THEATRE, NEW YORK, N. Y.

Eugene De Rosa, Architect.

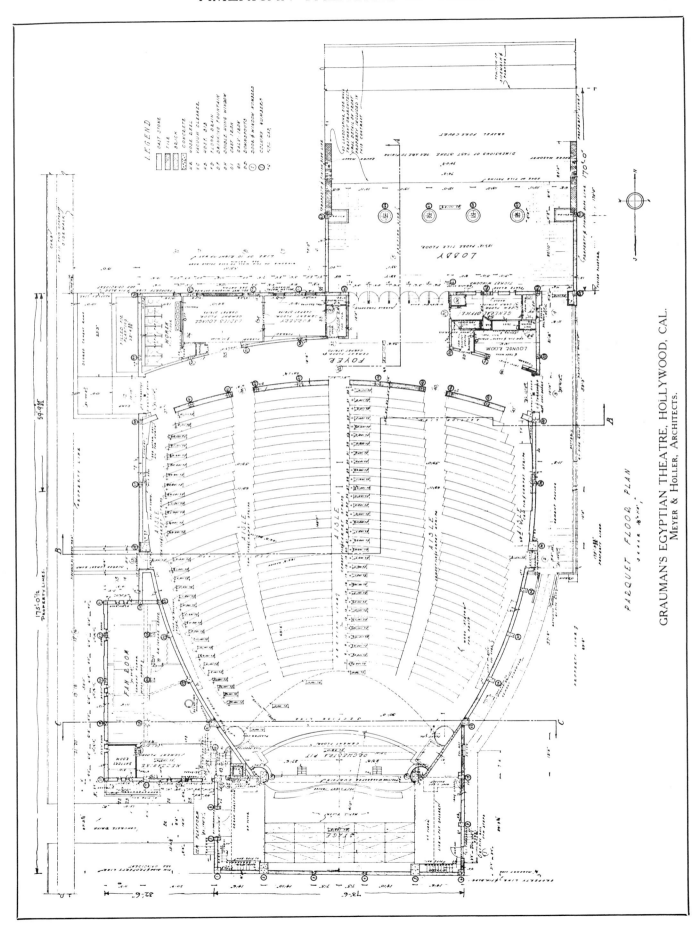

PARQUET FLOOR PLAN

GRAUMAN'S EGYPTIAN THEATRE, HOLLYWOOD, CAL.

MEYER & HOLLER, ARCHITECTS.

GRAUMAN'S EGYPTIAN THEATRE, HOLLYWOOD, CAL.

MEYER & HOLLER, ARCHITECTS.

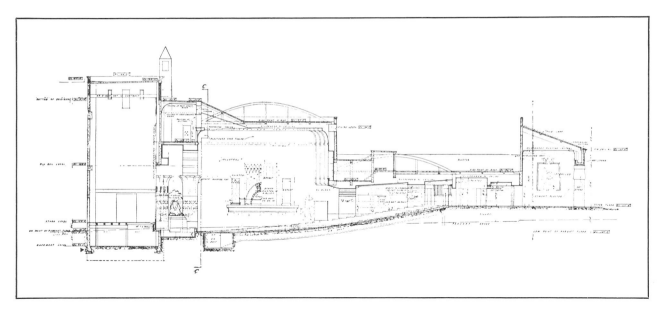

LONGITUDINAL SECTION

GRAUMAN'S EGYPTIAN THEATRE, HOLLYWOOD, CAL.
MEYER & HOLLER, ARCHITECTS.

EXTERIOR DETAILS

GRAUMAN'S EGYPTIAN THEATRE, HOLLYWOOD, CAL.

MEYER & HOLLER, ARCHITECTS.

MUSIC BOX THEATRE, HOLLYWOOD, CAL.
MORGAN, WALLS & CLEMENTS, ARCHITECTS.

MUSIC BOX THEATRE, HOLLYWOOD, CAL.
Morgan, Walls & Clements, Architects.

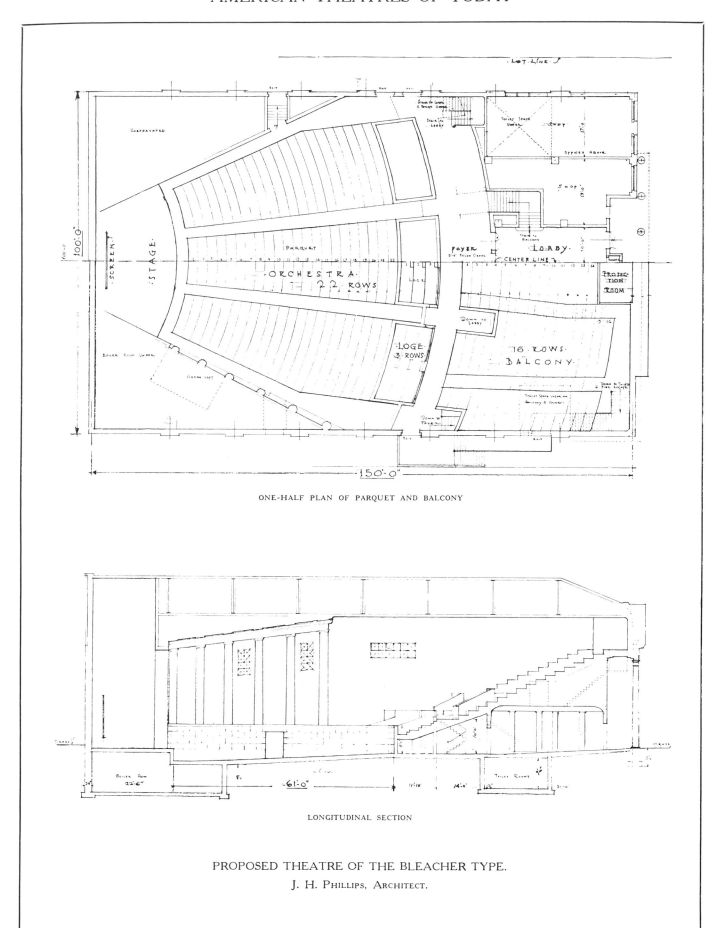

ONE-HALF PLAN OF PARQUET AND BALCONY

LONGITUDINAL SECTION

PROPOSED THEATRE OF THE BLEACHER TYPE.
J. H. Phillips, Architect.

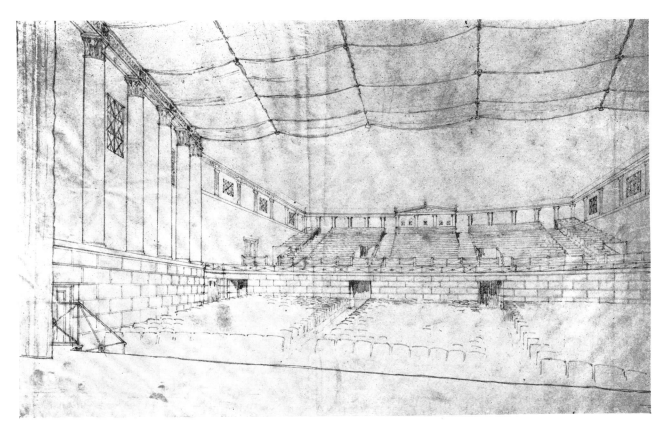

PROPOSED THEATRE OF THE BLEACHER TYPE.
J. H. PHILLIPS, ARCHITECT.

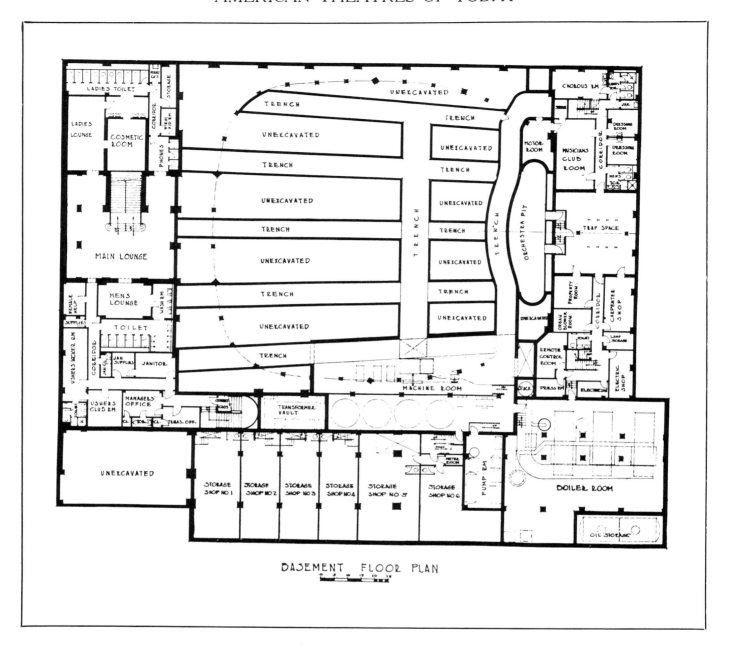

BASEMENT FLOOR PLAN

MINNEAPOLIS THEATRE, MINNEAPOLIS, MINN.

Graven & Mayger, Architects.

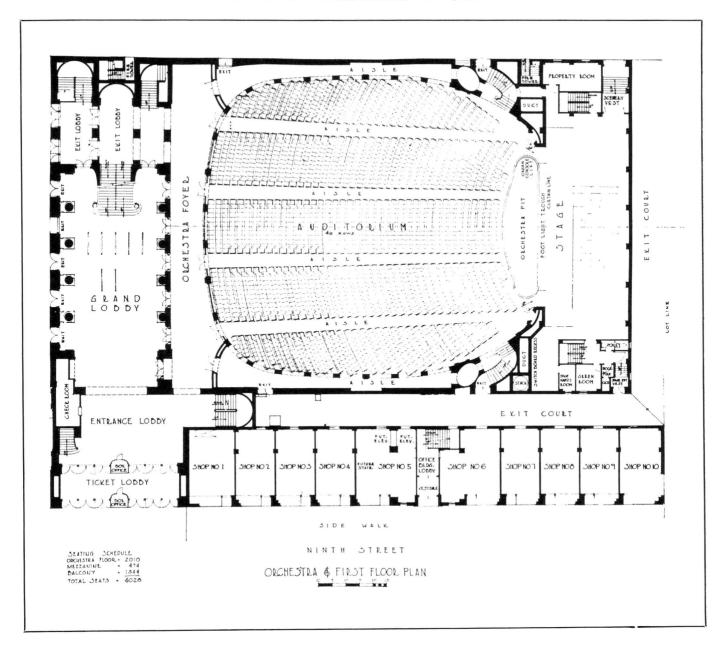

MINNEAPOLIS THEATRE, MINNEAPOLIS, MINN.

GRAVEN & MAYGER, ARCHITECTS.

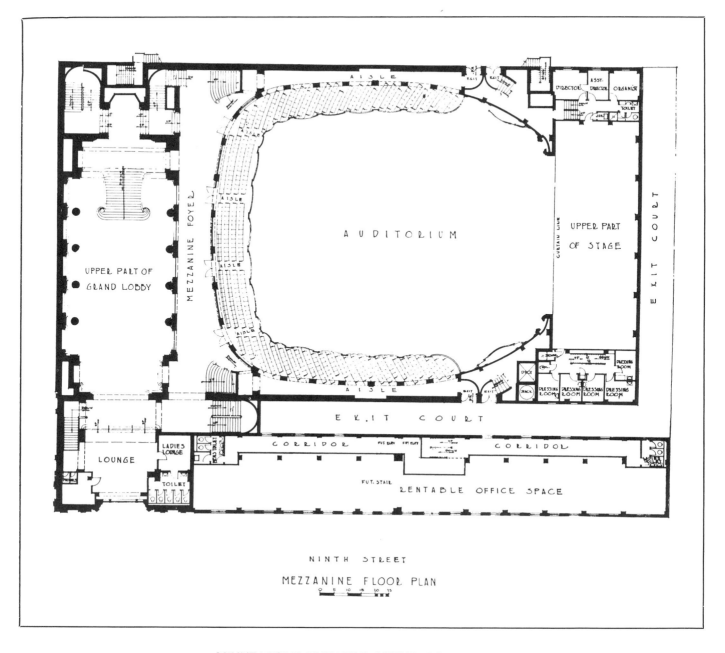

MINNEAPOLIS THEATRE, MINNEAPOLIS, MINN.
GRAVEN & MAYGER, ARCHITECTS.

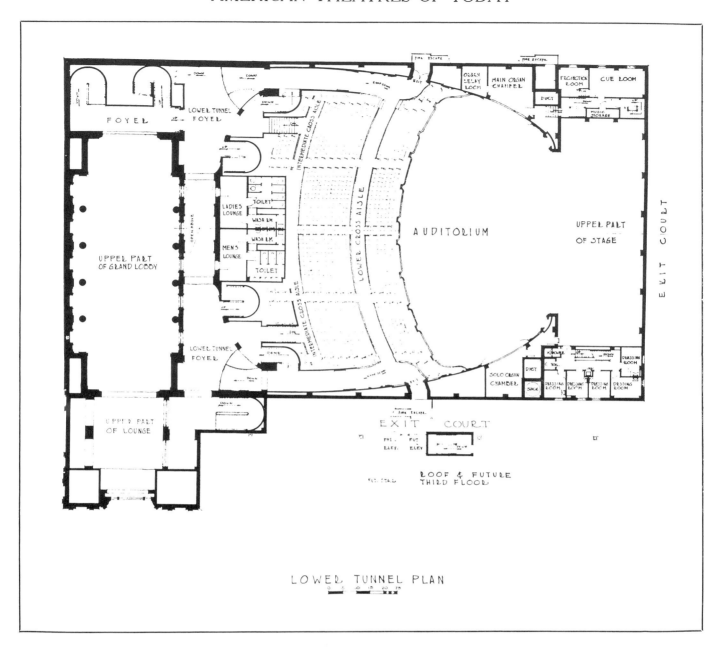

LOWER TUNNEL PLAN

MINNEAPOLIS THEATRE, MINNEAPOLIS, MINN.
Graven & Mayger, Architects.

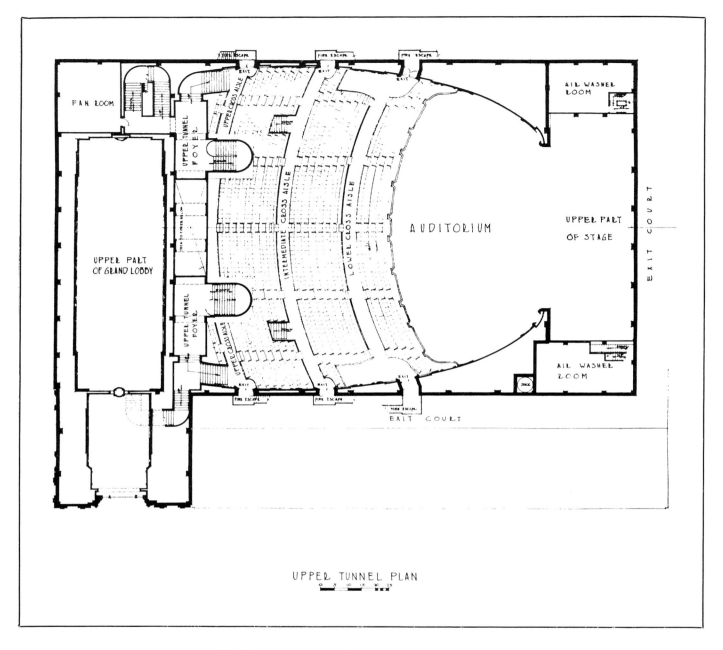

UPPER TUNNEL PLAN

MINNEAPOLIS THEATRE, MINNEAPOLIS, MINN.
GRAVEN & MAYGER, ARCHITECTS.

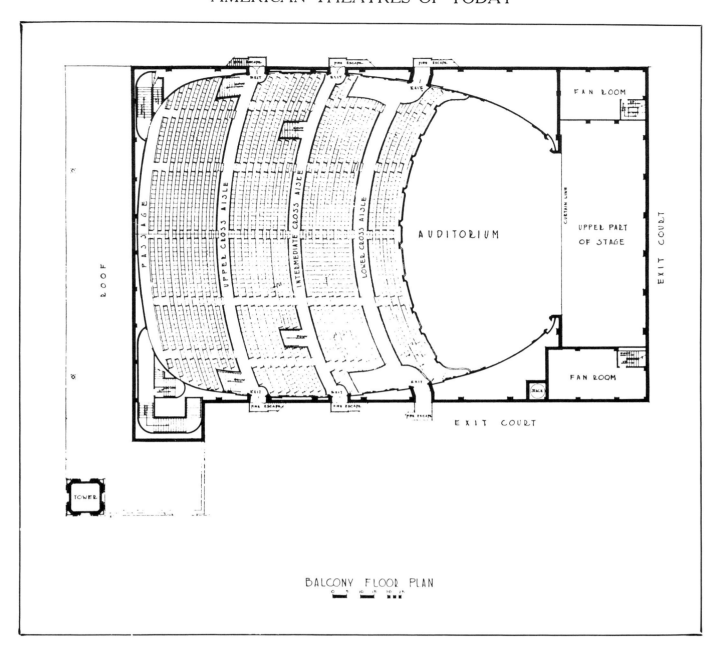

BALCONY FLOOR PLAN

MINNEAPOLIS THEATRE, MINNEAPOLIS, MINN.

GRAVEN & MAYGER, ARCHITECTS.

IMPERIAL THEATRE, JACKSONVILLE, FLA.

ROY A. BENJAMIN, ARCHITECT.

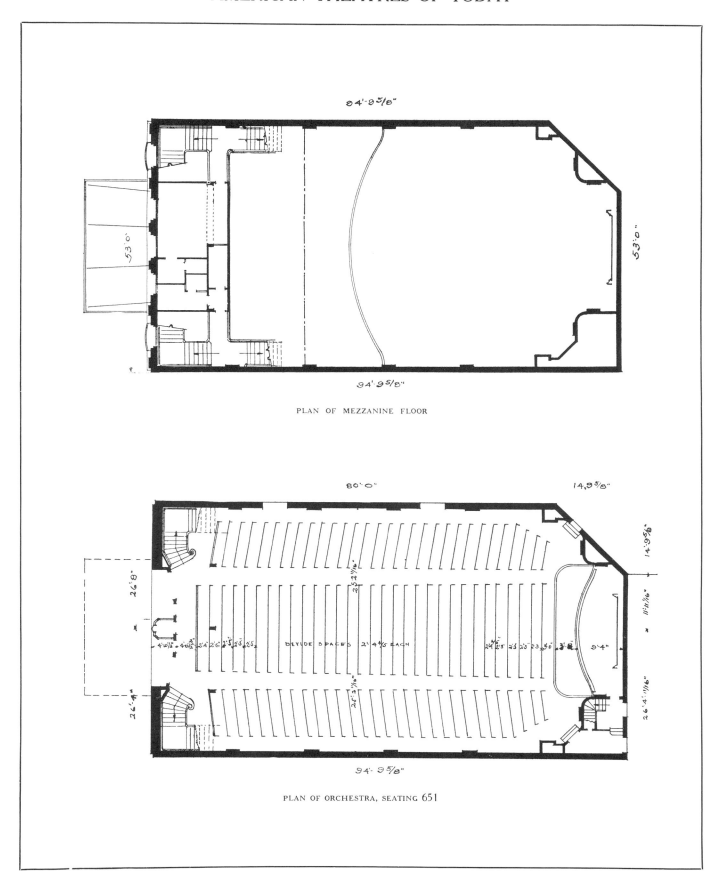

PLAN OF MEZZANINE FLOOR

PLAN OF ORCHESTRA, SEATING 651

IMPERIAL THEATRE, JACKSONVILLE, FLA.
ROY A. BENJAMIN, ARCHITECT.

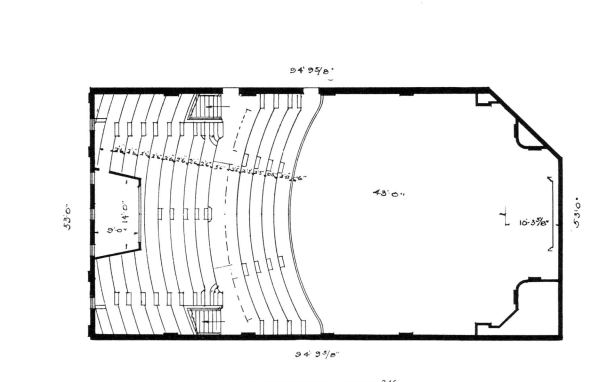

PLAN OF BALCONY, SEATING 346

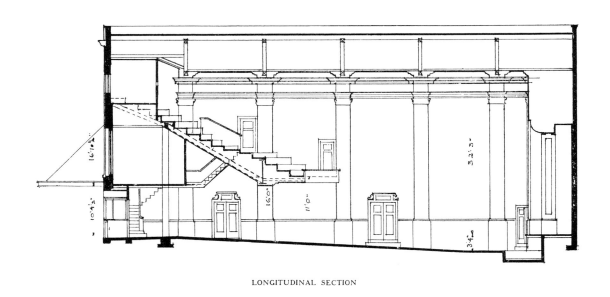

LONGITUDINAL SECTION

IMPERIAL THEATRE, JACKSONVILLE, FLA.

ROY A. BENJAMIN, ARCHITECT.

ROYALE THEATRE, NEW YORK, N. Y.
HERBERT J. KRAPP, ARCHITECT

RITZ THEATRE, VALDOSTA, GA.
Roy A. Benjamin, Architect.

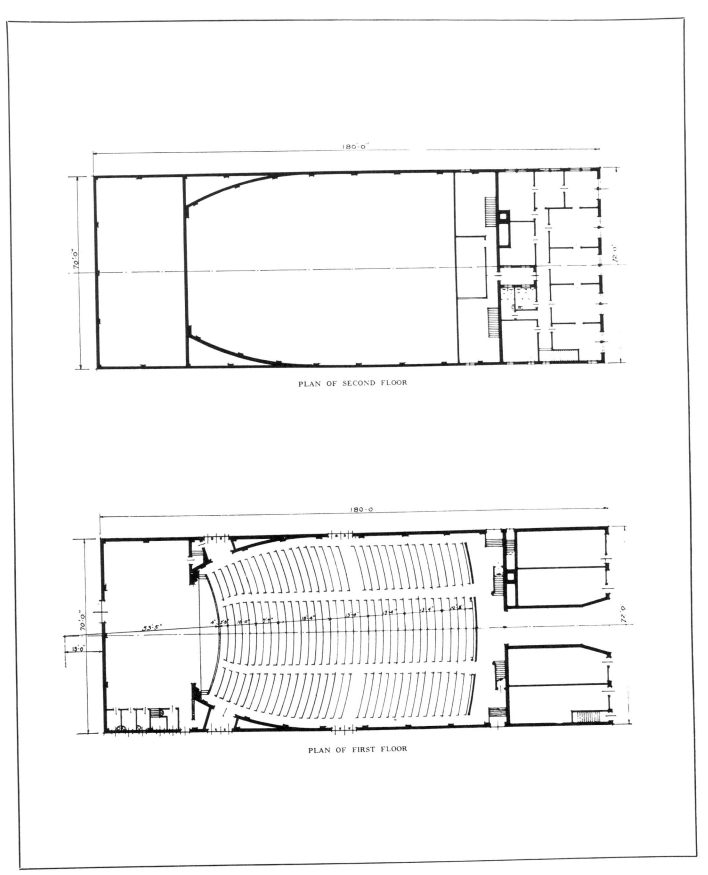

PLAN OF SECOND FLOOR

PLAN OF FIRST FLOOR

RITZ THEATRE, VALDOSTA, GA.

Roy A. Benjamin, Architect.

109

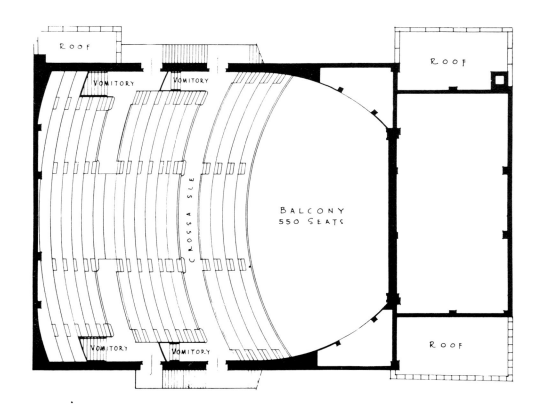

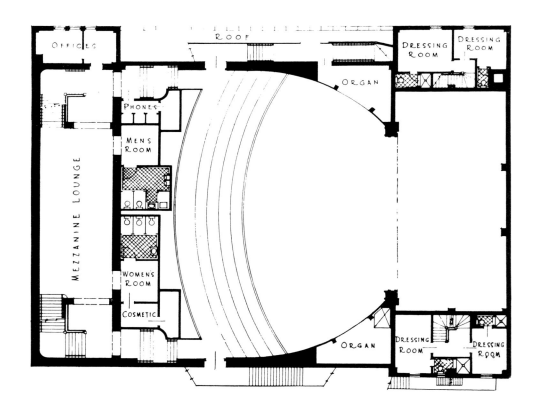

CAROLINA THEATRE, CHARLOTTE, N. C.

R. E. HALL & CO., INC., ARCHITECTS & ENGINEERS.

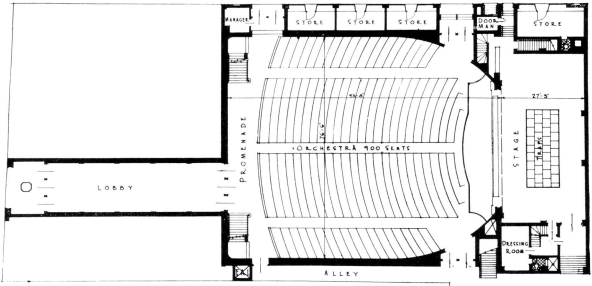

CAROLINA THEATRE, CHARLOTTE, N. C.

R. E. HALL & CO., INC., ARCHITECTS & ENGINEERS.

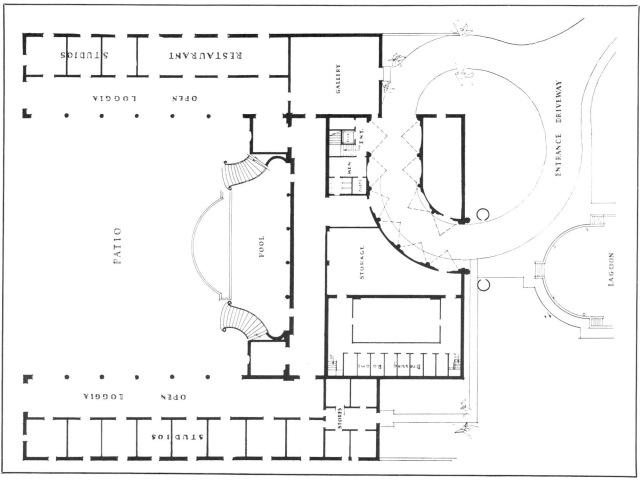

PROPOSED THEATRE, FLORIDA.

J. H. PHILLIPS, ARCHITECT.

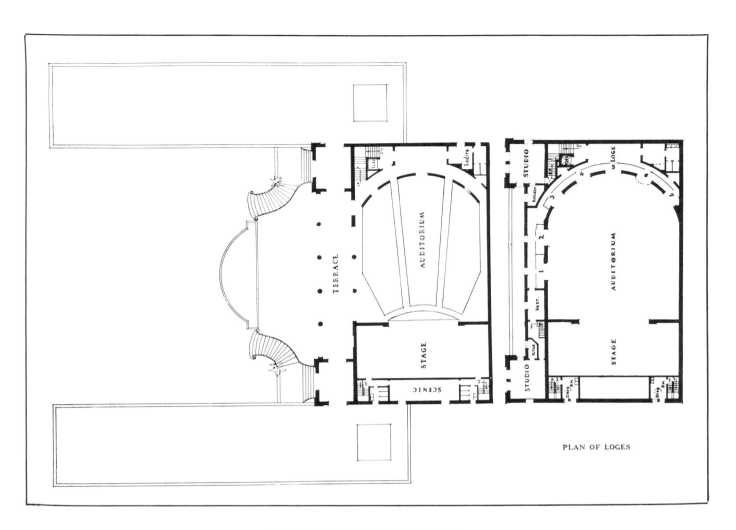

PROPOSED THEATRE, FLORIDA.
J. H. Phillips, Architect.

PLAN OF LOGES

113

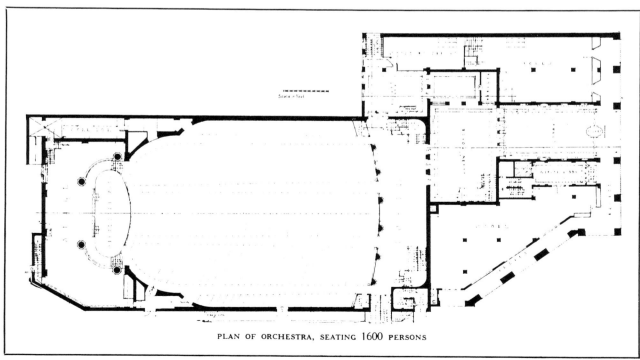

PLAN OF ORCHESTRA, SEATING 1600 PERSONS

TEXAS THEATRE, SAN ANTONIO, TEXAS.
BOLLER BROTHERS, ARCHITECTS, R. E. HALL & CO., CONSULTING ENGINEERS.

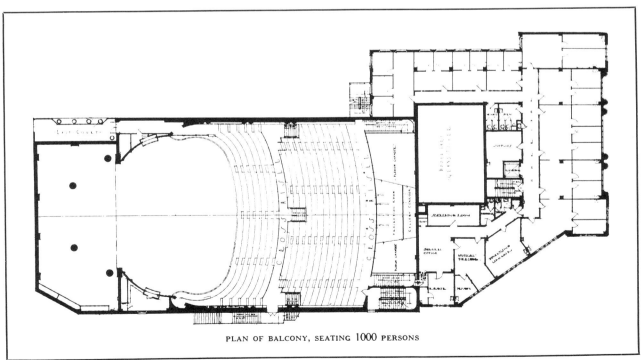

PLAN OF BALCONY, SEATING 1000 PERSONS

TEXAS THEATRE, SAN ANTONIO, TEXAS.
BOLLER BROTHERS, ARCHITECTS, R. E. HALL & CO., CONSULTING ENGINEERS.

THE MAIN FOYER

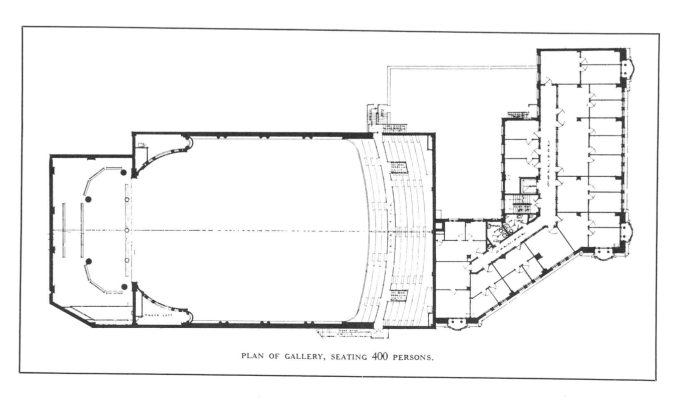

PLAN OF GALLERY, SEATING 400 PERSONS.

TEXAS THEATRE, SAN ANTONIO, TEXAS.

BOLLER BROTHERS, ARCHITECTS, R. E. HALL & CO., CONSULTING ENGINEERS.

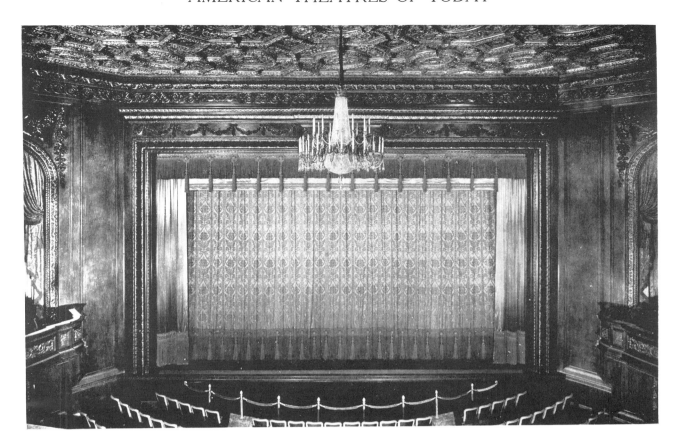

SELWYN THEATRE, CHICAGO, ILL.
C. Howard Crane & Kenneth Franzheim, Architects.

117

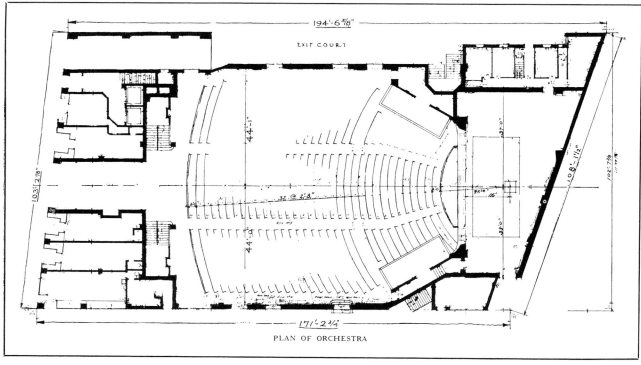

PLAN OF ORCHESTRA

LOEW'S CONEY ISLAND THEATRE, NEW YORK, N. Y.

Reilly & Hall, Architects, Samuel L. Malkind, Associate.

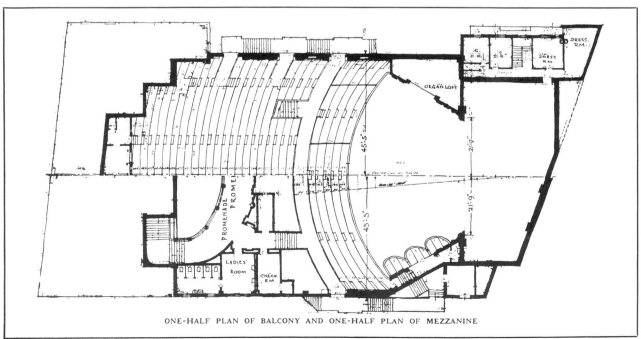

ONE-HALF PLAN OF BALCONY AND ONE-HALF PLAN OF MEZZANINE

LOEW'S CONEY ISLAND THEATRE, NEW YORK, N. Y.

REILLY & HALL, ARCHITECTS, SAMUEL L. MALKIND, ASSOCIATE.

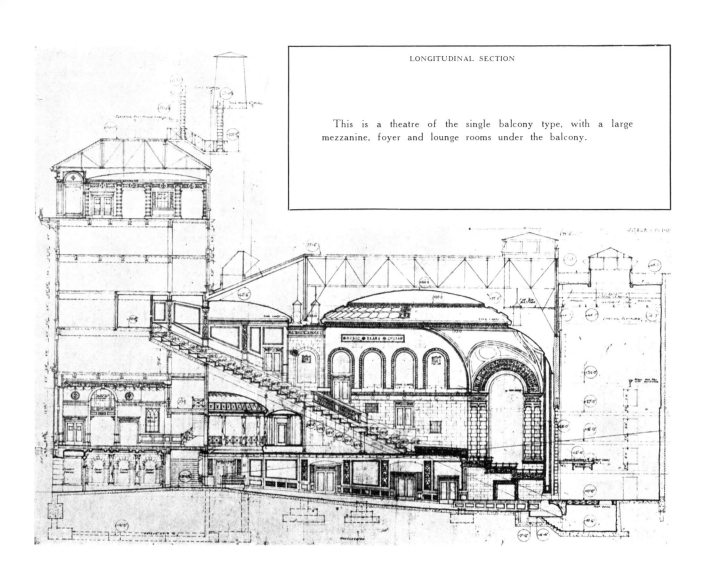

This is a theatre of the single balcony type, with a large mezzanine, foyer and lounge rooms under the balcony.

LOEW'S CONEY ISLAND THEATRE, NEW YORK, N. Y.
REILLY & HALL, ARCHITECTS, SAMUEL L. MALKIND, ASSOCIATE.

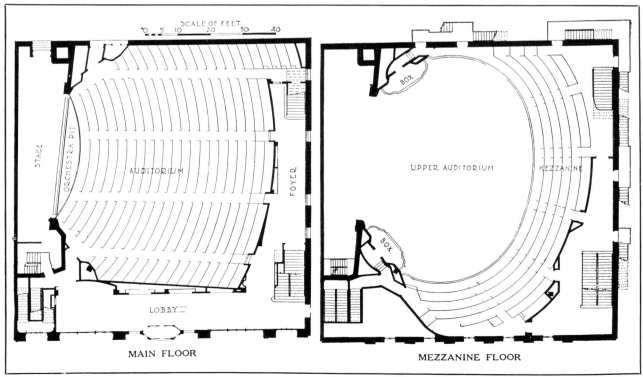

MAIN FLOOR

MEZZANINE FLOOR

ROOSEVELT THEATRE, CHICAGO, ILL.

C. Howard Crane & Kenneth Franzheim, Architects.

121

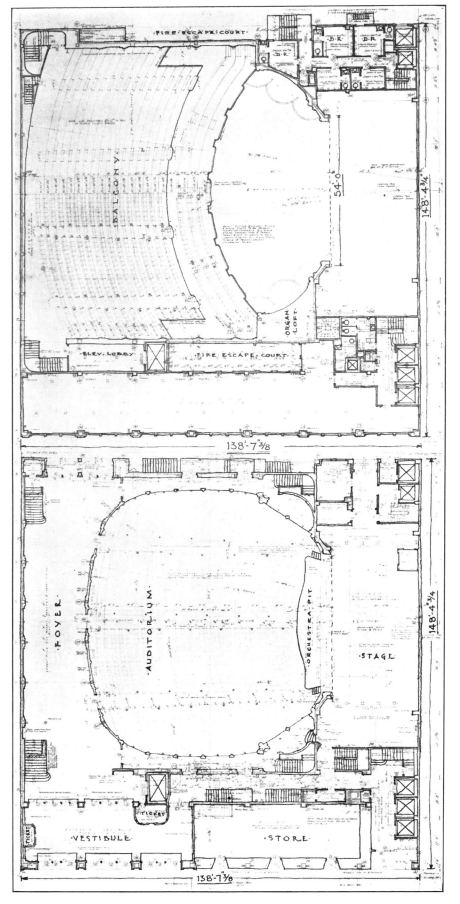

PLAN OF BALCONY

PLAN OF ORCHESTRA

This theatre is equipped for the presentation of the legitimate drama.

ORPHEUM THEATRE, LOS ANGELES, CAL.

G. ALBERT LANSBURGH, ARCHITECT.

ORPHEUM THEATRE, LOS ANGELES, CAL.

G. ALBERT LANSBURGH, ARCHITECT.

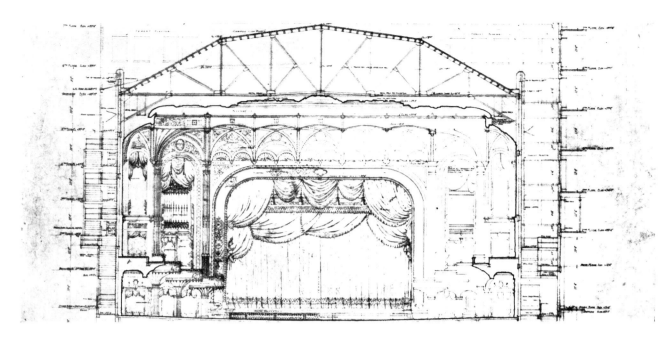

TRANSVERSE SECTION

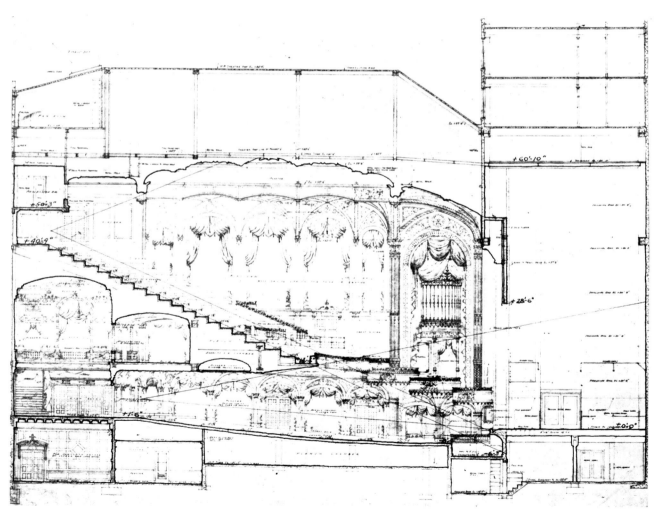

LONGITUDINAL SECTION

ORPHEUM THEATRE, LOS ANGELES, CAL.

G. Albert Lansburgh, Architect.

THE MAIN FOYER

BALCONY SOFFIT

ORPHEUM THEATRE, LOS ANGELES, CAL.
G. ALBERT LANSBURGH, ARCHITECT.

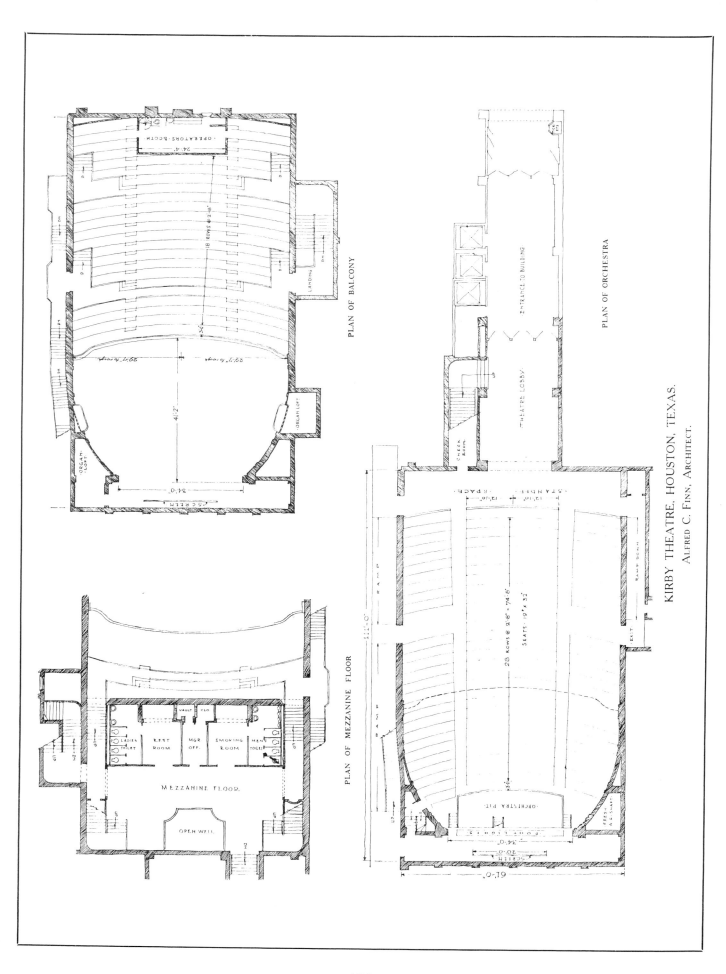

PLAN OF BALCONY

PLAN OF MEZZANINE FLOOR

PLAN OF ORCHESTRA

KIRBY THEATRE, HOUSTON, TEXAS.
Alfred C. Finn, Architect.

126

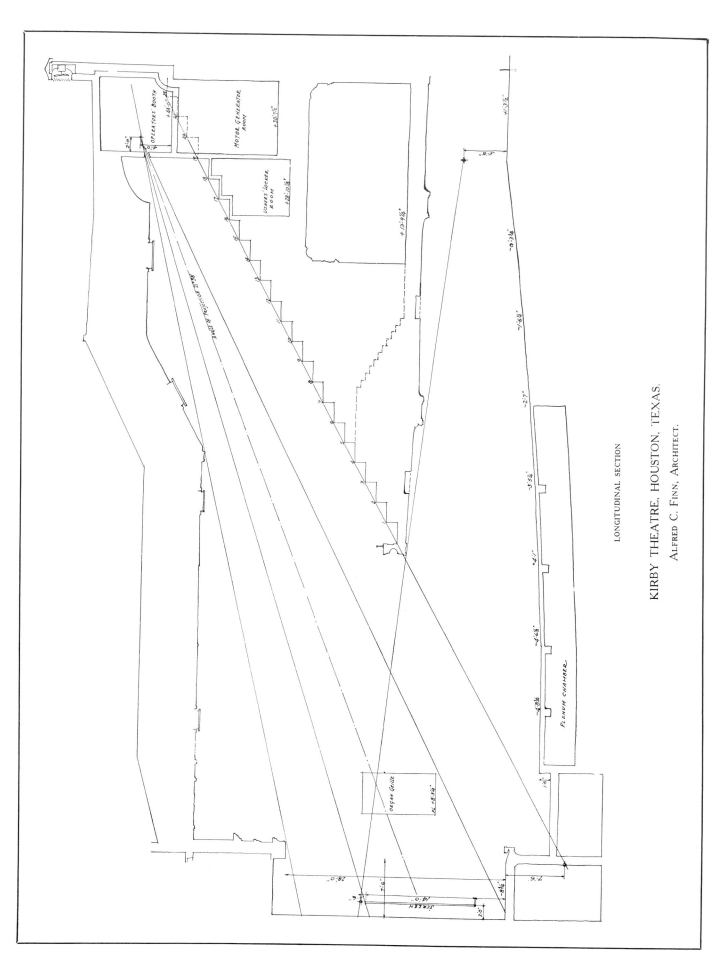

LONGITUDINAL SECTION

KIRBY THEATRE. HOUSTON, TEXAS.

Alfred C. Finn, Architect.

ZIEGFELD THEATRE, NEW YORK, N. Y.

Joseph Urban and Thomas W. Lamb, Associated Architects.

DETAILS OF THE FANTASTIC DECORATION WHICH COVERS THE ENTIRE WALL SURFACE

ZIEGFELD THEATRE, NEW YORK, N. Y.
JOSEPH URBAN AND THOMAS W. LAMB, ASSOCIATED ARCHITECTS.

LONGITUDINAL SECTION
ZIEGFELD THEATRE, NEW YORK, N. Y.
JOSEPH URBAN AND THOMAS W. LAMB, ASSOCIATED ARCHITECTS.

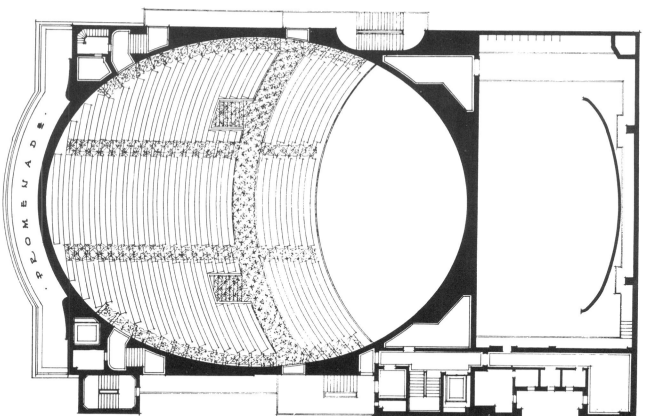

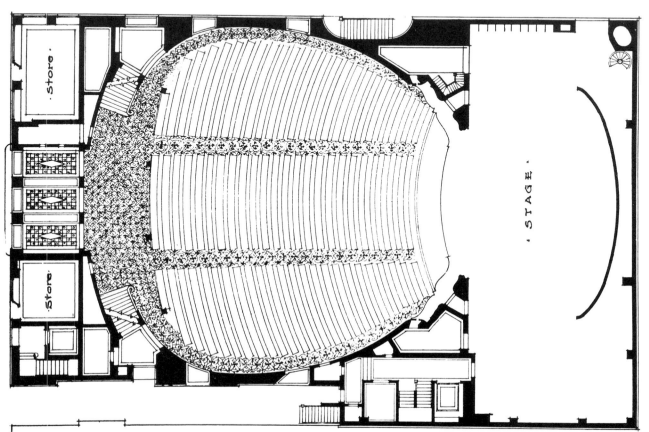

ZIEGFELD THEATRE, NEW YORK, N. Y.

Joseph Urban and Thomas W. Lamb, Associated Architects.

131

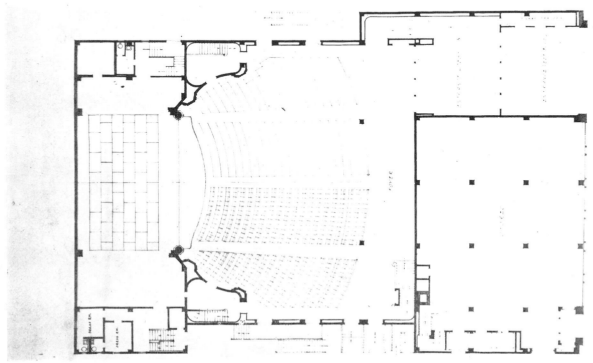

EL CAPITAN THEATRE, HOLLYWOOD, CAL.
G. Albert Lansburgh, Architect.

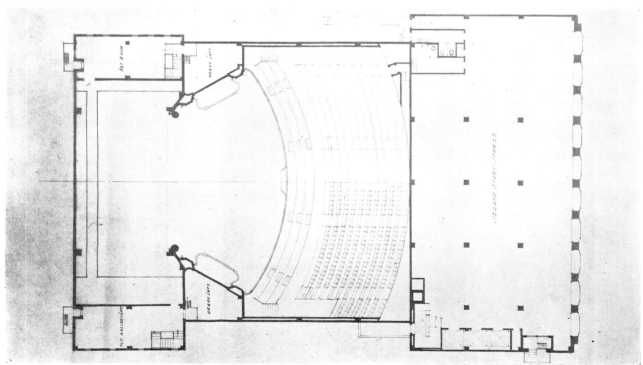

EL CAPITAN THEATRE, HOLLYWOOD, CAL.
G. ALBERT LANSBURGH, ARCHITECT.

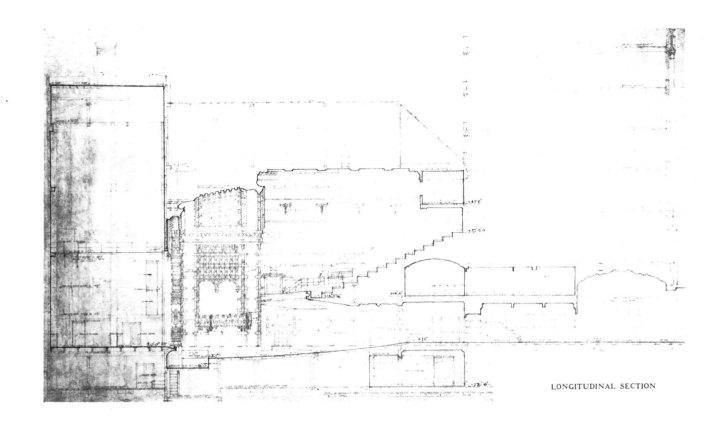

LONGITUDINAL SECTION

EL CAPITAN THEATRE, HOLLYWOOD, CAL.

G. Albert Lansburgh, Architect.

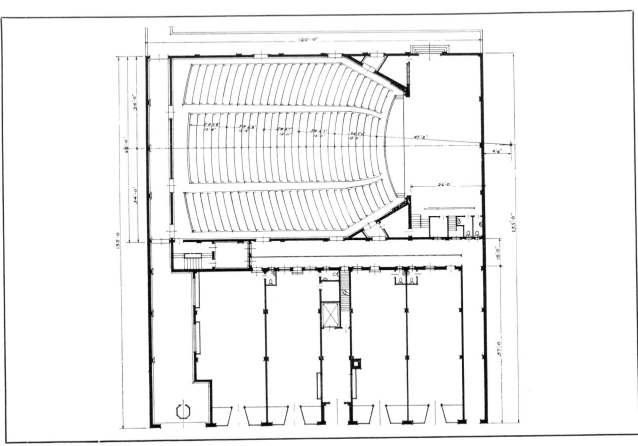

RIVERSIDE THEATRE, JACKSONVILLE, FLA.

Roy A. Benjamin, Architect.

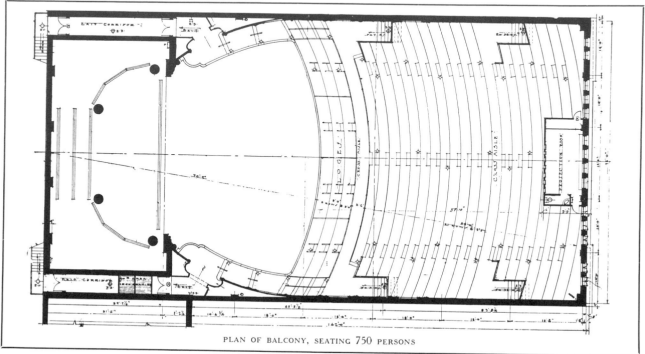

PLAN OF BALCONY, SEATING 750 PERSONS

LINCOLN THEATRE, LINCOLN, NEB.

BOLLER BROTHERS, ARCHITECTS, R. E. HALL & CO., CONSULTING ENGINEERS.

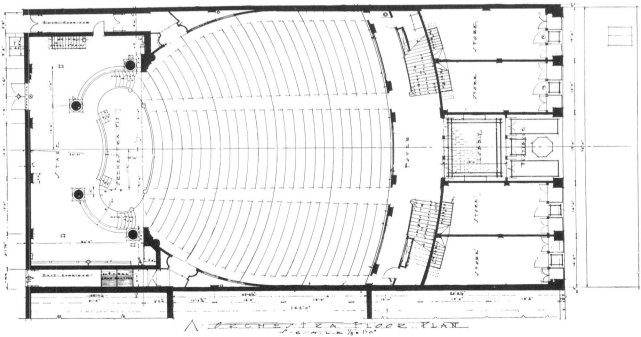

PLAN OF ORCHESTRA, SEATING 850 PERSONS

LINCOLN THEATRE, LINCOLN, NEB.
Boller Brothers, Architects, R. E. Hall & Co., Consulting Engineers.

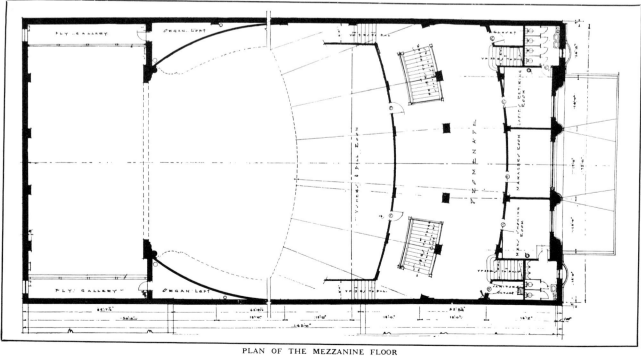

PLAN OF THE MEZZANINE FLOOR

LINCOLN THEATRE, LINCOLN, NEB.
BOLLER BROTHERS, ARCHITECTS, R. E. HALL & CO., CONSULTING ENGINEERS.

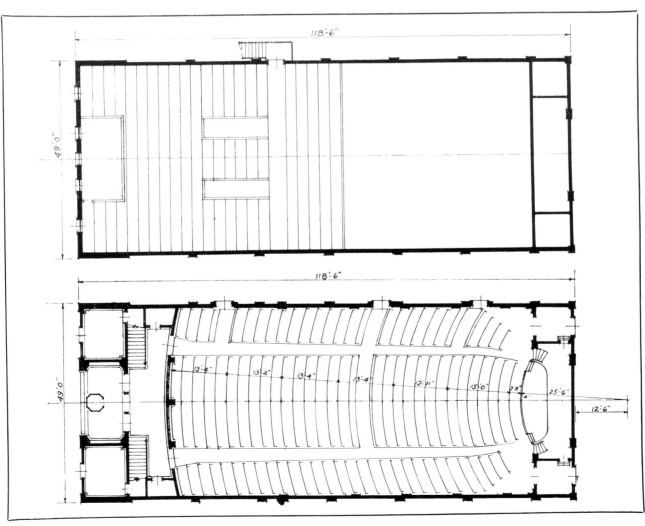

PALACE THEATRE, LAKELAND, FLA.

Roy A. Benjamin, Architect.

139

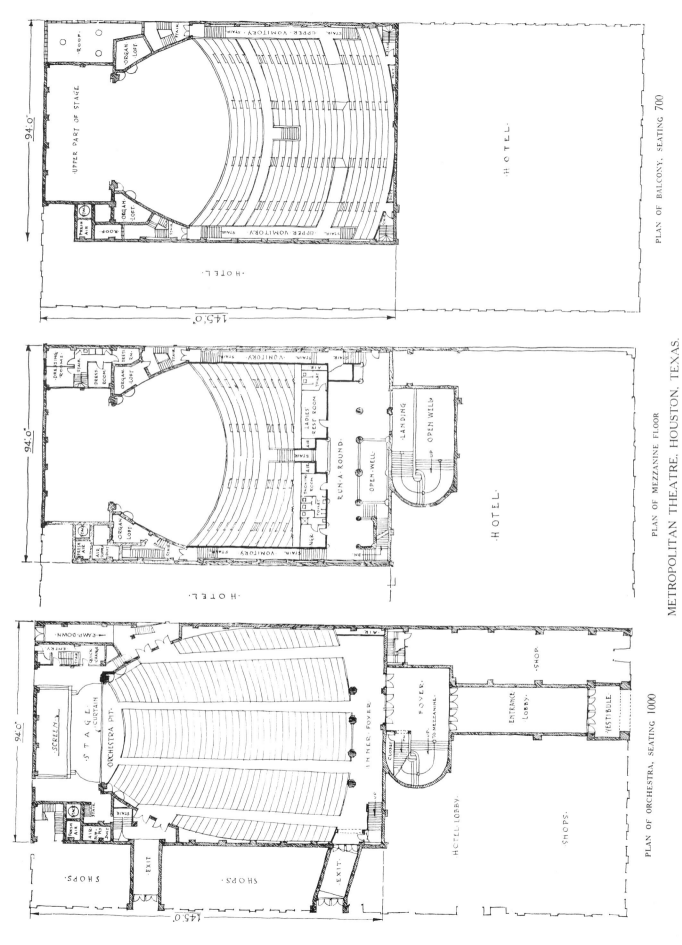

PLAN OF BALCONY, SEATING 700

PLAN OF MEZZANINE FLOOR

PLAN OF ORCHESTRA, SEATING 1000

METROPOLITAN THEATRE. HOUSTON, TEXAS.

Alfred C. Finn, Architect. R. E. Hall & Co., Consulting Engineers.

140

METROPOLITAN THEATRE, HOUSTON, TEXAS.

Alfred C. Finn, Architect, R. E. Hall & Co., Consulting Engineers.

141

METROPOLITAN THEATRE, HOUSTON, TEXAS.

Alfred C. Finn, Architect, R. E. Hall & Co., Consulting Engineers.

LAFAYETTE THEATRE, SUFFERN, N. Y.

Eugene De Rosa, Architect.

143

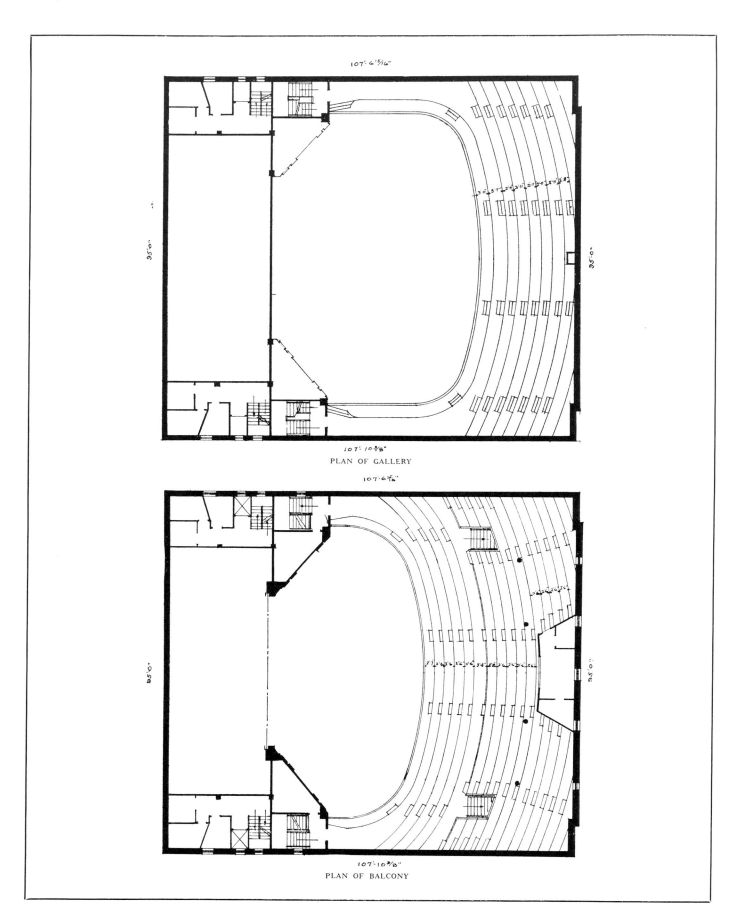

PLAN OF GALLERY

PLAN OF BALCONY

PALACE THEATRE, JACKSONVILLE, FLA.

Roy A. Benjamin, Architect.

144

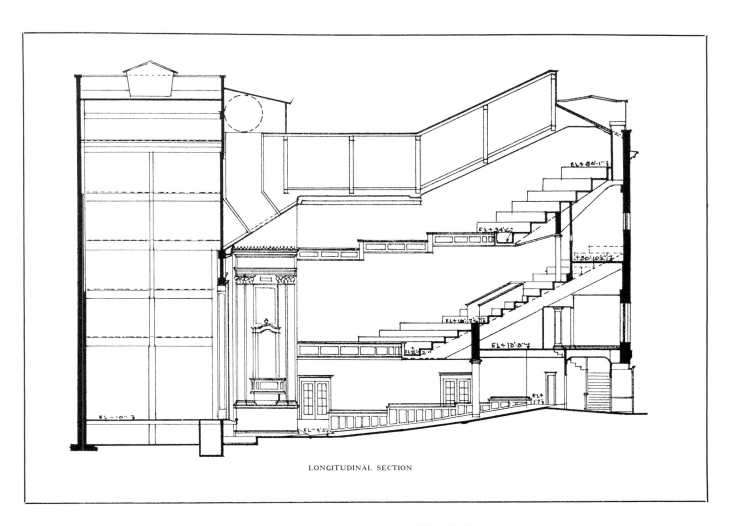

LONGITUDINAL SECTION

PALACE THEATRE, JACKSONVILLE, FLA.
Roy A. Benjamin, Architect.

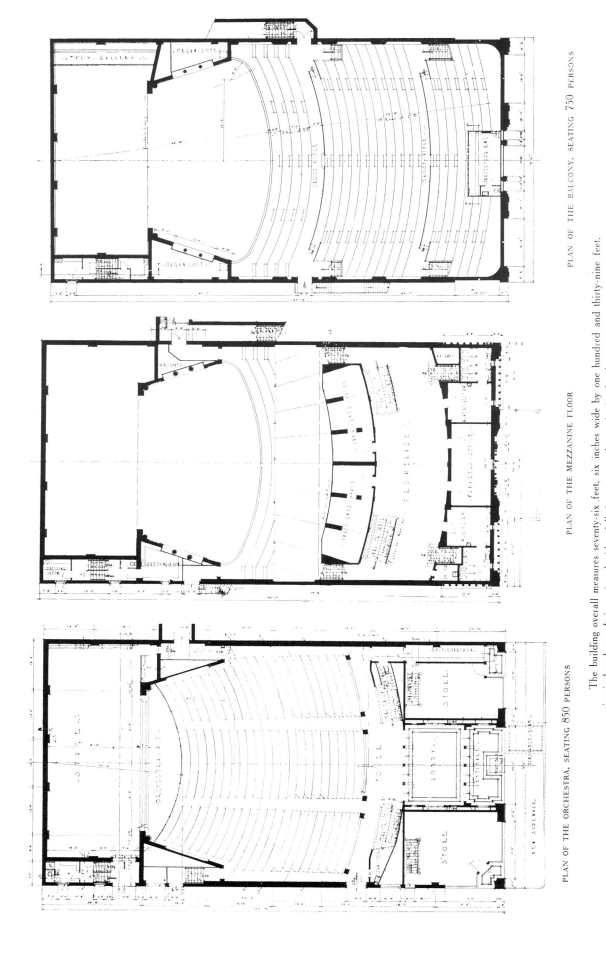

PLAN OF THE BALCONY, SEATING 750 PERSONS

PLAN OF THE MEZZANINE FLOOR

PLAN OF THE ORCHESTRA, SEATING 850 PERSONS

The building overall measures seventy-six feet, six inches wide by one hundred and thirty-nine feet, nine inches deep. It is equipped with a full size stage, and a projection booth.

MISSOURI THEATRE, ST. JOSEPH, MO.
BOLLER BROTHERS, ARCHITECTS.

MISSOURI THEATRE, ST. JOSEPH, MO.
BOLLER BROTHERS, ARCHITECTS.

A special effort has been made to create an exterior appropriate to the theatre. The electric sign
has been carefully considered as a part of the architecture.

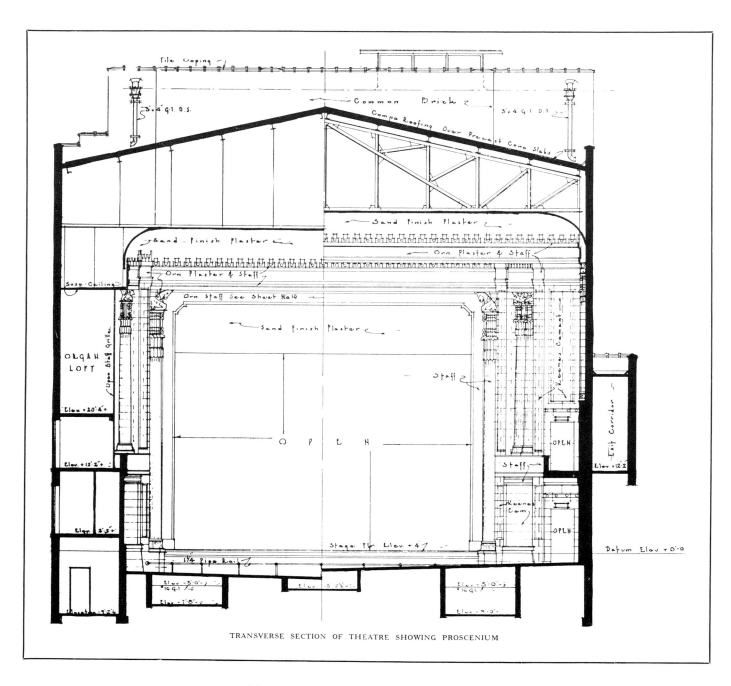

TRANSVERSE SECTION OF THEATRE SHOWING PROSCENIUM

MISSOURI THEATRE, ST. JOSEPH, MO.
BOLLER BROTHERS, ARCHITECTS.

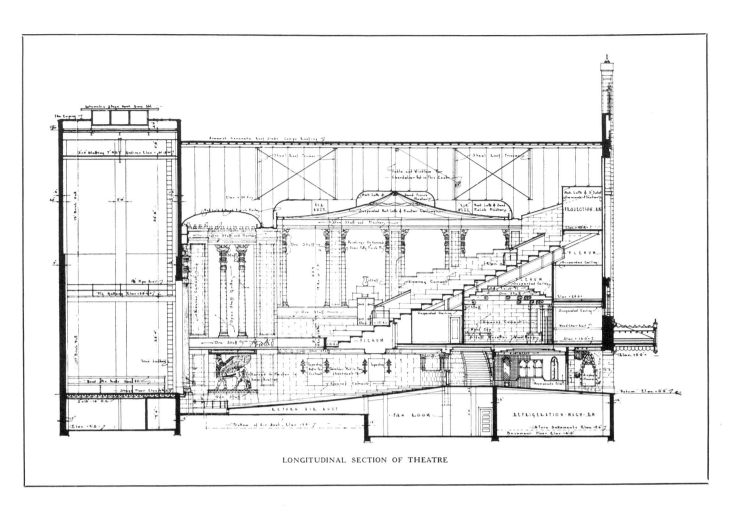

LONGITUDINAL SECTION OF THEATRE

MISSOURI THEATRE, ST. JOSEPH, MO.

Boller Brothers, Architects.

149

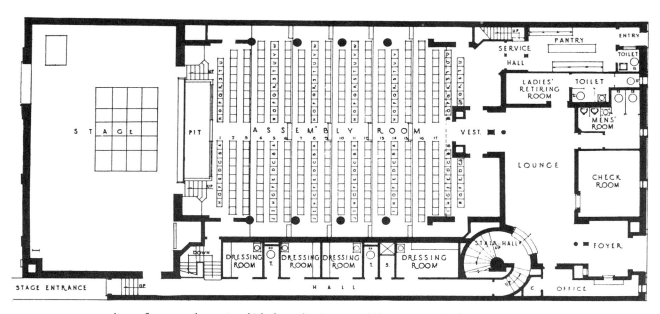

A one-floor type theatre in which the auditorium seats 350 persons, and a loge seats 35 additional.

THE PLAYERS' PLAYHOUSE, DETROIT, MICH.
Smith, Hinchman & Grylls, Architects.

THE LOUNGE SHOWING ENTRANCE TO ASSEMBLY ROOM

THE PLAYERS' PLAYHOUSE, DETROIT, MICH.

SMITH, HINCHMAN & GRYLLS, ARCHITECTS.

THE PLAYERS' PLAYHOUSE, DETROIT, MICH.
SMITH, HINCHMAN & GRYLLS, ARCHITECTS.
DETAIL OF THE INTERIOR OF THEATRE

HARRIS THEATRE, CHICAGO, ILL.

C. Howard Crane & Kenneth Franzheim, Architects.

153

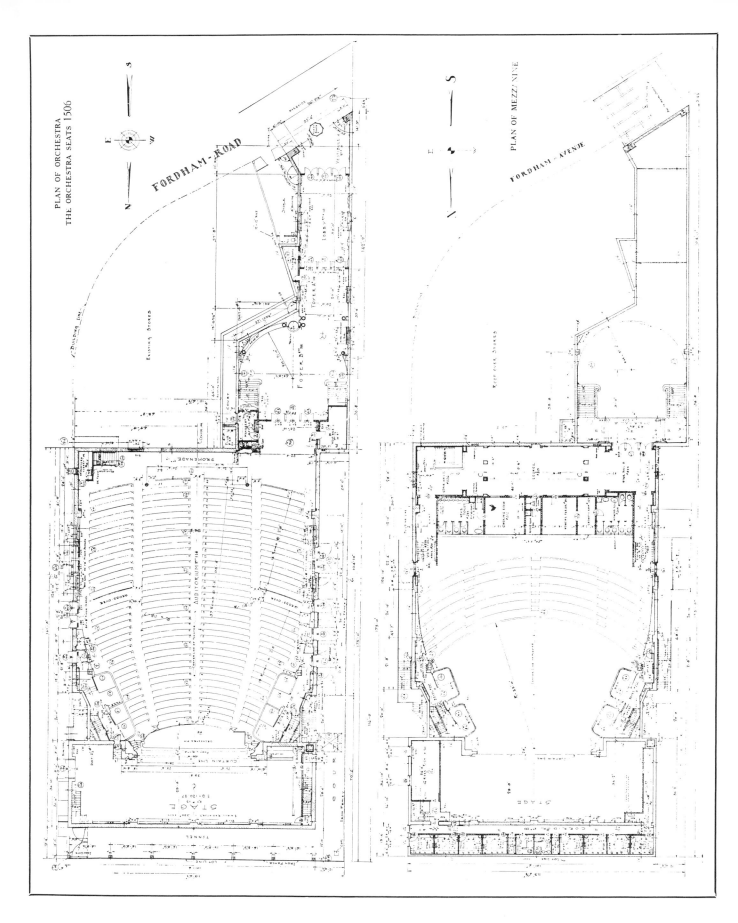

GRAND THEATRE, NEW YORK, N. Y.

Eugene De Rosa, Architect.

154

GRAND THEATRE, NEW YORK.

Eugene De Rosa, Architect.

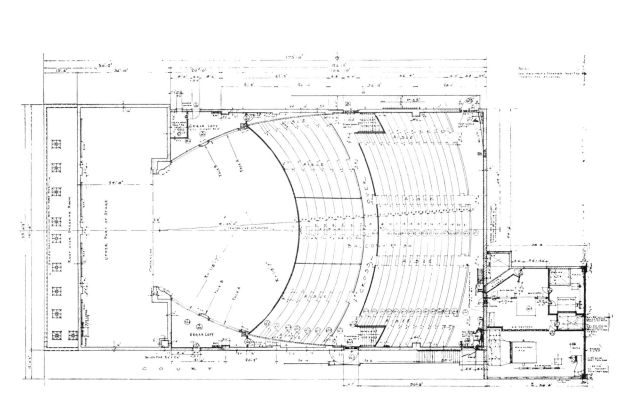

PLAN OF BALCONY
THE BALCONY SEATS 926

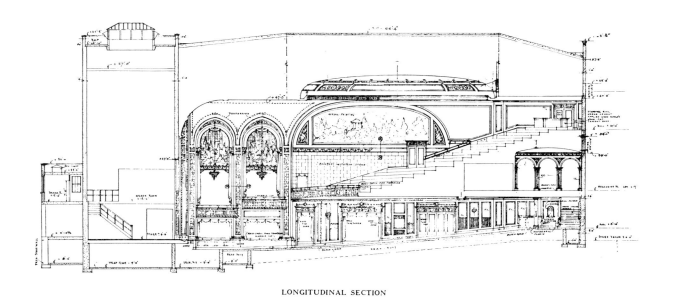

LONGITUDINAL SECTION

GRAND THEATRE, NEW YORK, N. Y.
Eugene De Rosa, Architect.

LOOKING TOWARDS THE STAGE

A DETAIL OF THE WALL TREATMENT

EMBASSY THEATRE, NEW YORK, N. Y.

Thomas W. Lamb, Architect.

(Courtesy The American Architect.)

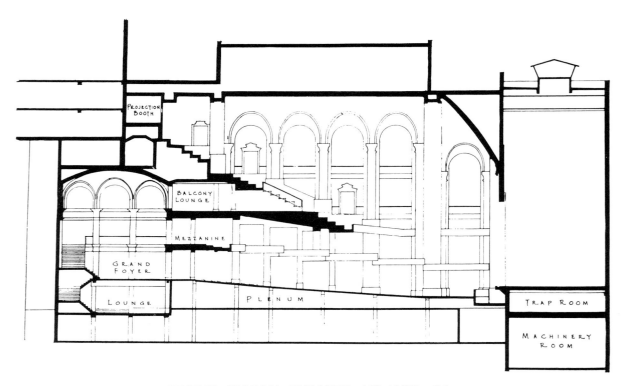

KEITH'S GEORGIA THEATRE, ATLANTA, GA.

R. E. HALL & CO., INC., ARCHITECTS AND ENGINEERS.

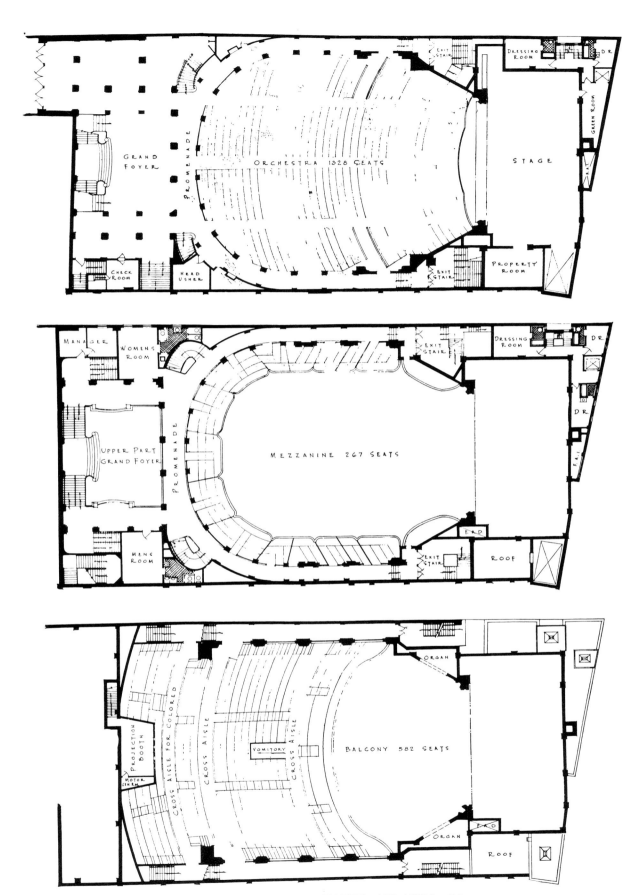

KEITH'S GEORGIA THEATRE, ATLANTA, GA.

R. E. HALL & CO., INC., ARCHITECTS AND ENGINEERS.

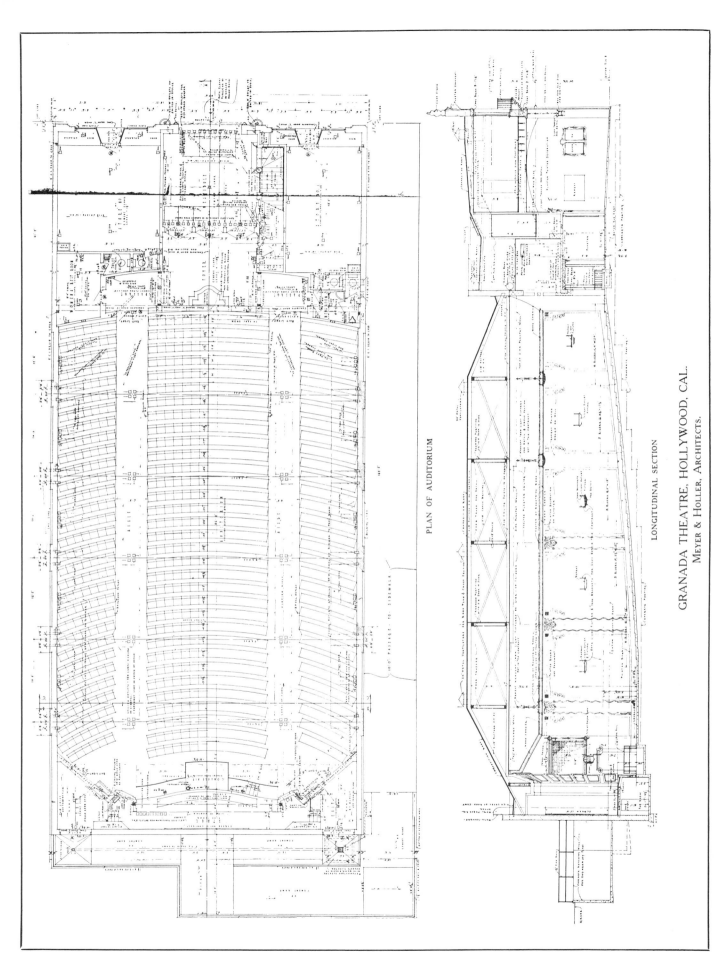

PLAN OF AUDITORIUM

LONGITUDINAL SECTION

GRANADA THEATRE, HOLLYWOOD, CAL.
Meyer & Holler, Architects.

GRANADA THEATRE, HOLLYWOOD, CAL.

MEYER & HOLLER, ARCHITECTS.

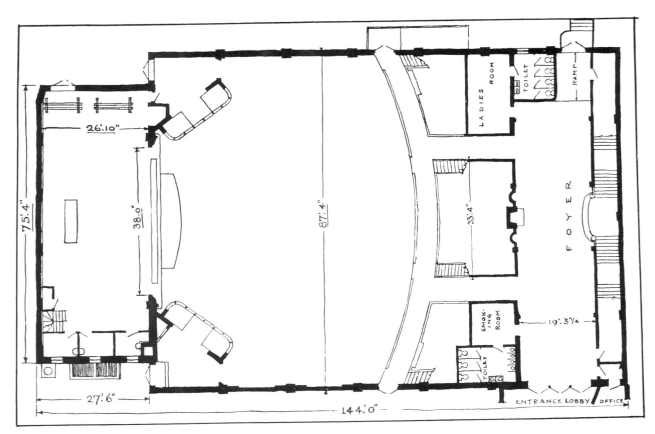

PLAN OF THE AUDITORIUM—THE STADIUM TYPE OF PLAN

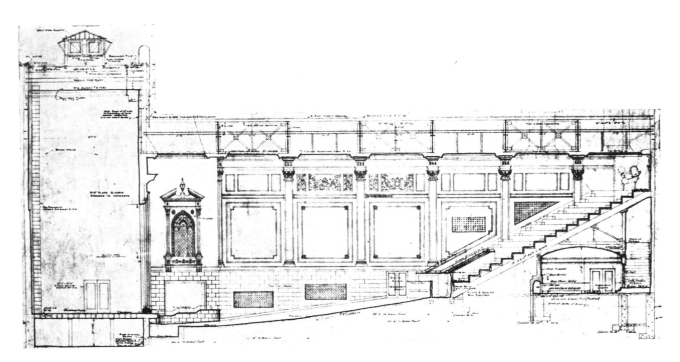

LONGITUDINAL SECTION

STADIUM THEATRE, WOONSOCKET, R. I.

FRANK B. PERRY, INC., FORMERLY PERRY & WHIPPLE, ARCHITECTS.

162

LOOKING TOWARDS THE PROSCENIUM

LOOKING FROM THE STAGE

STADIUM THEATRE, WOONSOCKET, R. I.
FRANK B. PERRY, INC., FORMERLY PERRY & WHIPPLE, ARCHITECTS.

MAIN FOYER OPPOSITE THE STAIRS TO REAR OF THEATRE

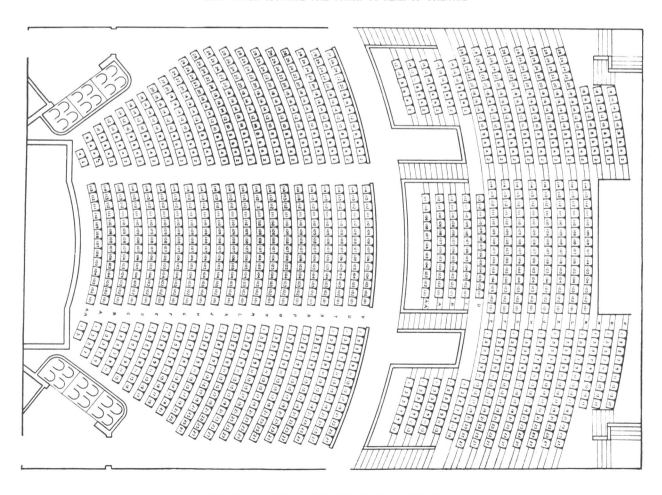

STADIUM THEATRE, WOONSOCKET, R. I.

FRANK B. PERRY, INC., FORMERLY PERRY & WHIPPLE, ARCHITECTS.

GUILD THEATRE, NEW YORK, N. Y.

C. Howard Crane & Kenneth Franzheim, Architects.

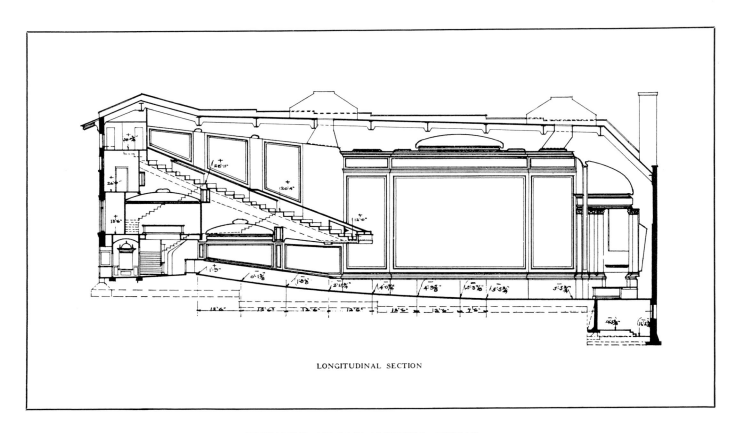

LONGITUDINAL SECTION

THEATRE AT SAN ANTONIO, TEXAS.

Roy A. Benjamin, Architect.

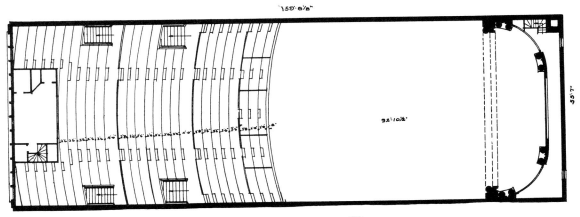

PLAN OF BALCONY, SEATING 498

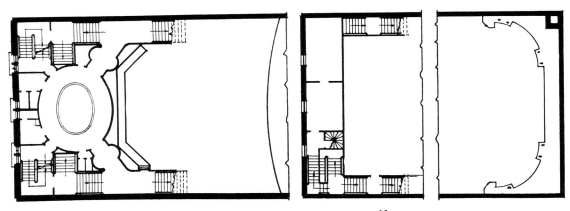

PLAN OF MEZZANINE.   BOXES SEATING 66

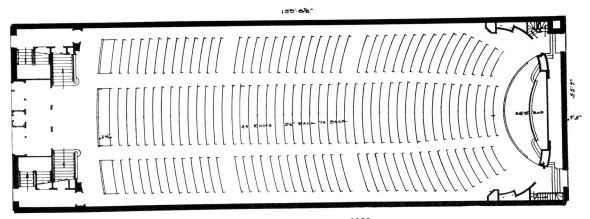

PLAN OF ORCHESTRA, SEATING 1038

THEATRE AT SAN ANTONIO, TEXAS.

ROY A. BENJAMIN, ARCHITECT.

167

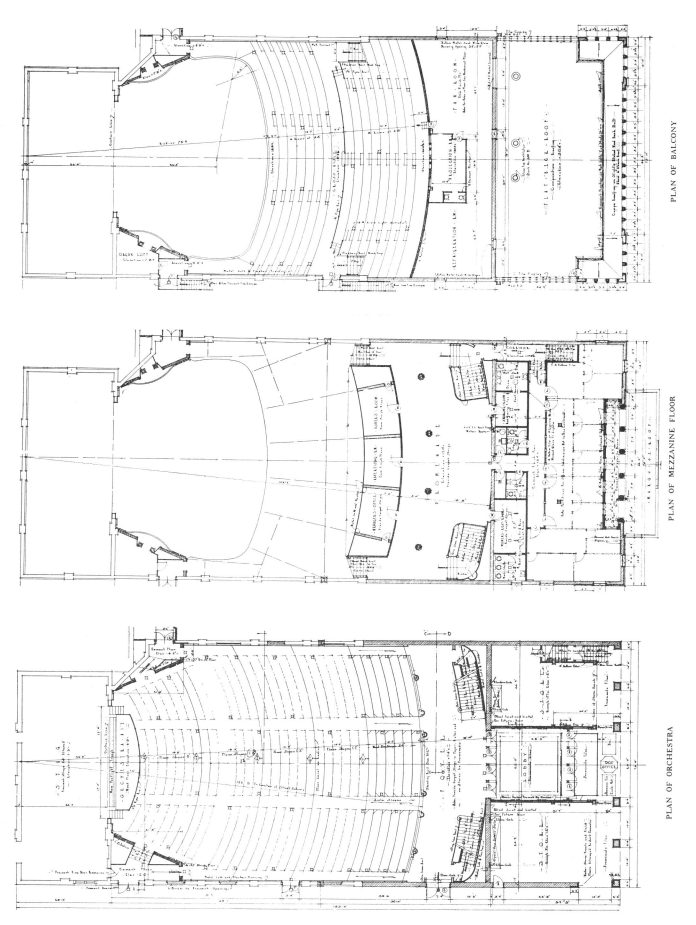

PLAN OF BALCONY

PLAN OF MEZZANINE FLOOR

PLAN OF ORCHESTRA

ELECTRIC THEATRE, ST. JOSEPH, MO.

BOLLER BROTHERS, ARCHITECTS.

ELECTRIC THEATRE, ST. JOSEPH, MO.
BOLLER BROTHERS, ARCHITECTS.

169

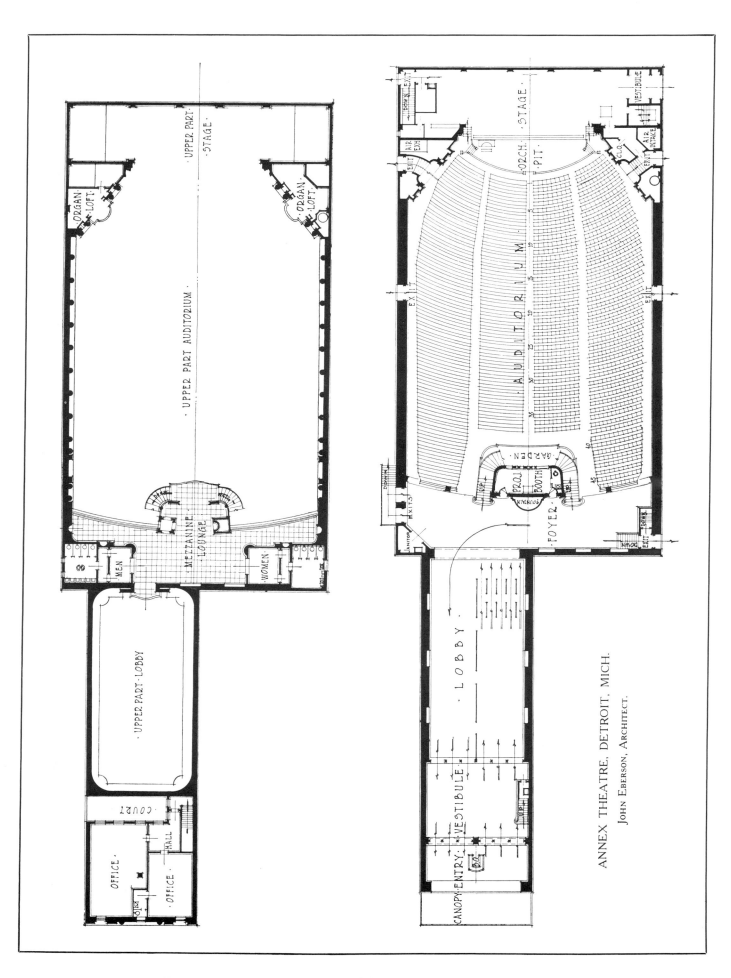

ANNEX THEATRE, DETROIT, MICH.
John Eberson, Architect.

170

ANNEX THEATRE, DETROIT, MICH.

JOHN EBERSON, ARCHITECT.

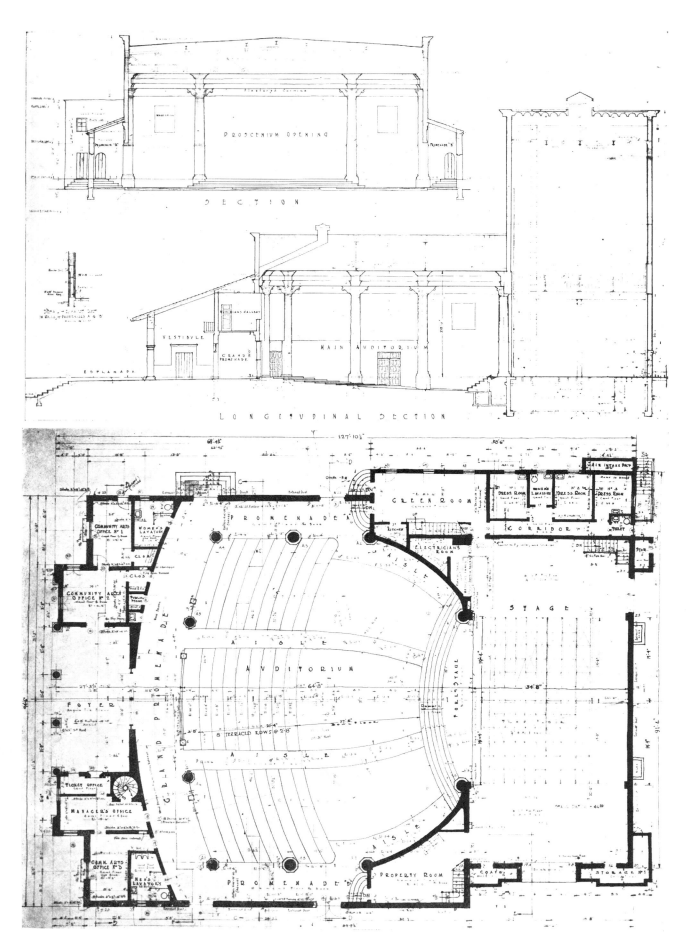

LOBERO THEATRE, SANTA BARBARA, CAL.

CEORGE WASHINGTON SMITH, ARCHITECT.

172

LOBERO THEATRE, SANTA BARBARA, CAL.

GEORGE WASHINGTON SMITH, ARCHITECT.

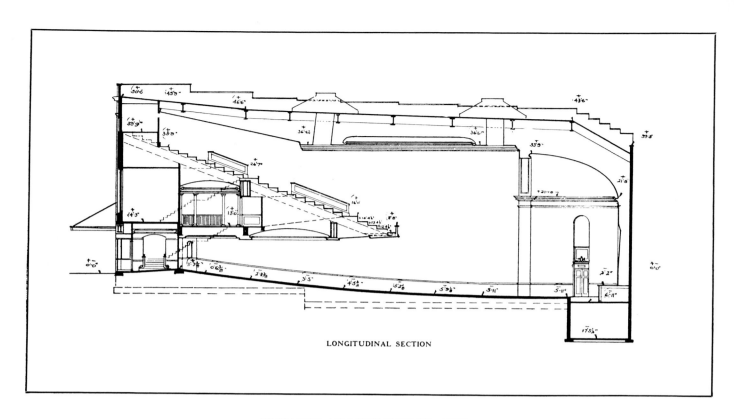

LONGITUDINAL SECTION

THEATER AT LITTLE ROCK, ARK.

Roy A. Benjamin, Architect.

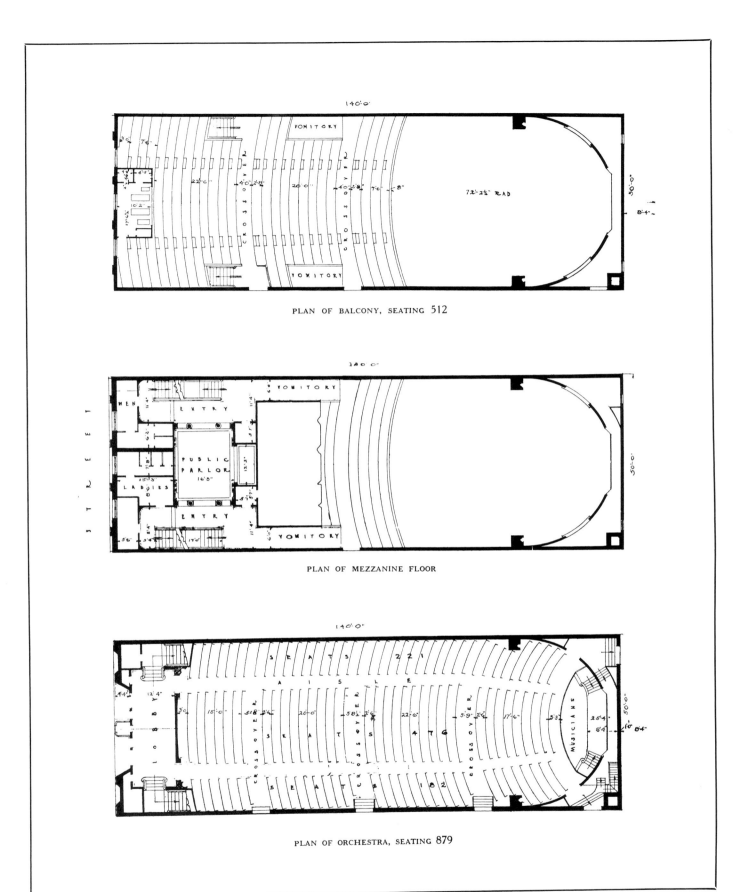

PLAN OF BALCONY, SEATING 512

PLAN OF MEZZANINE FLOOR

PLAN OF ORCHESTRA, SEATING 879

THEATER AT LITTLE ROCK, ARK.

ROY A. BENJAMIN, ARCHITECT.

AMERICAN THEATRES OF TODAY

VOLUME TWO

Preliminary sketch for a theatre for northeast Philadelphia, Pa.
Magaziner, Eberhard and Harris, Architects
The design is suggestive of the character of a modern theatre

AMERICAN THEATRES OF TODAY

PLANS, SECTIONS, AND PHOTOGRAPHS OF EXTERIOR AND INTERIOR DETAILS

Edited by

R. W. SEXTON

Author of "American Commercial Buildings of Today"
"American Apartment Houses of Today"
"American Country Houses of Today"
"The Logic of Modern Architecture"
"Interior Architecture"

VOLUME TWO

ARCHITECTURAL BOOK PUBLISHING CO., Inc.

108 WEST 46TH STREET

NEW YORK

TABLE OF CONTENTS

Page

AMERICAN THEATRES OF TODAY

CHAPTER I

TENDENCIES IN THE DESIGN OF THE PRESENT DAY THEATRE

By R. W. SEXTON

VARIOUS uncertainties that exist in the motion picture industry today are responsible for the fact that many plans for new theatres have been held up awaiting certain decisions of the industry regarding the size of the film, the size of the screen, the further development of sound pictures and the use of color. For, unlike most other types of buildings, the plan and other phases of the design of motion picture theatre is entirely dependent upon the technicalities by which the film is projected on to the screen. Theatre owners naturally hesitate to spend large sums of money on new buildings when the industry itself is so undecided as to what new steps it may take, for they run a chance that these new houses may be entirely inadequate for the presentation of the pictures which may be produced under the changed conditions. For example, there is talk of a wider film and a proportionately wider screen. In fact, the wide film has already been shown in certain theatres. But, in order to be of any particular advantage, a wider screen must be higher in proportion and this is impossible in the theatres as they are now planned, for the sight lines are drawn so tight that any addition

Sketch of exit door, Majestic Theatre,
San Antonio, Texas
John Eberson, architect

made to the height of the screen would be out of the vision of the majority of the audience in nine out of ten of our theatres today.

A higher and wider screen will undoubtedly affect the plan of a theatre by making the seats in the rear of the house much more desirable than those in the front. It will also mean the elimination of the mezzanine and will therefore increase the size of the balcony. The sound film has necessitated certain changes in the design of the theatre. It has brought the small theatre again to the fore, for the sound waves are often broken before they reach under the low projecting ceilings of the mezzanine and balcony. And it stands to reason that the deep coves in the ceiling of the auditoriums of so many of our present-day theatres are a hindrance to proper acoustics as are the various details of the ornament which project at such great distance from the walls.

Of late, there has been a tendency to design so-called "modern theatres." And yet we find on analysis that most of the modern theatres today are based on the same plan and section that has been adhered to so closely for the last fifty years. These theatres are modern in their decorative treatments because the de-

Study for front elevation for proposed theatre
Boller Brothers, architects

sign of their decorations does not suggest the influence of any one of the old styles and periods. But we still find the elaborate proscenium arch, the huge orchestra, the squeezed in mezzanine and the deep sloping balcony. The architects can hardly be blamed for the present state of affairs for it must be remembered that a great majority of the details of both the plan and section of our theatres of today are actually governed by building laws and fire codes.

So we might just as well admit now as any

Study of elevation for proposed theatre
Boller Brothers, architects

Preliminary sketch, Wyatt Park Square Theatre, Los Angeles, California
Morgan, Walls & Clements, architects

time that we have no new style theatre any more than we have a new style of domestic architecture. And no one needs to be shown, even if he comes from Missouri, that the old styles and periods dominate the design of our houses today. We are apt to forget that a style in architecture has its roots in structure, and the only buildings today that are actually designed in a style that is American are our skyscrapers, and they are modern because they are constructed of materials and in a method which originated in this age. Many of our theatres are embodied in steel and concrete skyscrapers, but the peculiar thing about those buildings is that although the architect has given the exterior of the building a character in keeping with its structure, when he comes to design the theatre he forgets entirely that it is part of a modern building, and falls back into the same old rut. The result is that you enter a thoroughly modern building at the first floor to reach a supposedly modern theatre and when you get there you find instead a Mayan, a Spanish or a French Renaissance theatre.

Here, again, I do not feel that architects must take the blame. Theatre owners, almost universally, are of the opinion that the average theatre-goer comes to the theatre to get the thrill of rubbing shoulders with the elite and basking in luxuries that their homes cannot afford. They claim that the audiences increase in proportion to the amount of ornamentation. They insist that a theatre designed in the character of one of the old styles and periods will immediately attract a regular following, while the house that lacks rich, elaborate and gorgeous ornamentation will be half empty at every performance.

This may account for their seeming lack of interest in the pictures which they show. If they can be so sure that they will have a full house at every performance because of the design of the theatre, it matters not at all what the attraction is. And sometimes we can easily think that they take this attitude.

So, then, too, certain theatre owners have allowed their architects to "go modern" as long as they keep the design elaborate enough. For they have seen that the public is quite interested in modern architecture, as expressed in our skyscrapers and in some of our shops and apartment houses. But they will not listen to anything that suggests a radical departure from what has been done before.

I think, however, that we will see in the next decade a tendency to discard the elaborate period theatre. I think that the people

Preliminary sketch, Hollywood Bowl Theatre, Hollywood, California
Morgan, Walls & Clements, architects

will shortly begin to show that they go to the theatre to see a good picture or a good show and not to give them the opportunity to kid themselves for the time being that they are millionaires. This is evidenced today in the full houses where some of the best old pictures have been revived. It is "better pictures" that the public wants and when the producers and owners realize this and allow their architects to design logical theatres for them,—theatres that center the interest of the audience on the screen and the stage rather than on the walls and ceiling,—then our architects will design houses for the showing of pictures that will be truly modern as are our skyscrapers today.

The theatre planned for the showing of motion pictures should naturally be a modern building. It cannot be compared with our own houses, for actually we live today very much as our ancestors lived. It is not strange that our houses follow certain lines of those that were built one and two centuries ago. But the motion picture is a purely modern invention. There is no precedent to guide us in the design of the motion picture theatre. There was a decided social aspect to the legit-imate theatre of fifty years ago. Only those who could pay well for a seat sat in the orchestra and those of us in more moderate means liked to look down upon the four hundred as they hobnobbed between the acts. But we have gotten more democratic of late. And we have gotten more prosperous, too. There is no four hundred anymore. We are all one class. But we are all moderns. We have our own modern customs, our own ways of living, and we will welcome our own modern theatres.

I see the modern theatre, then, built of steel and concrete, the ceiling supported by huge paraboloidal arches, or with visible steel columns, and the side walls only slightly decorated to focus the eye on the stage. The lighting of the modern theatre will be a feature of its design. The film itself may project on the walls and ceiling of the theatre decorative effects in keeping with the character of the picture being shown on the screen. In other words, every detail of both the architectural and decorative schemes will be worked out to allow the eyes and ears of the audience to enjoy to the fullest the picture that is being projected on the screen.

AMERICAN THEATRES OF TODAY

CHAPTER II

THE DESIGN OF THE MODERN THEATRE

By ARMAND D. CARROLL

WE naturally associate the modern theatre with the talking pictures, for the "talkie" or sound picture is our most modern form of theatre expression. And yet the modern theatre must be equipped and planned for the presentation of the legitimate drama, the silent motion picture and the talking or sound picture. This is largely a matter, however, of planning that part of the theatre that is not visible to the audience. For, from the point of view of those who come to the theatre to see the performance, the outstanding consideration is to give the occupant of each seat a clear and unobstructed view of the stage. This holds true whether the presentation be legitimate drama, silent motion pictures or sound pictures.

But it is natural, I say, that we speak of the modern theatre as the "talkie"—a most unsatisfactory term, but the only one that has as yet been devised. What can we call it? The word "movie" is not accurately descriptive; the word "cinema," used abroad, is not entirely expressive. Certainly a dignified name should be given to the theatre which houses our newest form of dramatic art and entertainment.

It may well be said that the modern theatre is the playhouse of the masses. Theatres are no longer gathering places merely for the elite. Every village and hamlet has its theatre and every member of a community has his favorite playhouse.

Prosperity has resulted in a demand for the erection of fine buildings for community use. Thus we have seen the demand for finer theatres—theatres that are architecturally correct.

And yet we cannot put our finger on any one type of theatre building as representative of the modern theatre. Changes in our political as well as in our social life, are so rapid in these days that it is impossible to cite certain definite ideas as modern. The important fact which we must face is that our life has been given a new impetus. New discoveries in science, the recognition of the importance of industrialism, the widening of our

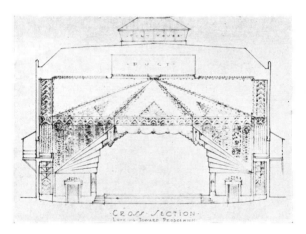

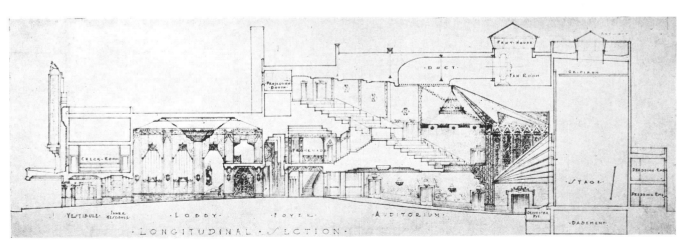

Sketches of proposed theatre, Philadelphia, Pa.
W. H. Lee, architect; Armand D. Carroll, associate

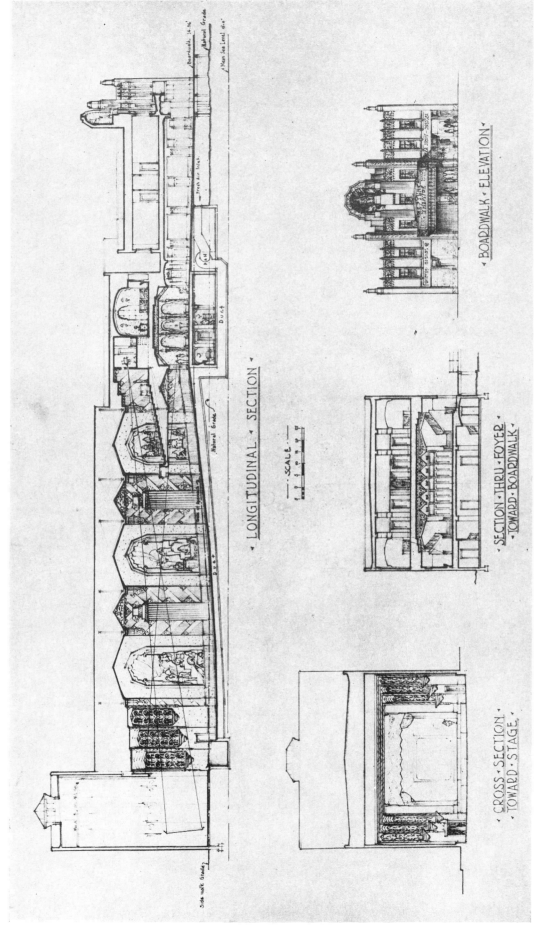

· LONGITUDINAL · SECTION ·

· SCALE ·

· BOARDWALK · ELEVATION ·

· SECTION · THRU · FOYER ·
· TOWARD · BOARDWALK ·

· CROSS · SECTION ·
· TOWARD · STAGE ·

Studies for a proposed seashore theatre—W. H. Lee, architect; Armand D. Carroll, associate

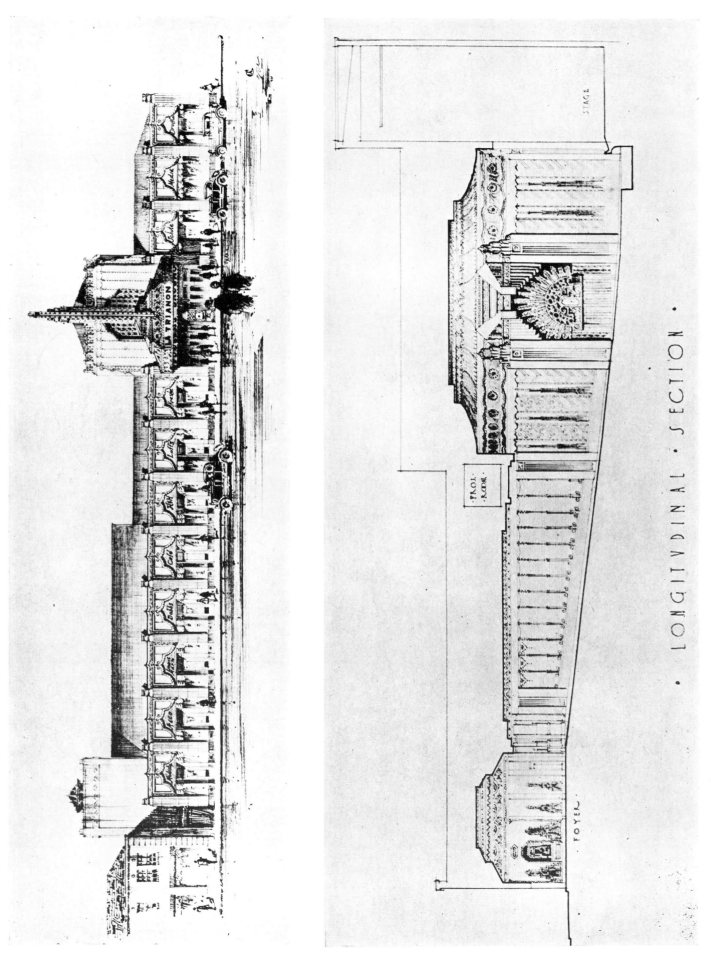

. LONGITVDINAL . SECTION .

Sketches for proposed theatre, Philadelphia, Pa.—W. H. Lee, architect; Armand D. Carroll, associate

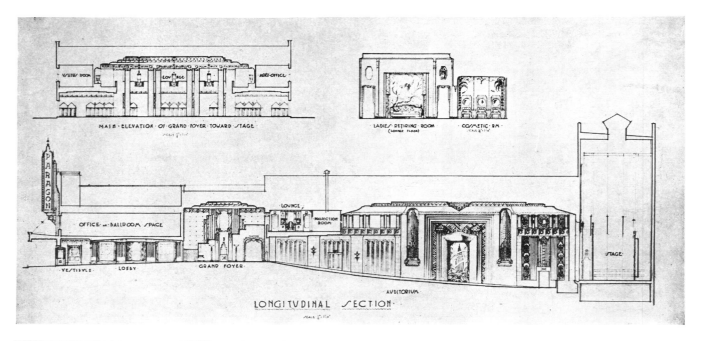

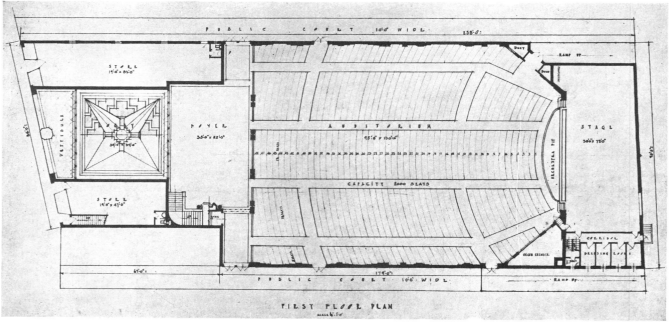

Sketches for proposed theatre, Philadelphia, Pa.
W. H. Lee, architect; Armand D. Carroll, associate

views through increased travel, these have all contributed to the modern movement. And this feeling of restlessness is reflected in our art and architecture today as it is in our own daily lives.

But let us consider briefly the contents of this modern "talkie" theatre. It is first of all a building dedicated to the presentation of a mechanical art. It is a building designed for the display of such marvellous inventions as moving pictures, sound pictures and color pictures, projected on a screen the dimensions of which approximate the legitimate stage of today. It is a building containing

scientific and mechanical perfection, enabling us to produce lighting effects and sound reproduction when and where desired.

Nor must we overlook our modern structural and decorative materials and the opportunities they afford us for creating a building that shall function more perfectly. Among these we find steel and reenforced concrete, the possibilities of which as they affect the design of the theatre are unlimited and still seldom thought of. And glass and the metal alloys, both possessing dramatic qualities, may be used to great advantage in the design of the modern theatre. And as these modern

8

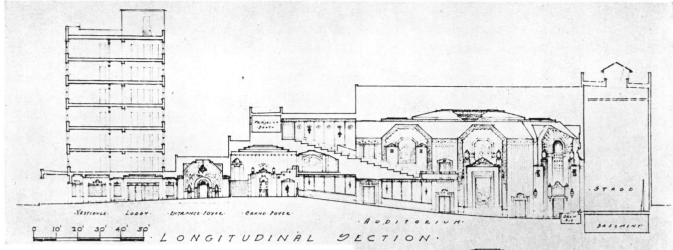

LONGITUDINAL SECTION.

Sketches for proposed theatre, Philadelphia, Pa.
W. H. Lee, architect; Armand D. Carroll, associate

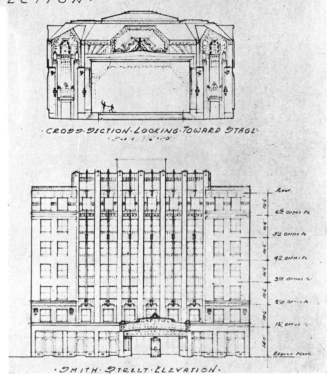

CROSS-SECTION LOOKING TOWARD STAGE.

SMITH STREET ELEVATION.

materials are given harmonious forms, the building will present an architectural style that will be at once reserved in color, graceful in line, and reflecting its purpose in every detail. These are the principles on which architectural design is established.

And this modern theatre building should not be merely a copy of some ancient structure which was designed to serve an entirely different purpose in an age when social and political conditions were vastly different from what they are today. It is appropriate to copy a building only when similar conditions are to be satisfied. Only in rare instances, if ever, does a Greek temple meet our modern requirements. On the other hand, a radical and conscious departure from tradition would not lead to the goal sought. An attempt to produce illusions is contrary to the spirit of architectural design in its serious aspect. It will not lead to permanently accepted standards, but a modification of forms to suit conditions will lead to new accomplishments for us and an architecture of our own in the same manner as that of other countries in previous history.

In the auditorium of the modern theatre we will find meaningless applied ornament and costly trimmings practically eliminated. The screen will be the only focal point. Replacing richly painted decoration by the simplest kind of ornamentation, decorative effects will be largely the result of lighting. Color lighting will be prominent, and the designer of the modern theatre will need to thoroughly understand color and color blending. He must be familiar with the visual effect of color combinations and colored lights

on colored surfaces. For, with a knowledge of light, emotions and effects can be expressed momentarily throughout the entire performance. In other words, the electric switchboard will serve as the means by which the walls and ceiling of the auditorium will be given various decorative treatments. The heavily laden proscenium arch will be eliminated and a method of treatment found to successfully bring the audience and screen players into one intimate room. This effect can be enhanced by a correct use of modern lighting when its relation to auditorium and screen platform is understood.

In general, then, the new theatre should express simplicity if it is to be modern. Some one once said that simplicity is the keynote of modernism. But there are certain other char-

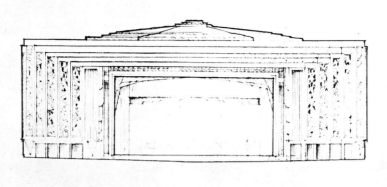

ELEVATION TOWARD STAGE

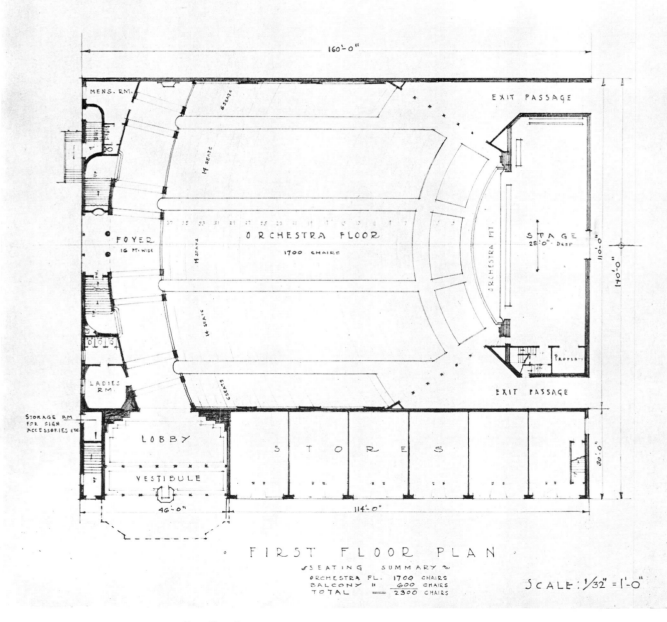

FIRST FLOOR PLAN

SEATING SUMMARY
ORCHESTRA FL. 1700 CHAIRS
BALCONY " 600 CHAIRS
TOTAL 2300 CHAIRS

SCALE: 1/32" = 1'-0"

Studies for proposed theatre, West Chester, Pa.
W. H. Lee, architect; Armand D. Carroll, associate

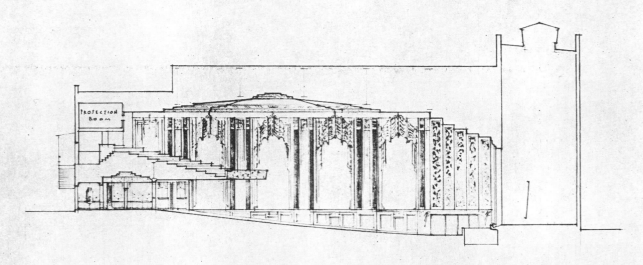

· LONGITUDINAL SECTION ·
SCALE 1/16"=1'-0"

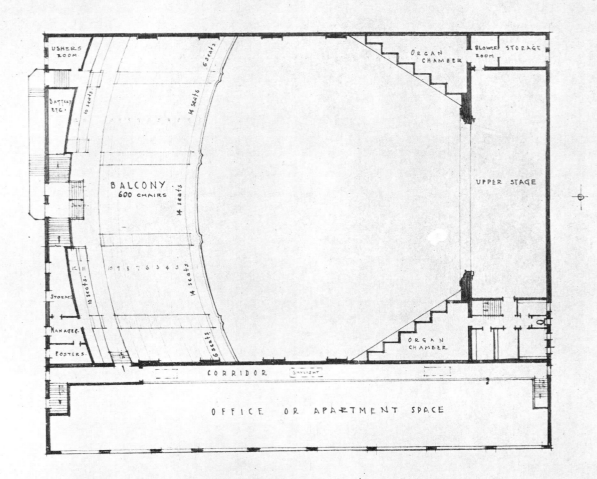

· BALCONY PLAN ·
SCALE 1/16"=1'-0"

Studies for proposed theatre, West Chester, Pa.
W. H. Lee, architect: Armand D. Carroll, associate

Final design was by Rapp & Rapp (BH)

Sketch of the Colonel Drake Theatre, Philadelphia, Pa.
W. H. Lee, architect; Armand D. Carroll, associate

acteristics that help to make a thing modern. These might be summed up as follows: continuity of line (as we find it in the stream line of an automobile or in the long unbroken lines in fashion); contrasts in colors; and sharp contrasts in light and shadow, created through definite angular mouldings and broken planes. Things modern also have in them a definite rhythm such as we find in modern dancing and music and in the frank accenting of form in fashion. They, too, avoid imitation in material.

So that while simplicity seems to be a characteristic of our time and should logically be reflected in our art, this is only a surface kind of truth. For simplicity is a kind of cover for the very complexity within us. It is true that our clothes and our buildings and our modern art are constructed on comparatively simple lines, with little ornamentation in detail. But actually life is more intricate and complex today than it ever was. So it is not so much simplicity that our modern architecture expresses, as it is logic. For a logical architecture is a simple architecture because it is so easily understood. The modern theatre, then, will be designed in a style of architecture that needs no explanation.

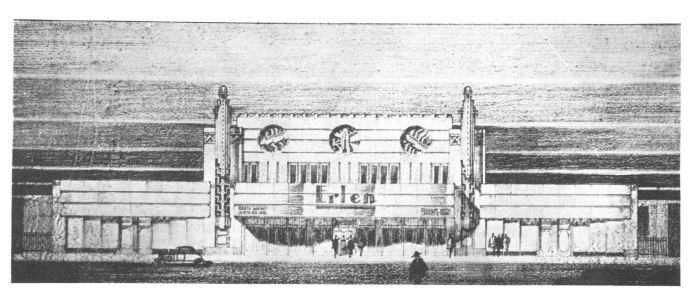

Sketch of Erlen Theatre, Philadelphia, Pa.
W. H. Lee, architect; Armand D. Carroll, associate

AMERICAN THEATRES OF TODAY

CHAPTER III

A STANDARD METHOD OF PLANNING A THEATRE
Showing the Effect of Sight Lines on the Plan and Section
By ALBERT DOUGLAS HILL, *architect*

THE showing of motion pictures has standardized the plan and general design of theatres to a very great extent, although we may not be aware of any similarity between the design of a small theatre that seats perhaps seven hundred persons and of one of the large "motion pitcure cathedrals" which boasts of a seating capacity of several thousand. Still it is true that the plans of both these theatres are based on the same principles. The problems which the planning of both theatres presents are very much the same, the difference being primarily in the size of the building, the number of seats desired, and in the fact that the small theatre may be a one-floor house, while the larger one may have one, two, or even three balconies.

Standardization is naturally due to the fact that in both theatres the same type of machine projects the pictures on to the screen; the films which record the pictures are of standard measurements; and even the screen on which the pictures are projected is thus standardized in its proportions—the relation of width to height—although the size of the screen may vary with the size of the theatre.

So it might be said that the problem of planning a theatre consists of arranging a certain number of seats, in a building of a certain size, placed on a lot of a certain size, so that a clear and uninterrupted view of the screen and of the stage may be had from every seat in the house. But there are many things to be considered besides merely arranging the seats. Space must be provided for the audience to enter the theatre comfortably; doors must be provided by which the theatre may be emptied in case of emergency; and very often the stage must be arranged for the showing of flesh and blood entertainment as well as for the projecting of motion and sound pictures.

Building codes and fire laws in operation in the various cities and communities regulate to a very great extent many of the details of the plan of a theatre. These codes and laws differ somewhat in different localities, but as a rule they govern the width of aisles, the width of exit courts, the space between aisles, the dimensions of steps in the balcony floor, and other details of a similar character.

When the prospective theatre owner calls in his architect he presents him with a problem to design a theatre on a lot of a specified shape and size that will seat a certain number of persons. Naturally the owner is anxious to provide as many seats as possible and very often he insists on more seats than the theatre can comfortably hold. This means that the architect must reduce certain sizes to a minimum—by making the stage slightly smaller than originally planned, cutting a foot or two off the standing space, or reducing the space between seats in certain parts of the house.

Let us assume that we have been commissioned to plan and design a theatre. The lot is in the center of a block, without any rear alleys, and only one frontage on a main street. It measures 110 feet wide by 185 feet deep. The owner wants the theatre to seat 2,500 persons. It stands to reason that a balcony must be provided to take care of probably one-third of the seats, making it necessary to provide for an orchestra of sixteen hundred seats.

It is necessary to determine the seating capacity of the orchestra approximately in order to proceed with the plan. For only on the basis of such a figure can we arrive at the amount of space that must be allowed for circulation and standing space: that is, sufficient space for the audience to enter and leave the theatre and necessary space for those who must stand while waiting for seats. Each person must be allowed one and one-half square feet of space for this purpose. Thus if there are to be seats in the orchestra for 1,600 persons, the number of square feet in the vestibule and standing space combined must total about 2,400 square feet. This is exclusive of the staircases leading to the balcony, but in-

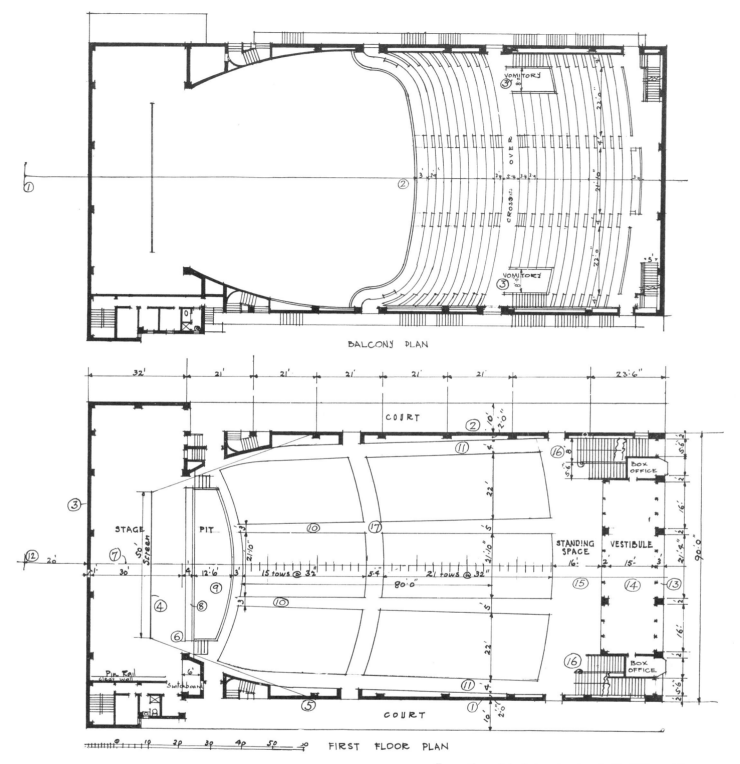

BALCONY PLAN

FIRST FLOOR PLAN

Diagram A

From the original drawing by A. D. Hill, architect

cludes, as I have stated, the outer vestibule.

Having the size of the lot, then, we mark off on both sides the proper width for the courts, which, as I said, varies in different localities. This I show on the diagram A as (1). Then we set off two feet inside that line for wall and column thickness (2). This establishes the width of the theatre as 90 feet. Now, to determine the distance of the last row of seats in the orchestra from the outer line of the vestibule, we divide 2,400 square feet, arrived at in the last paragraph, by the width of the house, on the inside—90 feet—which gives us 27 feet. This space is to be divided into the vestibule and the standing space at the rear of the orchestra. The outer vestibule may be anything you want to make it, and the standing space also is not fixed.

14

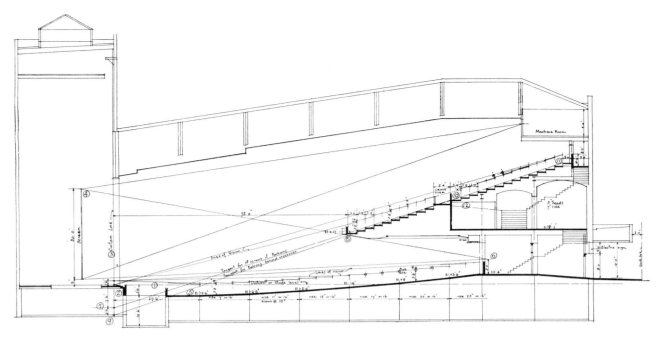

Longitudinal Section
Diagram B

But standing space is very important, as an admission is collected from every person, whether standing or seated.

Having established the point beyond which the orchestra seats may not extend, we are prepared to go ahead with the plan of the main floor according to diagram A. We draw the line of the rear wall of the stage, which coincides with the rear line of the lot and allows one foot for the thickness of the wall (3). Thirty-two feet from this line we designate as the center of the thickness of the proscenium arch. The jambs and head will be two feet thick over the plaster furring. From this point, which is the center of the columns that carry the proscenium arch, we mark off at every twenty-one feet the centers of the wall columns and trusses.

Now we draw the line of the screen (4), allowing at least six feet in back of the screen for horns. In order to provide for future developments in wide screens, suppose we make the screen fifty feet wide. From the center of the second wall column (5) draw a line to the edge of the screen on both sides of the auditorium to obtain the width of the proscenium (6). Now draw the center line of the orchestra plan through the center of the screen and proscenium (7). Allow four feet in front of the curtain line for footlights and apron (8). In front of this line set off 12 feet 6 inches for the orchestra pit (9) and three feet in front of the pit gives you the line of the first row of seats.

Now we are prepared to draw in the center block of seats. There is a law enforced in most cities that states that not more than six seats are allowed between any one seat and an aisle. This is generally interpreted to mean that a block cannot be more than thirteen seats wide. At twenty inches for each seat, the center block will measure 21 feet 10 inches wide. Now draw an aisle at either side of the center block (10), three feet wide at the pit line, increasing to five feet at a point eighty feet away from the first row of seats, or becoming wider at the rate of three inches in every ten feet. Now draw the side aisles (11) from three to four feet wide. On the center line of the plan strike off a point fifty feet in back of the curtain line (12). This point serves as the radius point for the seats. We can now line in each row, 32 inches apart, and determine approximately how many rows we can obtain allowing the necessary space for vestibule and standing space. And we are now able to calculate the width of each block of seats and therefore to determine how many seats in a row. The diagram indicates that each block is thirteen seats wide. In order to get the desired number of seats in the orchestra—sixteen hundred—on the basis that there are thirteen seats in each row, we must have about forty rows.

Now we go back to the plan of the entrance. The first five hundred people of a theatre audience need three doors, each five feet wide; each additional three hundred or

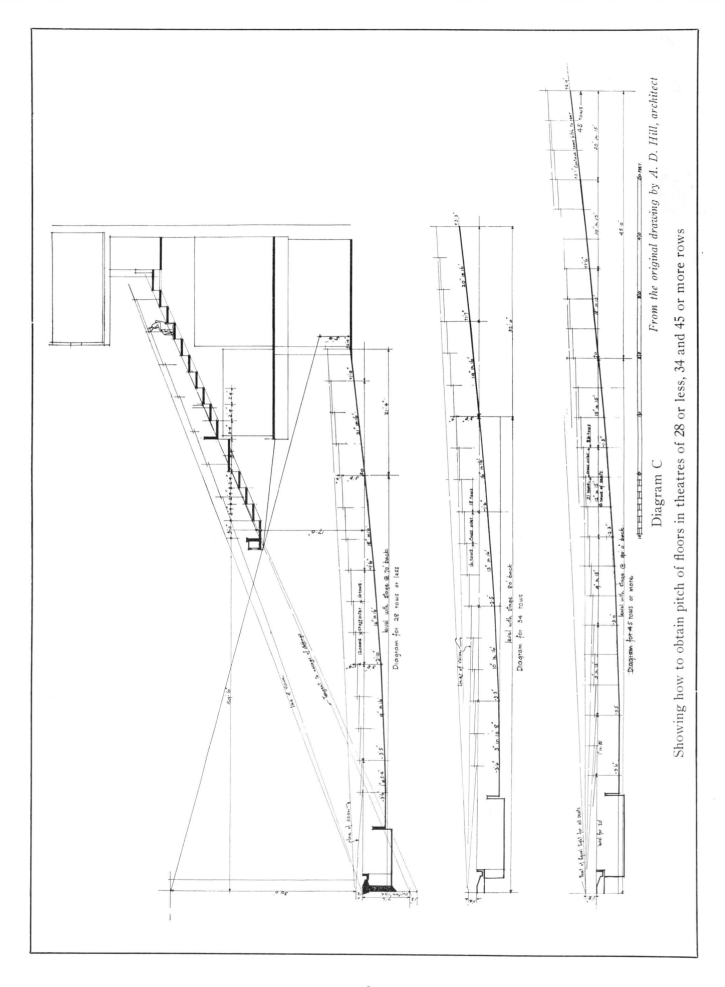

Diagram C

Showing how to obtain pitch of floors in theatres of 28 or less, 34 and 45 or more rows

From the original drawing by A. D. Hill, architect

fraction thereof need one more door; so that twenty-five hundred people (the seating capacity we are striving to attain) will require ten doors each five feet wide. So we mark off on either side of the center line of the plan these five doors, making ten in all, allowing for the doors to stand open without encroaching on the pavement (13). We then set off fifteen feet for the vestibule inside these doors (14). This may be a little larger than necessary, but ten feet is the minimum. Allowing two feet for another series of doors (it is even desirable to have three lines of doors between the rear seats and the street to keep out draughts) we give sixteen feet for standing space (15). This gives us, too, the rear line of the orchestra seats.

When we figured out above that the vestibule and standing space would take 27 feet, we were figuring rather closely, and so in the diagram we have increased the size of both spaces. Some architects might prefer to work from the pit out and see how much space is left for the vestibule and standing space, instead of, as I have done in the diagram, working from the vestibule in.

It is now necessary to determine the width of the stairs by which the remaining nine hundred people can reach the balcony. Fifty people require stairs four feet wide. The next fifty need six inches more, and so on, so that nine hundred people need a staircase 12 feet 6 inches wide or two staircases 6 feet 3 inches wide. I think it would be better to make the stairs eight feet wide and place an extra handrail down the center of each. This reduces the chance of a person falling, for a handrail is available for each one ascending and descending the stairs. Thus we draw in on the diagram the stairs (16). We notice that this reduces the size of the vestibule and standing space and for that reason these spaces have been made deeper than we originally calculated.

If, in counting the seats, we find that we are short, we can reduce in different places slightly. We can make the depth of the stage 27 feet instead of 30. We can take two feet off the standing space and we can set the front rows of seats 30 or 31 inches apart instead of 32 as shown on the diagram. When we count the seats indicated on the diagram we get a total of about fourteen hundred and ninety, perhaps a hundred less than we wanted. This takes into consideration, too, that we have allowed a cross over (17) and spaced all seats at 32 inches.

Now we turn to the section, as in diagram B. We first strike a point (1) which will serve as stage floor level and datum. We assume that the auditorium floor is level with the stage at a point 85 feet in front of the curtain line. From experience I have found that the point where the stage floor and the auditorium floor coincide in small theatres is approximately 75 feet in front of the curtain line. In large theatres this is increased to 95 feet so that in this case, as on the diagram, we may compromise at 85 feet. Now we draw the apron (2) and the pit, from measurements marked off on the plan. Then we establish the proscenium (3) and the line of the screen (4). The height of the screen must not be less than 22 feet, but we shall allow 30 feet to retain the proper proportion with the 50 feet width we show on the plan. Set off a point 3 feet 6 inches below the level of the stage as the floor level of the front of the orchestra (5). This floor level is retained for a distance of 27 feet 6 inches in front of the curtain line. From there on it rises 7 inches for the next 16 feet, and then 11 inches, 15 inches, 17 inches, 20 inches and 23 inches for each 16 feet. Now draw in from the plan the vestibule and standing space, and the line of the rear seat.

At this latter point, which represents the position of standing persons, we set up a point of sight 5 feet above the floor line at that point (6), the average height of the standee's eye. We draw a line between this point (6) and the top of the screen (4). The balcony must not project downward below this line at any point. On the curtain line extended, mark a point 7 feet 6 inches below the level of the stage (7). Draw a line at a distance about 75 feet in front of the curtain line; mark the point (8) one foot above the intersection of this line with the line already drawn connecting points 4 and 6.

Connect points 7 and 8 and continue for a distance of ten rows of seats and a cross over (to point 10 on diagram). Then from another point ten feet below the stage level on the curtain line, or two feet six inches below point 7, strike off point 9. Connect this point (9) with point 10 and continue to the rear of the house. All the steppings of the balcony must touch this line, 8—10—11.

Now we come to the balcony plan as diagram A. Extend from the plan of the orchestra, the rear line, the proscenium line, the line of the screen, and the front building line. Draw the center line and on it above point 12

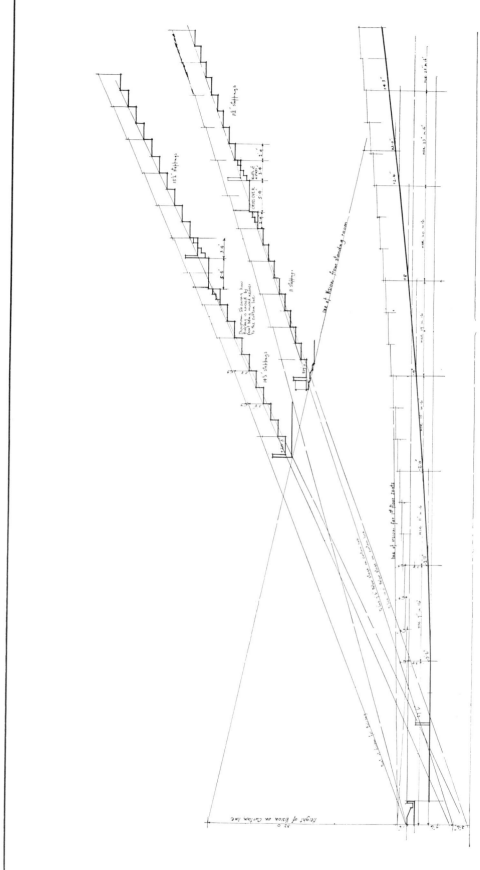

From the original drawing by A. D. Hill, architect

Diagram D

Diagram D shows how the balcony pitch is steeper and the theatre higher when the front of the balcony is moved nearer the stage. There is no fixed position for the front of the balcony in relation to the stage. For this point is fixed by the line from the eye of a person standing in the rear of the first floor to the top of the screen or to the fixed height of the proscenium. It must be remembered that the line extending from the points 7 and 9 on the section should not be at a greater angle than the ratio of 16 to 33 or there will be more than two steps on each stepping of the balcony and that is too steep for comfort.

in first plan, mark point 1, which is the radius line for balcony seats, also. Point 2 indicates the front of the balcony, established on the section. Locate vomitories leading to cross over, indicated on section, the vomitories being the same width as the stairs—8 feet (3). Draw in the blocks of seats as in the orchestra, with 21 feet 10 inches for the center row of 13 seats, and aisles 4 feet in the clear.

After counting the seats we find that the number is below that required, the same procedure is followed but the additional seats may be gained by moving the balcony forward, remembering that as we move it forward we raise the front of it too, because it must not project lower than line 4-6 drawn on section.

Diagram C shows how to obtain the pitch of the floors. It is necessary that the occupants of all seats have an equal view of the stage over the heads of people sitting in the next row but one in front. If the theatre is short, it is possible to make the floor steeper. If the floor rises too rapidly in the first twenty rows, however, the floor in the rear portion of the auditorium will have a pitch so great that one cannot walk comfortably in the aisles. We can safely begin by assuming that the floor of the stage will intersect with the auditorium floor at a point 70 feet in front of the curtain line, as in the diagram for a house of 28 rows. Through this point—the intersection of the stage level with the orchestra floor—draw a vertical line and on this line mark a point 3 feet 8 inches above the floor as the height of the eye of a person seated. Four inches above this point is allowed for clearance for those seated in the seats two rows back. From this same vertical line, both forward and backward, set up other verticals 5 feet 4 inches apart. Now, on the curtain line, establish a point 12 inches above the stage. Connect this point with the point on the first vertical 3 feet 8 inches above the floor until it cuts the other vertical 5 feet 4 inches in front. On this line drop down four inches to the eye level and repeat the opera-

tion. Then work backwards four inches above the original 3 feet 8 inches. After these lines of vision are complete, the line of the floor may be obtained by drawing a line parallel to the eye points, at a distance 3 feet 8 inches below them.

If the floor line thus obtained is too steep to suit other conditions that may prevail, then move the point of intersection of floor and stage datum line 10 feet to the rear and raise the point of equal vision on the stage four inches as shown in the diagram for 34 rows and proceed as before.

In the balcony we will assume that the desired point of equal vision is the interesection of the curtain line with the stage and proceed as we did for the orchestra floor. The balcony steppings should never be higher than 16 inches or less in width than 33 inches.

HINTS

Do not place steps in the vomitories which are dark during a performance or in any dark place if it is possible to avoid them.

The rows on either side of a cross over in the balcony must be wide enough for the number of steps required to reach the second row. Do not make these steps less in width than 10½ inches or higher than others in the balcony.

Place seats in the center of a theatre instead of an aisle. These make the best seats. Place aisles on the wall sides and do not have seats against a wall if avoidable. People passing in the center aisles obstruct the views of those sitting and the aisles must be placed so that this annoyance is reduced to a minimum. This rule holds good for balcony vomitories also.

Never place a seat with an impaired view of the stage. It will produce dissatisfied patrons. Better let the patrons wait for a good seat.

It is better to lose a row of seats than to crowd other rows and it is better to spend money on seats than on plaster and paint.

Pantages Theatre, Hollywood, California
B. Marcus Pritica, architect
The design follows modern lines

Pantages Theatre, Hollywood, California
B. Marcus Pritica, architect
Traditional motives have given way to modern forms

21

Main Lobby, Fox Theatre, Brooklyn, New York
C. Howard Crane, Kenneth Franzheim, architects
Traditional motives are given a modern interpretation

AMERICAN THEATRES OF TODAY

CHAPTER IV

THE DECORATIONS OF THE THEATRE

By HAROLD W. RAMBUSCH

IN discussing the problem of theatre decoration it is well to consider and analyze the problem of decoration in general and the purpose of theatre decoration specifically.

Decoration may be defined as the treatment of a room already built in such a manner that it should be adapted to its specific use. Decoration should make a living room quiet and comfortable; it should make a ballroom cheerful and gay and it should leave a lecture room neutral and quiet. Decoration is done to affect the comfort or mood of people. It is not a scientific profession such as engineering. It is not possible to calculate and figure out the effects of a certain color scheme or certain lighting effects. Clive Bell once defined the word beauty as "that which creates pleasurable emotion in a cultured mind."

In decoration the means at our disposal are lighting effects, the colors of ceilings, walls, ornamentation, drapes, carpets and furniture. In speaking of decorations we are speaking of something which has its effect on our public essentially through their eyes and not through their sense of touch on rugs, chair coverings and the like. But while we are catering to the eyes of man we should look beyond this to certain effects that we wish to create on the mind through his eyes. One feels comfortably at ease or, conversely, disturbed or uncomfortable as a matter of general feeling or mood, and it is his mood essentially that we wish to affect. It is our end to create a definite mood in a definite room. It must be done mainly through one's eyes and secondarily, through their sense of touch. In our

Showing the wall decoration of the auditorium of the 175th Street Theatre, New York
Thos. W. Lamb, Inc., architects
Decorations by Rambusch Decorating Company

modern theatre problem we might go so far as to say that ventilation and heating are a part of our decoration because they have an enormous effect on the mind of the public.

Discussing theatre decoration specifically we find that it falls under three broad headings: the entrance or approach rooms, the auditorium and the subsidiary rooms. Each has its specific problem. The auditorium is, of course, the most important in that the greatest amount of time is spent here. In the auditorium the public is mainly interested in the performance. This, however, does not prevent them from being subconsciously affected by the scheme of decoration. The decoration, although they are not specifically conscious of it, makes them appreciate the show either more or less. With the proper approach rooms it is easier to get the public into the theatres. This, of course, is of paramount importance in a commercial undertaking. The various lounges and rest rooms are also of importance in our modern theatres because we are gradually acquiring the European habit of visiting and lounging in these places.

The modern theatre is more than a house in which to see a picture or to produce an act. It has a very important place in our social and economic structure. The vast majority of those attending our theatres are of very limited means. Their homes are not luxurious and the theatre affords them an opportunity to imagine themselves as wealthy people in luxurious surroundings. They may come here as often as they please by paying a small fee within their means and feel themselves to be the lords of all they survey. In our big modern movie palaces there are collected the most gorgeous rugs, furniture and fixtures that money can produce. No kings or emperors have wandered through more luxurious surroundings. Emperors have been able to do no more than feast their eyes on pomp and luxury. In a sense these theatres are the social safety valves in that the public can partake of the same luxurious surround-

View of the proscenium of the Hollywood Theatre, New York
Thos. W. Lamb, Inc., architects
Decorations by Rambusch Decorating Company

ings as the rich and use them to the same full extent.

Many of the big producers today feel that it is necessary to be gaudy and vulgar in taste in order to satisfy the cravings of the public. They seem to assume that the public has a definite criterion of what the theatre should be. The best architects and theatre decorators disagree with them and believe that the public is fully satisfied with good taste provided it is sufficiently pompous and ostentatious. It is agreed that the theatre is not the place to demonstrate reserve and refinement in its most constrained form, but there is no objection to having it rich and in good taste.

The Roxy theatre is an example of Mr. Rothafel's (Roxy's) theory that you can give the public the very finest and best taste in both music and in art provided you give it to them in music in a slightly faster time and in art a trifle richer than you would in a home. The Roxy is an example of this because it is probably one of the best attended theatres in the country. In its scheme of decoration it has been held down to a very definite scheme of tones of gold, tans and browns, with rich wine-colored hangings and rugs of the richness of a Paisley shawl.

The theatre starts at the marquee and outer lobbies and here the showman's point of view must maintain. The people must be attracted to the place and lured in. We humans are, fortunately or unfortunately, like moths; we are attracted to the light and bright. Every effort should, therefore, be made to make the approaches as prominent and attractive as possible. We, the public of today, are perfectly willing to excuse or accept an exaggeration or an apparent deceit in an advertisement or billboard. We feel that it is legitimate, and the showman must hold sway at the entrance as well as on the stage. Our lobbies and entrance foyers are not meant to be quiet and restful places to linger. They should be bright and as prominent as possible. This is not exactly restful, but, after all, we must

Detail of auditorium decorations, Hollywood Theatre, New York
Thos. W. Lamb, Inc., architects
Decorations by Rambusch Decorating Company

remember that the public passing through these rooms has just come off the street and is very much keyed up by reason of the traffic, the noises, shop windows and the like. Even a very elaborate entrance and foyer has a certain easing effect after the excitement of the street. Lobbies may well be full of gold, mirrors and posters.

When we speak of the theatre in the United States today we are thinking mainly of a movie place. The legitimate houses throughout the country, except for those in two or three cities like New York and Chicago, are to all purposes and intent non-existent. The public sits most of the time in a dimly lighted space, but they are most conscious of the chair in which they sit and of the carpet on which their feet rest. In the best houses an enormous importance is attached to the seat.

The general tone of the auditorium must be what is technically called warm. The warm colors, as we understand them, are gold, orange, reds and tans when applied to materials or wall surfaces, and amber and straw when applied to light. After all, these two things of light and painted decoration of materials are closely associated because all that we see, we see by means of the light, and warm colors can only be lighted by means of

warm light. Blue or green bulbs played on yellow or tan colors give only dirty greys. A white light lights all colors. A blue light lights blues, and a red light lights reds. But a blue lighting scheme is ghastly; white light is good for an office or working space. A warm golden amber light in a color scheme is best for a living room, a theatre auditorium or in any other place where people have to spend much time at ease and in comfort. When we speak of these color schemes we speak of them as predominating. This does not mean that blue or green should not appear at all, because, used in limited quantities, these colors serve to accentuate the richness of the more golden colors.

Decoration is decidedly psychological and colors are of enormous psychological value. Our warm golden colors tend to make people glad and cheerful; our blues and greys tend to depress and unnerve. The metal gold has always spelled richness, not only because it is valuable but because it is pleasing to look at. Whether this instinct has been embedded in man from the earliest times when a wood fire meant protection and warmth we know not, but the fact remains that a lavish use of gold in our auditoriums is the best means of attaining richness and warmth.

Lobby of the Hollywood Theatre, New York
Thos. W. Lamb, Inc., architects
Decorations by Rambusch Decorating Company

Gold has another charm when used in the theatre auditorium. In these dimly lighted interiors the metal will pick up such little light as there is and make the most of it. The light from the few lamps that burn is reflected here and there on the various gilded ornamental features and the light bounds and rebounds and gives richness without glare.

In these days of the talking picture a profuse use of hangings and material on the walls is becoming more and more necessary. In the past hangings were used essentially as decoration. Now they are used to avoid echoes as well, and it will be found that the extensive use of materials will have a tendency to make our theatre auditoriums even richer than they have been.

Most of our theatre auditoriums have a balcony or two, and it is well to bear in mind that the space under the balcony, the space above, and the auditorium in front of the balcony are three separate entities. The space under the balcony must be treated as a complete interior by itself because the people sitting here are not conscious of anything but the orchestra floor, walls, balcony ceiling and, of course, the stage. This portion must, therefore, be treated so that it forms a complete scheme in itself. It must, of course, be in harmony with the balance of the theatre. Each man's world is that which he sees. The man sitting under the balcony soffit is not conscious of the main ceiling. He must, therefore, be considered and care must be taken that he views a complete and well balanced interior.

The people sitting in the balcony, of which the front portion is usually called the loge, have the best general view. They see the main ceiling, the side walls, box fronts and proscenium arch and, of course, nothing at all of the main orchestra. Here again care must be taken that all they see taken together constitutes a well-balanced scheme.

That part of the audience sitting in the front of the orchestra sees the least. Most of the time they see little but the stage and portions of the features on either side of the proscenium arch which in the old theatres conformed with the boxes.

It is necessary that the architect and the decorator consider these three distinct points of view in the theatre auditorium and recognize them as three separate parts. In studying the theatre auditorium in plan or in sketch it is easy to fall into the mistake of considering the auditorium as one complete scheme and feeling, as the gallery walls are vast, light and

General view from the stage of the auditorium of the Hollywood Theatre, New York
Thos. W. Lamb, Inc., architects
Decorations by Rambusch Decorating Company

27

large, they may be treated with goods and plaster ornament. It is natural to assume that the orchestra walls must be treated in the same manner but, of course, the problem is totally different, for the orchestra walls are only about eleven or twelve feet high, and the room created under the balcony is essentially a low room and it needs a much more intimate decorative treatment than the grander spaces viewed from the gallery. Generally speaking, the space viewed from the balcony needs an architectural treatment and the space under the balcony needs a more intimate and home-like treatment. The entresoles and grand lobbies are generally kept in the style of the auditorium. They are to a great extent the public places of assemblage and intimately related to the auditorium itself.

The lounges, cosmetic rooms, smoking rooms and rest rooms in general lend themselves to a more exceptional style. No one of them is to be used for any length of time and it is here that an opportunity presents itself to try out a more varied, interesting and exceptional form of decoration. Silver and blue or grey and blue schemes are most interesting

in the cosmetic room, for example, while to try these schemes in an auditorium might have disastrous effects. In such a scheme its greatest value lies in its uncalmness, in its peculiarity, in its eccentricity. Such schemes are continually proposed and considered for the large auditorium but almost invariably and, most fortunately, are abandoned for the final decision. As the public wanders through the various show-rooms, lounges and social rooms it has an opportunity to see all these exceptional styles. They are interesting and museum-like, but for a steady diet they are unsafe. For any room in which the public has to stay for any length of time these styles are rarely tried.

It would seem that the schemes laid out for the auditorium are extremely limited in the insistence on golden tones, and we must remember that the conditions in the auditorium are somewhat fixed. To all purposes and intents the audience watching a moving picture or an act is confronted with the same conditions in general in New York and in San Francisco, in the Bronx and in Brooklyn—last year and this year—and if the problem

Auditorium of the Kansas City Theatre, Kansas City, Missouri
Thos. W. Lamb, Inc., architects; Rambusch Decorating Company, decorators
Note how the walls under the balcony are treated in scale with their height

maintains the solution must also be the same. These general conditions are naturally affected by such large general changes as that from the silent picture to the talking picture, and any such change would immediately require a special solution which in this case means more goods and more sound-absorbing material. Human nature, however, does not change; people always want to be glad and cheerful and so they are in warm, golden surroundings.

The distinctly modern styles which are conventional and extremely geometric have found their best application in facades, entrance vestibules and lobbies. The various modifications of Renaissance, French, Italian and Spanish, are still the most popular.

The availability of the exotic styles, such as Persian, Chinese, Indian and the like, is somewhat limited. The desirability of carrying such styles through the entire scheme is fraught with many difficulties. We have magnificent examples of Chinese and Hindu architectural motifs and decoration but the furniture to round out these schemes is either unavailable or precedent for it is lacking. Of greater concern is the fact that such furniture, if it were possible to produce, would not conform with our modern ideas of comfort. These nations and tribes have not always used settees, lamps, ash trays and chairs in the way we have used them and are accustomed to use them. When we take their furniture and make our chairs we no longer conform to their styles.

The out-of-door interior, or that which is commonly known as the "atmospheric interior," has met with reasonable success. It has been done effectively and the public has taken to it, but it is essentially so sophisticated and unnatural that there is grave doubt that it will long survive.

A strenuous effort is being made throughout the country to create something symptomatic of our age; to create something distinctly and exclusively modern seems to be the ambition of our modern designers, but they are setting themselves an enormous problem and one which can hardly be accomplished in a lifetime. They might find a new treatment for a ceiling or wall or a new treatment of a vestibule, but the style of decoration and ar-

Auditorium of the Pitkin Theatre, Brooklyn, New York
Thos. W. Lamb, Inc., architect; Rambusch Decorating Company, decorators
An example of the so-called "atmospheric interior"

Detail of wall treatment in the auditorium of the Kings Theatre, Brooklyn, New York
C. W. & Geo. L. Rapp, architects
Decorations by Rambusch Decorating Company

chitecture requires an enormous vocabulary to be thorough. The form and proportions, detailed ornament, the color scheme and the hangings, both in material and in drape formations, the chairs, the carpets and all the furnishings would have to be of a style. New styles like these are not created of a desire to create a style; they are created more by new requirements and every new requirement will be reflected in a new solution which means a new form of treatment.

Success seems to be more near through the modern Renaissance; that is, the use of the historic styles in their main form and propor-

tion, interpreted in a modern accent or dialect, keeping the entire vocabulary of the past and interpreting it in the vernacular of the day. And let us all remember that the showman insists on the spectacular; he insists on the gorgeous and the rich, but he does not insist that it be done in bad taste. He does not always recognize the bad taste but it becomes a problem for the architect and the decorator to fulfill the showman's requirements and still keep within the bounds of good taste, because the public has no objection to beauty or good taste provided they satisfy the yearning for luxurious surroundings.

AMERICAN THEATRES OF TODAY

CHAPTER V

ELECTRICAL INSTALLATION IN THE MODERN THEATRE

By EDWARD B. SILVERMAN, *Electrical Engineer*

ELECTRICITY is the valuable servant upon which the theatre is dependent for its satisfactory operation.

The electrical plans and specifications for the modern theatre are rather intricate, and for that reason, the architects who specialize in such work have found it profitable to include on their permanent staff an experienced electrical engineer. To those who are occasionally confronted with a theatre project it would prove to their advantage to employ the services of a professional engineer who has made a specialty of theatre work. The author, however, will endeavor to enumerate and describe the different phases of this work in the forthcoming pages.

In designing the electrical installation of a theatre it is important that thorough knowledge of the client's requirements be given first consideration, particularly when the project is being done for the operators of chain theatres. To this end it is advisable that a form questionnaire including all items of importance, such as stage equipment, projection booth equipment, sign lighting, communication equipment, and so forth, be prepared. If such a questionnaire is submitted and properly signed, it will relieve the designer from any responsibility should his client, according to a common practice, change his wishes after the award of the contract.

Whether the architect or engineer secures an answered questionnaire or the installation is left to his own judgment, it is necessary in either event that the installation designed, while economical, shall be adequate to provide for flexibility of the entertainment policy.

If the theatre is for a small operator, it should be taken into consideration that this theatre may eventually be operated by larger companies and the installation, therefore, should be designed accordingly.

In order to properly present for estimating a description of the electrical installation, a set of wiring plans is essential which shall indicate the location of all outlets, panelboards, motors and other equipment complete with the diagrams of connections and the indications of circuits and feeders. The specifications should include a thorough description of the type, quality and arrangement of all electrical apparatus and the labor in connection therewith. There should be only a single interpretation possible.

In addition to being familiar with the installation of electric work in theatre buildings, the designer should acquaint himself with the laws, rules and regulations of the municipal or district departments having jurisdiction, with the requirements of the Board of Fire Underwriters and the company supplying the power.

It is also important that every consideration be given to provide facilities to maintain the equipment; and, in such locations as main ceilings, where concealed lighting sources exist, access ladders and platforms properly arranged and lighted should be included. Absence of such accommodation would give the maintenance man sufficient reason for neglecting this equipment.

SERVICE ACCOMMODATIONS

The accommodations and location of the service room should be determined after a fair analysis has been made of the amount of lighting and power equipment followed by a discussion with the company supplying the power. It is a general practice that a large service room be located in the basement at a point economical to the installation and acceptable to the utility company.

The majority of installations today are served with alternating current and the loads in connection with the theatre are of sufficient magnitude to require the installation of a transformer vault. This vault should be of fireproof construction and arranged with an exterior access door and area at one end to permit the removal of any equipment. The vault should also be provided with a vent area at the opposite end to permit a natural circulation of air in the vault. A secondary exit door opening into the building can be included in this vault provided there are no local rules to the contrary. Figure No. 1 shows the scale plan of a typical transformer vault. At the street grade over the main areaway, a removable grille should be provided having a hinge section for access. The vent area should also have a removable grille at the street grade for cleaning purposes. Both areas should be well drained and the vault proper should be

required by local ordinances should be included for public safety and so arranged that, in the event of the failure of the normal lighting service, the emergency equipment could be instantaneously brought into operation until restoration of the normal service.

Emergency lighting applies to such locations to which the public has access and is normally used during the performance, and definitely includes exit lights, aisles in the auditorium, corridor, stairs and lobbies. The

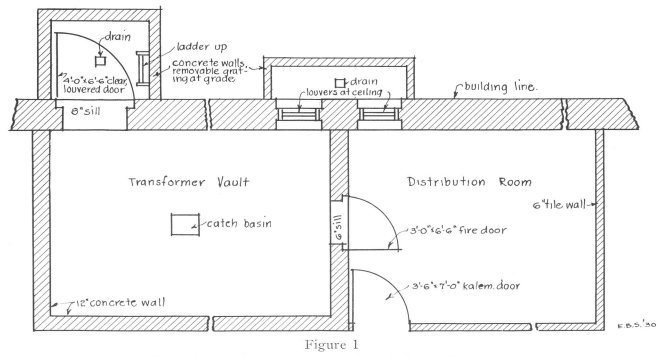

Figure 1

Plan of typical transformer vault and distribution room

equipped with a catch basin for any oil that may leak from the transformers. The size of the vault varies and should be determined by the requirements of the utility company.

Immediately adjacent to the vault and within convenient access to it, an additional room should be provided for the distribution of the electric service and the accommodation of the meters and miscellaneous equipment. This room can be built of hollow tile blocks and should be equipped with a 3 feet 7 inches by 7 feet calumein door. The average size of such a room is approximately 12 feet by 20 feet, with a headroom of 9 feet.

A distribution switchboard, preferably one of the "dead front" safety type construction is the important feature of this room. The entire electrical system is fed by arteries or feeders emanating from the switchboard to the various lighting and power load centers.

An emergency lighting system of the type

system may be supplied by a separate service to the building or an emergency battery system, the latter equipment being mandatory by law in many of the states.

THE STAGE

"Light" is the valuable medium for creating effects upon the stage and therefore the utmost consideration is required in the selection and location of the operating and producing equipments. These equipments vary according to the type of theatre and may be divided in two principal classifications, namely, the combination or variety policy, which provides for sound pictures, presentations, vaudeville and legitimate entertainment, and the straight sound-picture policy. The former type requires a full stage of 30 feet or more depth and the latter a platform of sufficient depth to accommodate the picture sheet, a stage setting and the speaker units.

In this discussion the author is eliminating the large operatic stage and public auditoriums as each case is of special nature; however, the two arrangements covered by the following paragraphs may be applied in proportion.

The combination stage should be completely equipped to provide for any change in entertainment as the time for such changes is generally limited.

STAGE SWITCHBOARD

For the operation of the combination stage equipment a stage switchboard provided with operating switches and dimming controls for each of the lighting units is required. The proper location of the board is at the side of the stage where the rigging operating classified as Remote Control and the Mechanically Interlocked types. The former, which is now the more extensively used, is a system by which pilot switches on the stage board operate singly or collectively, through set up combinations, magnetic switches mounted on a switchboard in a ventilated room, preferably in the basement, beneath the stage board, affording economy in wiring. The mechanical board is a system whereby the switches on the stage board act as direct disconnects for the lighting units. This board, standardized by various manufacturers, is of "dead front" safety type construction having operating handles at the face of the board and the switches at the rear are operated by rods protruding through the front of the board. In either type of board the dimmers and switches should be compos-

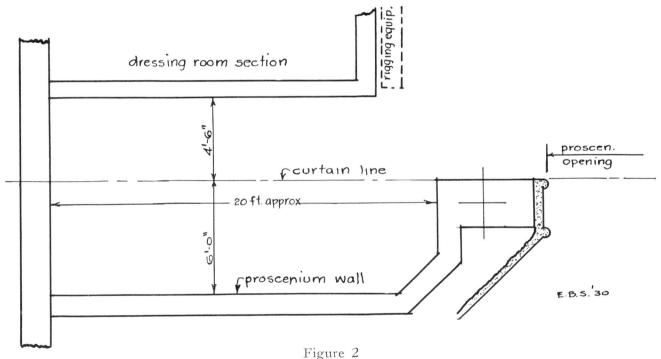

Figure 2

Plan of typical stage switchboard recess

equipment is located. A six foot recess should be provided in the proscenium wall so that the face of the switchboard will not extend beyond the curtain line. The width of these recesses depend upon the number of controls, but twenty feet can be considered as an average. A greater width is preferable if the layout permits A space of 4 feet 6 inches should be allowed at the front of the board for the operator. Figure 2 shows the plan of a typical switchboard recess.

There are many types of switchboards but the two principal standard systems can be itely constructed so that each switch has its respective dimmer control directly over it.

STAGE EQUIPMENT

A well lighted stage is essential and for its accomplishment sufficient overhead lighting is required. This lighting is provided by borderlights which consist of a continuous metal troughing housing individual reflectors or compartments, wired alternately for different colors, which, in general practice, are white or amber, red and blue. Standard clear lamps are used and the color effects are obtained with the use of glass roundels or framed gelatine mediums.

These borders are horizontally supported to the riggers pipe batton by means of adjustable chains and are electrically connected by multi-conductor cables to the overhead gridiron, where the wiring is continued to the stage board. The borders are hung by steel cables of the rigging system and can be lowered to the stage floor, for maintenance, or raised to the grid when not in use, for clearance of the stage scenery.

The following borders are necessary for the average 32 foot deep stage:—One (1) Valance Border located at the proscenium arch soffit, two feet shorter than the width of the proscenium opening. Four (4) other borders each six feet shorter than the width of the proscenium opening. The first border should be located approximately three feet from the curtain line and the remaining borders approximately six feet six inches on centers.

A complete stage should be equipped with a light bridge wired with separable pin plugs and mountings for spot units and effect machines. The location of this bridge may be over the second or third border light.

Efficient footlights are essential for good stage lighting. The equipment consists of a continuous metal troughing with hood and gutter, housing individual reflectors wired and equipped as described for the border

lights. The trough length should be approximately six feet less than the proscenium opening.

Care must be taken in designing the re-

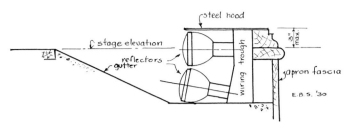

Figure 3
Detail of footlight recess

cesses so that the top of the footlights do not exceed three inches over the stage floor, a factor that should also be considered in figuring the sight lines. To conceal the footlight construction, the fascia of the stage apron should be built to the top of the equipment as shown in Figure No. 3.

To provide electrical service to the various portable lighting and effect units at different locations away from the switchboard, plugging pockets are necessary for the stage. When these units occur in concrete slabs, a slot should be formed before pouring. The pockets are located at the sides and rear of the stage. Figure No. 4 shows a typical stage electrical layout.

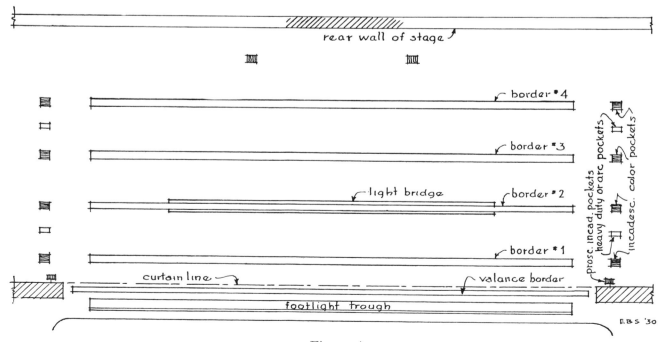

Figure 4
Plan of stage lighting equipment

STAGE PLATFORM

For the theatre equipped with a platform for presenting only sound pictures, the lighting equipment consists of footlights, one border and a plugging pocket at each side of the stage. The footlights can be either of the fixed type, as described for the stage or of the disappearing type, which is equipped with a wooden cover and frame set flush with the floor when not in use. The control of the lighting is arranged from a switchboard located in the projection room and within convenient distance of the projectionist.

THE AUDITORIUM

In creating effects and atmosphere in the auditorium and public spaces of the theatre, here again light is an invaluable medium.

In addition to visualizing the aesthetic effects in connection with the design, the architect should furnish the inspiration for the decorative lighting scheme. The engineer can then develop the necessary details for the arrangement and the accommodations of the equipment and fulfill the architect's desires. It is essential that this information be incorporated on the drawings before the building is too far advanced.

The modern inclination is to create innovations in lighting and we find a tendency towards Spanish, Chinese, rich Romanesque and modernistic schemes being applied.

THE ATMOSPHERIC HOUSE

There is also a recent innovation known as the "atmospheric style," with its sky effects and side walls indicating gardens, interiors, patios, and so forth. In this style of design lighting effects are generally concealed from public observation. In all cases where concealed lighting is provided, sufficient accommodations should be made for maintenance and concealment of the units.

In the atmospheric style of house, platforms should be provided behind the architecture of the side walls. To produce satisfactory lighting for the great span of the sky in this type of house, efficient reflectors should be used at the source of light of the type that would furnish proper diffusion and elimination of shadows.

Accommodations should also be provided on these platforms for the installation of cloud machines. It is also advisable to intro-duce a number of individual lighting units in the furred space above the main ceiling (sky), arranged with small openings in the ceiling for producing a star effect. These units should be arranged in accordance with the natural constellations to meet with the interest of the patrons.

These holes are generally about ¼ inch in diameter and fitted with a dew drop crystal to take the reflection of the fixtures. If it is desired to produce the twinkling effect to these fixtures, the thermostatic sockets can be used to supplement a constantly burning lamp.

COVE LIGHTING

The main dome cove, which is so often found in the theatre of Adams design, is the effect that will undoubtedly remain for some time to come as it creates a beautiful tone of warmth and color. These domes, whether they occur as the main motif of the ceiling or are in secondary locations, should bear a true parabolic curve starting from the cornice line. The architect should bear in mind that

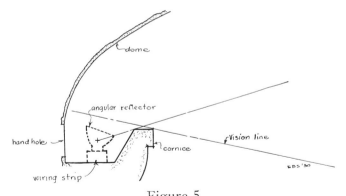

Figure 5
Detail of lighting cove

the higher the crown of the dome, the more even is the distribution that will be obtained. In this way the brilliancy of the source can be avoided. The accompanying figure No. 5 indicates the proper design for cove lighting. Full size architectural details should be made for the plaster contractor for all coves. The domes should have a mat finish to avoid the reflection of the lighting source.

LIGHTING FIXTURES

Where the design requires the use of lighting fixtures, sufficient accommodation should be made in the electric wiring. The fixtures should contain sufficient lighting receptacles to properly illuminate the area, giving consideration to the absorption of the surrounding decorative color scheme, the glass or material enclosing the lighting source and the maintenance. Where glass enclosures form a part of the fixtures, lamps should be so arranged as to conceal the glare of the lamp filaments. There is nothing so unattractive as a spotted lighting fixture which is caused either by the lamp being too close to the glass or when the glass is a medium insufficiently transfusant.

When the main fixture is to be used in the auditorium or foyer ceilings, exceeding 20 feet in height, the windless and platforms should be located in the attic space and provided for in the ornamental iron specifications. These machines should be of the worm gear type and of sufficient capacity to withstand the weight of the fixture and its trimmings. The cable should be of sufficient length to permit the lowering of the fixture for maintenance.

In establishing the length of the large chandelier, suspended from the auditorium ceiling, care must be taken so that the bottom of the fixture will not occur within the area of the picture projection. A limit for its length can be established by drawing a line of demarcation from the projection openings to the top of the finished stage opening.

It is just as important that the architect include with his plans a schedule and details of the lighting fixtures as it is for him to make the details and schedules of the draperies and hangings. In this way proper proportions and harmony in design will result in this important item.

In determining the intensity of lighting we should start from the very brilliant vestibule and taper down in brilliancy as we come from the lobbies to the foyers, until we finally arrive at the auditorium where there should be a warmth in color. This also shows consideration for the patrons when leaving the subdued light of the auditorium during the picture and eliminates the discomfort of eyestrain caused by glare.

AISLE LIGHTING

In the selection of the chairs for the balcony and orchestra, the end castings that occur at the aisles should be designed to provide for lighting fixtures that reflect the light downward upon the aisles or steps. In the orchestra these lights should be located at every third row and in a staggered arrangement. In the balcony where the steps occur the lights should be located at every row also in a staggered arrangement. It is standard with many seating companies to include lighting accommodations in their castings; otherwise, there are standard fixtures that are made for mounting on these castings.

As explained in the previous paragraphs, this lighting is to be a part of the emergency lighting system.

BALCONY FLOOD LIGHTING

Balcony flood lights are a very satisfactory supplement to stage lighting. They consist of an arrangement of lighting units at the balcony fascia, the enclosure of which forms a permanent part of the architecture. This equipment consists of adjustable spot flood lights that are mounted on flat iron or pipe supports and focussed through plaster openings at the front of the enclosure and upon the stage. It provides an excellent opportunity for avoiding face shadows and offers excellent provisions for effective illumination of the curtains. It frequently substitutes the flood lighting from the projection booth. In addition it can be used for illuminating the musicians' pit, particularly when the theatre is featuring an elevating platform.

An average installation of this equipment would be 18 units arranged in 3 colors of pro-

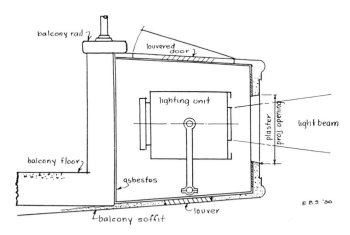

Figure 6
Balcony floodlight enclosure

jections. The plaster openings vary between 10 and 12 inches, according to the range of projection from the front of the pit to the top of the proscenium drape. The accompanying figure 6 shows the arrangements of this lighting.

Projection room, Kings Theatre, Brooklyn, New York
C. W. and Geo. L. Rapp, architects

The enclosure should be lined with asbestos board or asbestos plaster and ventilated either through the auditorium proper or in connection with the auditorium ventilating system. The access doors for the maintenance of these units should be located at the top so that they can be handled from the balcony. These units do not require the use of an operator as they are electrically controlled from the stage switchboard.

PROJECTION BOOTH

The motion picture projection room should be centralized about the axis of the theatre, either at the rear of the auditorium over the balcony, or at the front of the balcony. The first has its advantages over the latter location inasmuch as it provides better construction and affords access to it with no loss in seating. In establishing its location, special care should be taken so as not to permit an angle of projection exceeding 26 degrees. This angle, which corresponds to the inclination of the projector, is measured between the horizontal and the line joining the projection lens and the centre of the screen.

The construction of the projection booth may be summarized as follows:—

(a) Steel framing with supports between rear wall and roof trusses.

(b) Partitions and enclosures, hollow-tile blocks with Keene cement finish.

(c) Floor, cement on concrete arches with coved cement base, colored.

(d) Doors, fire-proof with combination metal buck frame and trim.

(e) Windows, hollow metal double-hung, with wire glass.

(f) Furred lath and plastered ceiling with ventilation grilles into ducts.

(g) All openings in port wall, metal sleeved, of given size.

(h) All sleeves to be splayed down at top and bottom, equivalent to angle of projection.

(i) Spot and effect machine sleeves also splayed out at sides.

(j) Rewind-room requires an 18 inch x 60 inch kalamein shelf or work bench.

(k) Rheostat-room requires an angle iron frame supporting slate slabs on which should be mounted the rheostats.

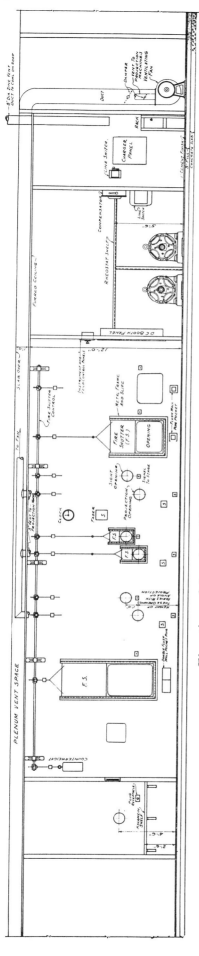

Elevation of booth looking towards stage showing port holes
S=Sound Equipment

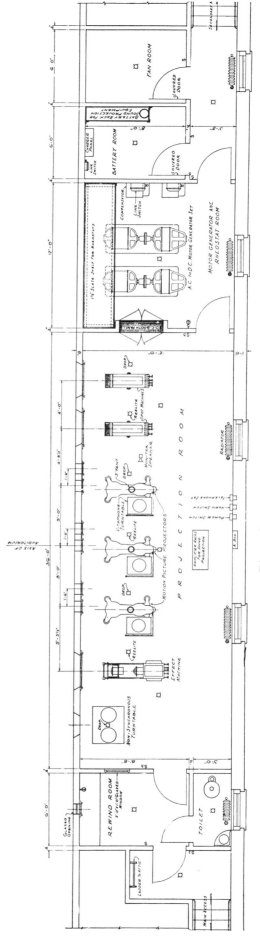

Plan of projection booth equipment

Figure 7

Typical plan of a projection booth in a modern theatre

This drawing was prepared in the office of Thos. W. Lamb, Inc., architects, under the direction of Edward B. Silverman.

Courtesy "Architecture"

38

A brief summary of the methods of safety and sanitation of the projection booth is as follows:—

(a) All port openings should be protected with asbestos shutters in metal slides, counter-weighted and with underwriters' fusible link control.

(b) Two means of access preferred, at opposite ends of the booth.

(c) Fireman's equipment, chemical extinguisher and sand pails.

(d) Water-closet and lavatory within convenient distance of projection-room.

(e) Mechanical and adjustable ventilation, with separate system for the rooms and projection equipment.

(f) Proper heat radiation at exterior windows.

(g) Diffused lighting.

The accompanying plan, Figure No. 7, indicates the required equipment for the average 3,500 seat theatre having a picture, vaudeville or combination presentation policy, complete with the modern sound-projection equipment of the Movietone and Vitaphone systems.

In cases where direct current is not available, motor generator sets are indicated for converting the alternating current supply to direct current, which is in turn distributed at the panel-board to the various projectors and their respective rheostats in the rheostat-room. These generators may be located remote from the booth, when space is not available.

The location of the non-synchronous turntable, used in connection with sound projection, is also optional. This equipment may be located away from the booth, such as in the rear of the balcony or in some side auditorium recess.

The electrical wiring is somewhat complex, owing to the special nature of the equipment and the requirements of the municipal and underwriters' inspections.

Expert advice is necessary in planning this wiring so that the termination of the conduits are properly indicated and all work concealed.

EXTERIOR LIGHTING

Exterior lighting plays an important part as a medium for increasing the patronage of the theatre and should therefore be attractive, brilliant and pleasing in design.

There are three major divisions of such lighting:—

Marquee Lighting
Upright or Wall Signs
Flood Lighting

THE MARQUEE

The marquee is the canopy embracing the entrance and extends from the face of the building. Its purpose is not only to protect the patrons from the weather, but to indicate to the public at large the current presentations and features. Accommodations are necessary on the three available sides for changeable signs. These signs should be featured with ornamental corner posts, animated lighting borders around each sign and the name of the theatre.

All the metal work should be of No. 20 ounce copper, artistically painted. The metal work should be properly reenforced to withstand severe weather conditions.

A room approximately 6 feet x 8 feet should be provided adjacent, if possible, to the marquee to house the animation equipment and distribution fuses. The control panel for these signs should be located in the lobby section.

A sign under the marquee over the entrance is advisable. A 5 inch recess should be provided in the construction so as to permit the sign to be flush with the facade.

The marquee soffit should sparkle with brilliance as it also lends itself to the attraction of the people. An artistic and pleasing design is advisable at this location and it should be equipped with an abundance of lighting receptacles.

The construction may be all metal (No. 20 gauge galvanized steel) or plaster cement, with metal ribbing for the receptacles. Ribs forming octagons, squares or any other pleasing geometric form, can be used and may be supplemented with flush opalescent glass fixtures. Coved domes with contrasting colors in lighting add to the warmth of the soffit and are very effective.

ATTRACTIVE SIGNS

In many instances, local ordinances prohibit the use of extended signs or marquees. In such cases, an attractive flush sign on the face of the building over the entrance should be used. This type of sign should be very ornate and active in animation. It should be equipped with a changeable letter section and a fixed monogram section.

Where commercial stores are a part of the theatre building, recesses should be provided over the store fronts for uniform signs. The recesses should be six inches deep, two feet high and the approximate width of the store and should be lined with copper. Hinged covers can be included, built of heavy gauge bronze, which may be cut to receive glass letters as required by the tenant.

The upright or vertical sign should be attractive, distinct and animated with plenty of action. A room should be provided in the building for housing the animation equipment and distribution fuses. Access ladders, foot and hand grips should be provided on the sign for maintenance.

FLOOD LIGHTING

With the present improvement of the incandescent lamp and the development of commercial floodlighting equipment, night illumination can be obtained at comparatively small cost. Such lighting contributes greatly to the contours and architectural beauty of the building and undoubtedly results in making the theatre a more imposing structure. As each building presents its own problems in flood lighting, the arrangement and requirements should be determined by the engineer or the manufacturers' specialists.

SOUND PROJECTION SYSTEMS

There are a number of sound projection systems available for use in theatres, each one involving its own technical problems. Only a casual reference to this new development is being made so that the architect should not overlook the urgent need of expert advice. There are certain designs, methods of construction and electric wiring requirements that vary with the system employed.

Pellissier Building and Theatre, Los Angeles, California
Morgan, Walls & Clements, architects
G. Albert Lansburgh, architect, associated as architect for theatre

AMERICAN THEATRES OF TODAY

CHAPTER VI

THEATRE ACOUSTICS

By Edwin E. Newcomb, A.I.A.

DURING the past few years a relatively new science has appeared upon the horizon to confound the already overburdened architect. With the advent of the "talkies", this new science, appearing under the impressive title "Acoustic Analysis", becomes of paramount importance to architects who specialize in the design of theatres. Theatre acoustics in the past was largely a matter of selecting, from a limited number of materials tested for sound absorption coefficients, some hair felt or wall board that might more or less detract from architectural charm and design. But with the knowledge disseminated by such pioneer devotees in the field as the late Professor Wallace C. Sabine, of Harvard University; Dr. F. R. Watson, professor of experimental physics at the University of Illinois; Dr. Paul Sabine, Mr. Clifford M. Swan, and others, theatre acoustics is now considered as a highly specialized profession. The architect has at his disposal today a large new list of materials with attendant sound absorption coefficients properly recorded, compiled with no less a guarantee than that of the Government Bureau of Standards in Washington, D. C. This list of materials ranges from marble to hair felt.

The question often arises as to why there are so many old examples of auditoriums, cathedrals, music halls, theatres, etc., which are considered good acoustically and yet no one ever heard of acoustic treatment at the time they were built. There are several answers to that question. In the first place, one must consider the properties of the materials used for building purposes at the time.

Steel, reinforced concrete, hard white plaster and heavily varnished woodwork, notorious reflectors of sound, were not used until comparatively late times. We find the old plaster and stone vastly more porous and, therefore, possessing more sound absorbent qualities.

The acoustics of the present New York Metropolitan Opera House could scarcely be anything but very satisfactory since its architects automatically and unwittingly did many of the very things that a good acoustical engineer would recommend now. The auditorium contains a multiplicity of shallow sound pockets formed by the loges and balconies, which, in turn, are heavily draped at the sides, thus forming virtual sound traps. The well-upholstered seats are another help; the perpetual capacity audiences still another. The auditorium is also high, rather than deep, allowing the preponderance of melody from a multitude of voices and musical instruments to rise and blend into a pleasing consistency before reaching the listener. The sound absorbent materials are, for the most part, distributed well away from the stage, thus allowing resonance about the performers that they may not tax their energies in order to build up the desired tone intensity to "fill" the auditorium. Pioneer attempts at acoustical correction in many theatres were very objectionable and were decried by many performers because they were forced to "work too hard to put things across the footlights". Especially is this condition discouraging to those of really sensitive temperament. The usual trouble lay in the injudicious disposition of sound corrective materials.

On the other hand, there are great cathedrals, built these many years, in which the acoustics are bad and yet these are considered very satisfactory for their respective uses; the reason being that the excessive reverberence therein is a positive aid to the clergy during the intonation of chants and to the aid of the choir in its singing. No one is really expected to understand the words, usually uttered in the Latin, or the responses, by the congregation, which were well timed through extreme familiarity with the services. However, one notices that the congregation is generally closely grouped about the pulpit that it might actually understand a brief sermon spoken with words of their own tongue.

But let us turn to more definite and desirable information relating to the architect's connection with the subject of theatre acoustics. Let us suppose that an architect has just been confronted with a commission to design a theatre. Naturally, his mind first turns to the plan and section of the auditorium proper. He must evolve a pleasing design for both. Finally, after the usual struggle for something good, he arrives at a more or less definite conception and the result attains the status of a "working sketch" upon which the final working drawings will be based.

At this point, for the sake of a minimum amount of "grief" to follow, he calls in a competent acoustical engineer. Not only should this man be competent but also disinterested as to what materials that he might be permitted to use. This allows greater free-

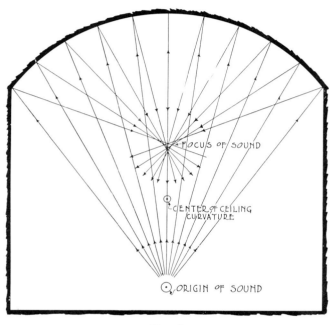

FIG. 1.

Figure 1 shows a diagram of a simple cross section of an imaginary theatre auditorium. The ceiling, a segment of a true circle, having a radius which is more than one-half the ceiling height, causes the elements of sound to converge and form a focus of sound in the usual balcony region

dom and facility for working out the problem. The first step for the engineer will be to examine the plan and section for proper surface profiles to gain the most desirable acoustic qualities and to make his recommendations accordingly. This will necessarily be a rough preliminary examination for the purpose of general criticism with refinements to follow before the working drawings are completed. In many instances, he will tender an immediate O.K. without reservations and, in others, he may recommend that the entire ceiling be lowered or raised, as in the case of the Eastman Theatre in Rochester, N. Y.; he

may modify the shape of the ceiling; he may change a few wall curvatures to eliminate sound foci or dead spots; or he may advise a certain amount of open grille work for some specific exigency which he may know will arise later. These things, considered at the proper time, may save untold expense and dissatisfaction at a later stage of the work. In a majority of cases, some of the above defects, if not remedied in the beginning, cannot be improved by the addition of sound absorbent materials. Any revision of surface profiles is usually referred to as the "surgical phase" of sound correction. It is a sad but true fact that this part of acoustical correction is generally the consideration that it most neglected, not from the standpoint of the acoustical specialist, but because of a lack of realization on the part of the architect. Of course, when the engineer is called upon to correct an auditorium after completion, the "surgical method" generally becomes prohibitive and he must do the best he can by the disposition of acoustic materials, often under an unsurmountable handicap.

Many designers, like opera singers, possess very tender sensibilities and are often very much chagrined at having an "outsider" meddle with their handiwork. For this reason it would seem best that they become acquainted with a few elementary essentials regarding the major limitations of certain surface profiles. For example, the designer should know that segments of true circles are dangerous things to use. These are constant sources of sound foci and "dead spots" if given the wrong radii for the size of the room. Should he insist upon a smooth vaulted or "dished" ceiling, he should know that the radius of such a ceiling should be less than one-half or more than twice the length of the distance between the highest point of the ceiling and the average main floor height. Otherwise, some of the audience will be harassed by an overpowering intensity of sound in the center of the room along its axis and "dead spots" will be evident elsewhere. In some cases, a ceiling with the wrong curvature may be coffered or its surface broken with ornamental projections to minimize the bad effects.

If, then, the acoustical engineer finds in the architect's design a smooth vaulted ceiling that is contrary to these requirements, a conceivable procedure would be to change the profile from the 'one center' arc to one having three centers; that is, so that the large central portion will have a radius equal to more than twice the ceiling height and the smaller portions at either side will have radii less than one-half of the ceiling height. With care, the original profile may be reasonably approximated. An elipse approximating this profile would present another possibility.

To be on the safe side, a designer should employ curved surfaces very sparingly. Especially does this apply in the design for the walls. Irregular curvatures are much to be preferred over circular segments if curves must be used. It is tremendously interesting, with the aid of a few principles remembered from the physics of reflected light rays,— principles which are applicable to the action of sound waves as well in-so-far as diagramatic studies are concerned,—to diagram a section or plan of some auditorium. These diagrams will show, to a great extent, where sound foci are likely to occur. One has only to remember, in making such diagrams, that the reflected element makes an angle, to a line drawn normal to any surface, equal to the angle of the incidental element which strikes the surface in question at its intersection with the same normal. Having followed this procedure, e.i., drawing the incidental and reflected paths of sound from the same source at the proscenium to several points about the room, one can, by inspection of the shape formed by the intersections of the reflected elements, diagnose the location of possible sound foci. If a round wall surface of unsatisfactory radius be mandatory for the purposes of design and a diagrammatic study indicate an objectionable sound foci, the trouble must be taken care of by other means, such as the employment of many deflecting ornamental projections and indentations or heavy sound absorbing materials or both. The specific problem alone tells its own tale and gives the engineer his clues. No two problems will be identical.

Much more could be written regarding the "surgical phase" of acoustic analysis. But let us now consider some of the essential facts governing the more usual side of sound correction, commonly termed the "medical phase."

The "medical phase" is based entirely upon correcting the time of sound reverberation; reverberation being defined here as the "prolongation of sound due to reflection of its elements." Should the period of reverberation be too prolonged, succeeding sounds will merge into inarticulate noises and more

or less confusion will result depending upon the period of reverberation. The confusion is caused by an overlapping of sounds. This is understood when we consider that sound travels at the average speed of 1120 feet per

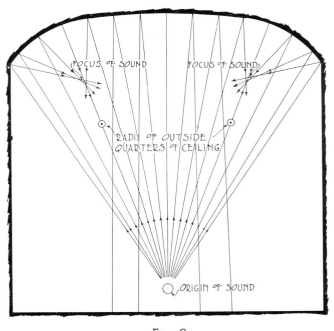

Fig. 2.

Figure 2 also shows a diagram of a simple cross section of an imaginary theatre auditorium. The ceiling has the same height as the section shown in Figure 1 and the side walls have the same vertical height as the first example. Unlike the ceiling of Fig. 1, the ceiling profile is formed from a three centered arch. The radius of the middle portion is more than twice the ceiling height and the radii of the portions at either side are equal and less than one-half the ceiling height. The diagram indicates small sound foci near the ceiling on either side. While this is not a perfect solution for changing the ceiling shown in Figure 1, it eliminates the trouble partially. A true elipse would disburse the sound foci more efficiently.

second at a temperature of 70 degrees and the average speaker utters from three to four words per second. With a long period of reverberation, these words are prone to bound about from wall to wall and finally reach the hearer some time after the direct sound has reached him, and thus the words will overlap with other words and "jumble" a conversation or lecture. In the case of music, one harmonious effect will be tangled with another just as harmonious and, if the two harmonies do not belong to the same chord, a dischord will be the result. On the other hand, a slight overlapping of sounds is necessary for the best psychological effects. This slight overlapping produces a certain pleasant resonance. A room that is too "dead" is

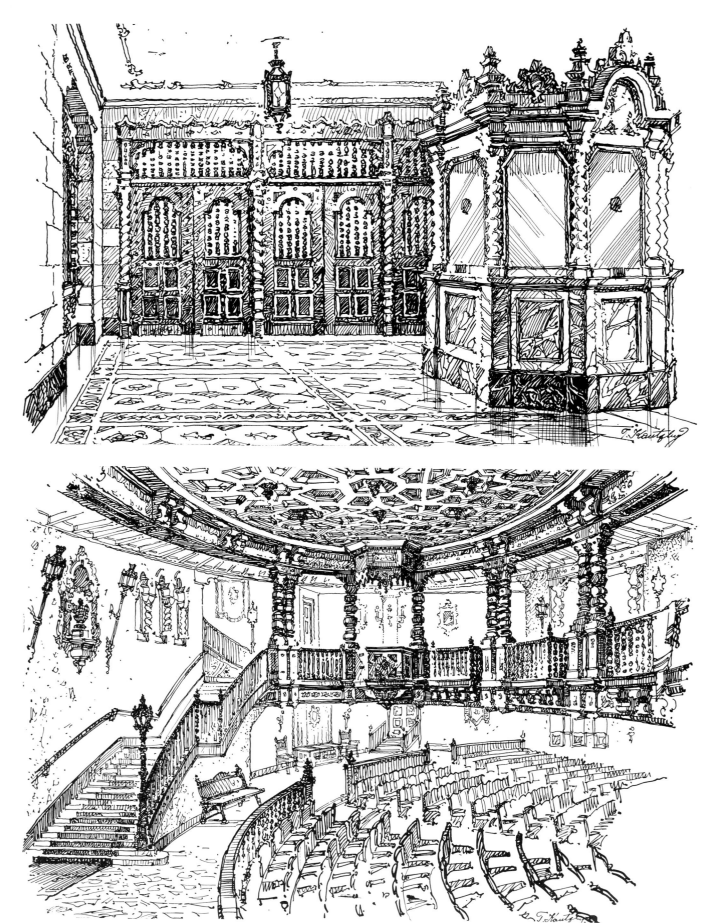

Majestic Theatre, San Antonio, Texas
John Eberson, architect
Above, the Lobby, and below, the Foyer

44

hard upon both the performer and the hearer causing depression and fatigue in both cases.

By comparison of many auditoriums which were considered excellent acoustically, standard periods of reverberation were determined to suit given free volumes of rooms. These comparisons were made for speaking, music and a combination of both, and charts were made which give the proper reverberation for any size of room. Before the advent of the "talkies", a theatre was usually designed to take care of both music and speaking in the presence of about one third of a capacity audience. This practice has since been revised for the "talkies" and we shall speak more in detail of this later on.

The usually accepted formula, used to express the period of reverberation in terms of the properties of a room, is the formula developed by the late Wallace Sabine;

$$t = .05 \frac{V}{A}$$

in which t is the time of reverberation in seconds (selected from the proper reverberation chart for the particular room in question); .05 is a constant value; v is the volume of the room in cubic feet, (free air space); "A" is the total sound absorption value of all objects and materials in the room in terms of "coefficient units", a unit being the value of the amount of sound absorbed by one square foot of open window space.

It has been determined by laboratory tests that the average absorption value of an adult person is given as 4.7 units and calculations of absorption value in a room are usually based upon one-third capacity audience minus the absorption value of the seats which it occupies. Upon determining the number of units absorption already present in the uncorrected room, that number of units is subtracted from the number of units required as found by means of Sabine's formula above in which t and V have been predetermined. Obviously, the result is the number of units of materials to be added to the room minus the absorption value existing in surfaces which the new materials will cover. In other words, having chosen a certain material to be added on account of its absorption coefficient, which we will say is .35 units per square foot, and the surface which it will cover might have a coefficient of .04 units per square foot, the coefficient value of the new added material would be considered as .31 units per square foot. Dividing the amount of the absorption

needed by the coefficient (.31), we arrive at the number of square feet of new material to be added.

Various opinions have been advanced as to the distribution of sound corrective materials but it has been finally conceded, for the sake of acoustical uniformity in the room, that it is much better to use greater amounts of corrective materials having comparatively low coefficients and being more or less uniformly distributed, than to use less of a material with a higher coefficient and confining it to widely separated positions. The judicious disposition of materials is a most important factor in theatre correction. There is, however, one rule that must invariably persist for obtaining satisfactory results. This has to do with an element which we will term "resonance aura". (The expression is as good as any and really seems most descriptive for explanatory purposes.) The best acoustical practice eliminates all sound absorbent treatment from a stage, rostrum or chancel, the ordinary wall surfaces being sufficient to preclude an excess of resonance. Many devices, such as painted cloth ceilings (ceiling flats) for stage sets are often employed to prevent the stage lofts from becoming "sound traps" and also to deflect more sound toward the audience. Of course, in the case of the horns and loud speakers used behind a screen for the "talkies", this consideration is not so important since the loudness (volume) may be regulated electrically from low to great power. The tone from the loud speakers, however, seems much better if it is not forced. It has been observed by the writer, especially in a very large theatre which requires a maximum of power from the loud speakers, that hearers sitting in a direct line with the screen are subjected to an "overdose" of volume and such a condition is very unpleasant. This leads one to believe that loud speakers should be shown much of the same consideration accorded an actual performer. In order to prevent "forcing" a loud speaker, it should be augmented by means of reflecting surfaces designed to throw the preponderence of its output toward the audience and keep the heavy leakage from the loft and wings.

It is hardly necessary to say that the loud speakers must produce a volume of sound proportionate to the size of a person on the screen as compared to the size of an actual person. To assume a volume of intensity through the screen to fit the size of an actual person would be rather ridiculous. The question then arises as to how much more sound absorbent material should be added for a "talkie" theatre than for a theatre used for general purposes. Let us consider a screen which would portray an average height of a human figure to be about twice the height of an actual person. We certainly would expect to hear a voice of at least twice the loudness of the ordinary voice. If such a volume be attained and the reverberation be kept at the proper time duration for the volume of the room, it is natural to assume that more sound absorbent materials should be used. In fact, if the loudness of sound were made twice that of the average human voice, the formula would mathematically show that a double quantity of acoustic material should be used.

The calculations would demand so much deadening of reverberation that a compromise of 50 per cent more absorbent material, instead of twice the usual amount, should form a reasonable conclusion. The subject of theatre acoustics is so new that the element of personal judgment is still an important one. Various acoustical engineers have their pet practices. New theories resulting from personal research are constantly being advanced. A recent theory is that invented by the late Emile Berliner, also inventor of the microphone transmitter. He claimed that the main cause of bad hall acoustics was due to the rigidity of the usual brick or stone walls and that where an auditorium had wooden walls, notably pine or spruce that would vibrate freely, there would be good acoustics. He thus developed the "acoustic tile," made of porous cement, hard, but possessing the resonance of wood when vibrated by a tuning fork. These tiles are semi-hollow and when cemented to the walls of an auditorium in a sufficiently large quantity the center of each tile forms a vibratory diaphragm. Unlike the usual sound absorbent materials, it presumes to absorb sound waves by means of vibration and transmission into wall surfaces. Other materials rely chiefly upon their porosity to assimulate sound energy, and then transmit sound waves through wall surfaces.

The method advanced by Mr. Berliner seems a rather unique one in that, by distributing tiles of various sizes indiscriminately over large areas, it is claimed that an auditorium may be "tuned" for all frequencies of pitch and thus absorb an even proportion of low, intermediate or high pitched sounds. The usual acoustic materials tend to absorb the high frequency sounds to a greater degree than others which are lower in pitch. It is also claimed for Mr. Berliner's method that the quality of reflected sounds is changed, so that should the hall be too reverberant (due to a small audience or other reasons), the changed reflected sound does not interfere seriously with the direct sounds.

These tiles have been used with great success by Magaziner, Eberhard and Harris, architects, in the new Uptown Theatre in

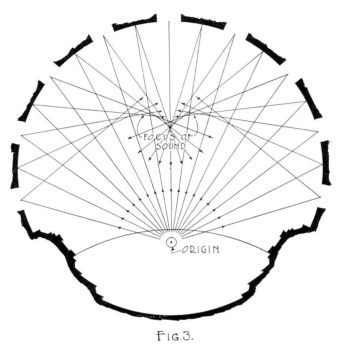

FIG. 3.

Figure 3 shows a plan diagram of an imaginary theatre auditorium having circular walls. An auditorium done in this manner presents one of the worst acoustic conditions possible, as shown by the large area occupied by the focus of sound. Figures 1 and 3 illustrate only a few of the dangers encountered by the use of true segmental surfaces.

Philadelphia, Pa., illustrated on other pages in this book.

The most favorable consideration of the Berliner method seems to lie in the fact that it is an entirely concealed treatment, and is also a permanent application of an acoustic material. It would make little difference how many times the hall might be redecorated. In that way, one would be warranted in stating that it is "fool-proof." In specifying an acoustical treatment for a certain job, one often hesitates to use draperies or heavily upholstered seats. These portable objects will do the work allotted to them but one never knows when they may be exchanged for some other kind of material by some energetic person failing to consider that these were for sound absorption as well as for other uses.

AMERICAN THEATRES OF TODAY

CHAPTER VII

HEATING AND VENTILATING A THEATRE

By EDWIN A. KINGSLEY, *Consulting Mechanical Engineer*

SOME one once said that there are five requisites to the design and construction of a successful theatre: safety, good acoustics, good vision, comfortable seats, and pleasant surroundings. I would add one more: good air. In fact, it might be better to substitute the word "comfort" instead of "comfortable seats" and list the other requisites as they are. For comfort includes the seats, the space between the seats, the size of the lobby and foyer and the matter of heating and ventilating as well. For a theatre patron cannot be comfortable, no matter how comfortable the chairs may be to sit in, if the theatre is not properly heated and ventilated.

Naturally these days when architects and engineers work in such close cooperation, the theatre architect almost invariably entrusts the heating and ventilating of a theatre to an engineer who specializes in this field. He therefore puts up to another the problem of the installation of apparatus, by which fresh air is brought into the building and distributed and foul air is taken out. But I think it is advisable for the architect to familiarize himself with the fundamental principles

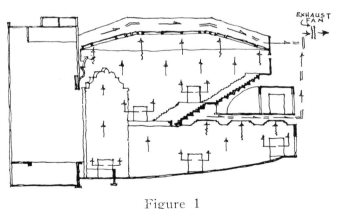

Figure 1

The exhaust system

which guide the heating and ventilating engineer in his work so that the necessary appliances may be installed with the least effort and to the greatest economy for the owner. So I will write only in generalities rather than going into the subject in too great detail. Besides, each problem has its own solution and

what might be desirable in one theatre would not apply at all to another.

Generally speaking, then, we might say that there are four systems by which a theatre may be heated and ventilated. They are (1) the exhaust system; (2) the supply system,—down-feed; (3) the up-feed system;

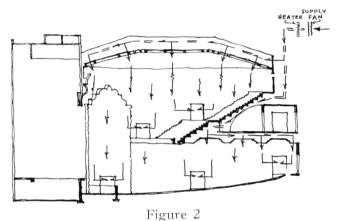

Figure 2

The supply system—down-feed

and (4) the air-washed cooling system. The first or exhaust system is the simplest, the cheapest and the least effective. It is used in small, cheap houses. Fresh air is supplied only by means of open doors, windows, and so forth. There is no supply fan or fresh air intake other than these. The air is exhausted by means of ducts which lead to an exhaust fan. Grilles in the soffit of the balcony and in the ceiling of the auditorium lead to these ducts and so the foul air is taken out of the theatre and the doors and so forth, open again to let in more fresh air. The supply system is almost the reverse of the exhaust system. Fresh air is brought in through an intake and a supply fan; it then passes through a heater which gives it the desired temperature, and is distributed downward throughout the theatre by means of ducts in the ceiling and in the balcony soffit. The foul air is then forced out through the doors and other openings. It may be said here that about 50 to 75 per cent of the air can be used in recirculation, the amount being governed by thermostatic controlled dampers. In some cases, too, the air

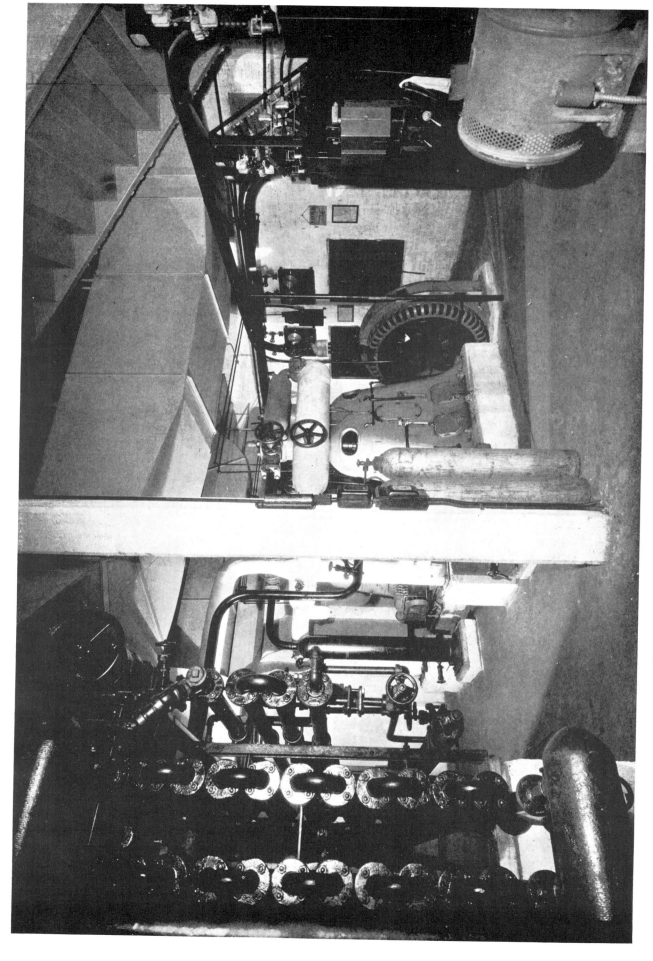

Refrigeration plant, Kings Theatre, Brooklyn, New York
C. W. & Geo. L. Rapp, architects

is partly purified by filters before it passes through the heaters.

The up-feed system is more complicated. A supply fan located near the fresh air intake duct brings the air through the filters, passes it through the heaters and it is distributed by ducts to floor mushrooms or aisle hoods in the orchestra and mushrooms, aisle hoods or step grilles in the balcony. The foul air is let out through grilles in the auditorium ceiling and balcony soffit and carried by means of exhaust ducts to the exhaust fan and then outside. In this system also 50 to 75 per cent of the air can be used in recirculation.

The air-washed cooling system is generally a down-feed system. Between the supply fan

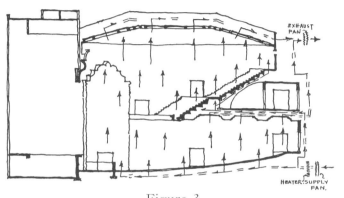

Figure 3
The up-feed system

and the heaters is an air washer. Ducts lead to grilles in the auditorium ceiling and in the balcony soffit and thus the air is distributed downward throughout the house. The foul air leaves by means of floor mushrooms or aisle hoods in the orchestra and step grilles or mushrooms in the balcony, and is taken to the exhaust fan by means of ducts. About 50 to 75 per cent of the air is recirculated by means of a by-pass damper placed in the exhaust fan, thermostatically controlled. Where it is desired to install an air conditioning system, a refrigeration plant is added to this air-cooling system. This plant is usually located in the basement of the building and it supplies cold water to the air washer so that fresh air is cooled to the desired temperature as it is led to the ducts by which it is distributed throughout the house. Where air cooling or air conditioning plants are installed it is necessary to also install wet and dry blub control.

In every case, supply and exhaust fans may be located wherever is most convenient. It is sometimes thought that fans must always be in the top of a building. This is not always

desirable or convenient. It is interesting, perhaps, to note that all basement rooms are heated and ventilated separately. The dressing rooms, too, are controlled by another system. In some cases this is a supply and exhaust system and in others an exhaust system only. A separate exhaust-only system is also installed for the toilets. It is also necessary that projection booths have a separate exhaust system of ventilation.

The size, amount and location of supply and exhaust grilles, mushrooms, aisle hoods and step grilles is determined by the amount of air in cubic feet supplied to each person in the house per minute (C. F. M.). In cheap houses this generally runs from 20 to 30 C. F. M., 20 being the minimum. In medium priced houses the rate is apt to be increased to 25 to 30 C. F. M., while in the better class houses 30 C. F. M. is generally found to prove more satisfactory.

In all cases where fans are installed it is essential that the fans have proper sound deadening foundations and that all ducts and grilles are properly sized so as to prevent noise from entering the theatre, as well as to prevent annoying drafts. In first class houses the spaces used for ventilating apparatus are soundproofed.

Where refrigeration is used it is also essential that spaces assigned to the refrigerating apparatus be entirely enclosed with sound-

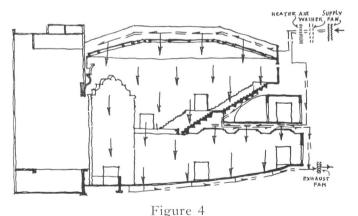

Figure 4
The air-washing cooling system

proofing material. Where cooling and air conditioning systems are used it is sometimes necessary to install a cooling tower, but this greatly increases the cost and the only justification for the use of cooling towers is in those cases where the city or municipality will not otherwise allow the use of water. The cooling tower is generally located on the roof of the theatre.

AMERICAN THEATRES OF TODAY

CHAPTER VIII

THE THEATRE OWNER AND THE ARCHITECT

By LEON FLEISCHMANN, C.E.,
Executive head of Construction Department, Loew's, Inc.

THE Theatrical Industry as it stands today is far different from that of years ago. One of the most important steps to be considered by the owner when contemplating the erection of a theatre today is the selection of an architect who by knowledge and practical experience is fully qualified to furnish proper plans and specifications for the enterprise.

Theatrical construction has followed the trend of the times, having become a highly specialized art, requiring a thorough knowledge of not only the component parts which enter into all construction, but also a knowledge by experience of air conditioning, sound effects, acoustics, sight lines, comfort to patrons, economy in construction, and in general a slight knowledge of theatre operation. Only an understanding of these several subjects would qualify an architect to successfully design a modern theatre building.

The equipment of a modern theatre intended for the exhibition of motion pictures is vastly different in many respects from the house in which drama or opera is presented, although the principles of both are identical. It seems strange, considering the great number of structures erected within the past ten years and the enormous sums of money expended therefor, that the architectural profession, which consists of so many able and high-class individuals and firms, should have permitted a comparatively few architects to practically monopolize all this class of work.

The demands and requirements of the public of today, whose patronage of theatres has so vastly increased within the last period of years, and the progress made in the nature and class of entertainment, as they are offered today, stipulates conditions not thought of formerly.

I have been asked what in my opinion the qualifications of an architect should be in order to qualify him to produce an intelligent set of practical working drawings and specifications for a theatre building and what I say to him when engaging his services.

Owners are interested first in the experi-ence that a particular architect may have had in designing theatres as this seems to be the more conservative and offers the line of least resistance. If his past performances have been successful, he is given the proper consideration to which he is entitled.

He is then given instructions as to what the type of building should be, about what seating capacity is required, the width of the chairs for the comfort of patrons, and, in general, an outline of the policy of the house, so as to enable him to provide for all contingencies for practical and economical operation.

Balcony vibrations are very important and should also enter into conversation, as excessive vibrations is the cause of much grief and in many cases reacts against the successful operation of a theatre.

Assuming that the architect has a thorough knowledge of sight lines and acoustics, there remain but three other essential and important necessary items which are all the public is vitally interested in to make the proposition a financial success:

1. A good and pleasing show.
2. A comfortable seat in which to sit.
3. Proper air conditioning to create a comfortable feeling.

The large sums of money invested in individual theatre operations in the past eight or ten years in certain so-called de luxe theatres of today, have not been warranted. Whereas they may be beautiful to look at, they bring very little or no return on the additional capital invested and are not appreciated by the public at large.

Only those directly associated with the theatrical industry are familiar with the vast amount of what we call "shopping" that is done by the public at large before selecting their theatre and those that make up the average theatre audience are never ready to pay admission unless you offer them the three and only important privileges they are interested in: A GOOD SHOW, A GOOD SEAT AND COMFORTABLE AIR CONDITIONS.

AMERICAN THEATRES OF TODAY

CHAPTER IX

THE THEATRE OF TOMORROW

By BEN SCHLANGER, *Architect*

WHAT form will the theatre of to-morrow assume—the theatre structure that must practically and aesthetically house the ultimate medium of expression in the theatre arts? The motion picture should become this ultimate medium of expression for two distinct reasons: first, because it receives financial support as it is so well patronized by the masses; and second, on account of its technical developments, which not only increase its popularity, but which also heighten its standards of production . These technical advancements—the introduction of sound effects and dialogue synchronized with the film, the inevitable enlarging of the screen, the use of color, and the unlimited possibilities of three dimensional photographic effects which recent experiments have assured—make this the most flexible and expressive medium to which the theatre arts could turn.

The theatre buildings as they exist today are structurally safe, and free from fire and panic hazards; they are equipped to be comfortably warm or cool, as the need may be; and the air within them is kept in constant circulation. With the exception of these comforts, these structures are inadequate to serve the theatre of tomorrow. The theatre industry is tremendously busy keeping up with the constant developments in production in the studio, yet it neglects the fact that it is as equally important to properly exhibit a production as it is to make one.

How large should theatres be? What should be their seating capacity? And just where should they be located, locally or centrally? Such questions are important and must be answered before attempting to design any one individual theatre. Very few people lived nearby the larger show-houses in the theatrical centers, but it was quite natural for them to travel to these centralized theatres because special music, dancing, vocal and other entertainments were presented in the flesh and blood performance. This was something more than could be seen in the local theatres within walking distance of their places of residence. This caused the building of the very large seating capacity theatre.

The smaller local theatres thus suffered while the larger ones prospered. This condition has not now necessarily reversed itself, but it is quite evident that the ability to hear and see in the smaller theatre, on the screen, almost everything that the larger ones previously presented in the flesh and blood performance, has noticeably increased the popularity of the smaller local theatre. These natural tendencies should point to a better understanding as to where theatres should be placed, and how many seats they should contain. Should they be centrally located, built on land so valuable that it reflects on the price of admission in the box office? Are we paying for entertainment or helping pay a large land rental? The possibility of placing an income producing structure directly above a theatre, to help offset the large rental fee of the land, is prohibited by the building departments of most every city.

It would also be reasonable to ask how small can a theatre be—or should there be many smaller theatres in preference to fewer larger ones? More theatres carefully placed and sized according to the communities they serve seem necessary. There is no longer any excuse for the very large theatre involving useless repeated costs of flesh and blood performers, stage hands, and so forth. It is becoming more and more possible to see and hear on the screen the most costly production, whether it be music, drama, or comedy, in every theatre regardless of its size. This should encourage more reasonable admission prices and a still larger and more interested theatre going public.

What really caused all the theatre industry to spend vast sums of money to change its policy of production by introducing sound pictures at a time when it was seemingly enjoying financial stability? It was one of the smaller producing companies, sorely in need of a business stimulant, that started something by producing the first practical sound accompanied film. The others had no choice but to follow.

If a change in the theatre as a structure could come about in just some such manner, the solution would be arrived at more quickly and appropriately, but the situation is somewhat more complicated than that. Unless some interested individual with sufficient financial standing, who is conscious of all the needs of a new theatre structure, ventured to erect such a building, we can look only to the producing industry that now controls the building of theatres for recognition of this problem. Sound accompaniment with the film as developed to date is not sufficient to demand the inadequacy of the theatre structure. It is the enlargening of the screen, together with the three dimensional effects, that will substantiate the dire necessity for a complete new aspect of the problem. To try to exhibit the well proportioned enlarged screen with effects of depth in our trite theatres would limit and stagnate its purpose.

Like most everything else, set rules for planning the lines of a theatre, both in plan arrangement and in section, have now for a long time almost standardized its shape; balconies are still used exactly as they were when they first originated; the sight lines are fixed so that you can just about see the top of a screen fourteen feet high from sitting in the rear of the orchestra; and the balcony sight line forms a sharp enough angle to necessitate an uncomfortable climb to the different levels of seats that are really poor seats looking down into a veritable well-hole, giving a distorted view of the screen. The architect receives a commission to design a theatre; he carefully plans along the lines prescribed by his predecessors, and then ventures forth expressing himself on the side walls of the auditorium in some Spanish or French historical palatial style of architecture, or in some modernistic ornamental mode; and we have what is now known blindly (both to the public and the theatre industry) as the modern theatre structure.

These large over-ornamented theatres, commonly found in all big cities, are intended to create a sumptuous feeling, and to intrigue the beholder with their glittering gold cornices, huge imitation marble columns, and excess of ornamental plaster, used in their grand lobbies, foyers, stairways and auditorium. Thus the theatre industry has arrived at a combination of an exhibition of palatial architecture and motion pictures. It assumed that these show places would be well patronized irrespective of the quality of performance given in them. The trick worked; but a trick stops working.

The public, or the layman, or even more specifically, the patron of the theatre, is seemingly the most disinterested and least helpful towards realizing the relation which the theatre structure holds to the theatre arts. This is largely due to the fact that publicity and criticism in the newspapers and periodicals is usually limited to the plays and films shown, but the facts regarding the theatre as a structure appear before the public only when a theatre opens its portals for the first time: and then it is in the same trite manner that the draperies, gold ornament and gorgeous lighting fixtures are breathlessly written about. Numerous articles have appeared in theatre art magazines and books written by able critics; they well pointed out the need of doing away with the ballroom style of auditorium in a theatre, and looked to the architect with great hopes for a change. To say that the architect has failed to advance is incorrect; the architect who has a keen appreciation of the needs of the modern theatre has as yet not been given the opportunity. But the theatre architects must stop designing in the architectural decorative manner. The problem must be attacked with a new impetus created by the technical resources of the film presentations which are developing with extraordinary rapidity.

The theatre structure of tomorrow must become more a part of the art which it is serving, and not be separated, as it is now, into an auditorium and a stage. The line of division between these two elements is usually marked off by an architecturally burdened proscenium frame, flanked by unused elaborate box treatments and obsolete ornamental organ grilles—a treatment which is religiously adhered to in most all theatres on record. It is here that the slaughtering should begin and concentrate itself. This is the part of the auditorium which is most visible to the viewer, where the transition from the auditorium to the presentation takes place. It is here where the mood is determined. It is mostly this transition that should enable the viewer to feel as little conscious of the surrounding walls and ceiling as possible, so that he can completely envelop himself in that which he is viewing. This portion of the auditorium should be flexible, and there is no reason why

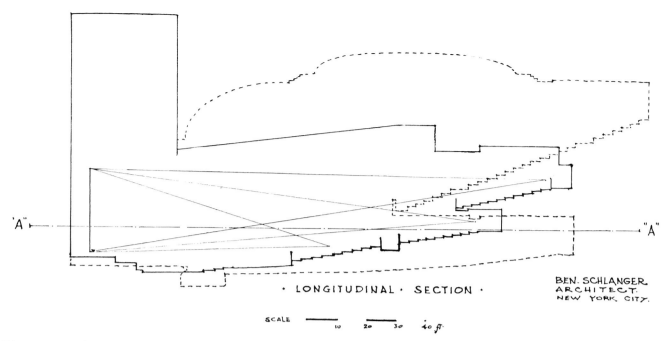

· LONGITUDINAL · SECTION ·

BEN. SCHLANGER.
ARCHITECT.
NEW YORK CITY.

SCALE ———— 10 20 30 40 ft.

The dotted lines on the diagram indicate the longitudinal section through the average large seating capacity theatre. Its dimensions are increased to acommodate the sight lines needed for the large screen. The usual large overhanging balcony is retained, but it starts approximately fifteen feet back of the point where most balconies in existing theatres start, and its lowest point is raised. The bowled orchestra floor is also used. There is only one supposed advantage in retaining the form of our trite theatres, they allow a very large seating capacity. Beyond this questionable need of seats, it has only disadvantages. The last ten rows of seats in the balcony are beyond a point of good sight and hearing of the film presentation. Most all of the balcony seats are too much above the screen and practically all of the orchestra seats are at too low a level, to be within fairly comfortable vision of the screen. The unnecessary height in these theatres is an absolute waste, in addition to causing poor acoustics. The pocket under the overhanging balcony is also troublesome acoustically.

The solid outline on the diagram indicates the longitudinal section through a proposed theatre that would not have as large a seating capacity, yet have many more choice seats. It is a very economical unit to build, and would prove to give more seats per dollar expended. Note how every seat level is kept close to line "A—A" where most of the action on the screen takes place.

its form cannot be changeable, and its lighting effects varied, to suit the tempo of what is being presented. The knowledge gained from the legitimate stage about rigging, coupled with modern electrical engineering, makes this more than possible.

The usual treatment of the rest of the auditorium might also come in for some slaughtering. The ornamental side walls, which are always treated vertically with columns, pilasters, arches, and so forth, defeat the purpose they might so well accomplish by having a symmetrical repetition of motifs from the proscenium to the rear of the auditorium, which causes a disturbing pull of the eye away from what should be the main focal point. These walls should have a gradual simplification and omission of forms as they recede to the rear of the auditorium; the forms used should have strong horizontal direction, instead of vertical emphasis, fastening the eye to the screen, the focal point, at the front of the auditorium. The ceiling, even

more so than the side walls, should be left as simple as possible, depending on lighting to vary the effect which can be made to give an impression of indefinite height, or of a lower intimate feeling, as the need may be. The usual domes, suspended from above and resting on air, not only are entirely unrelated to the walls, but also give no impression of height or intimacy regardless of any lighting that could be employed.

The suggestions made to simplify the interior of the auditorium need not be construed to mean that the effect produced by this simplification would be bare or cold in feeling. On the contrary the introduction of directional lines, both in the very structural breaking-up of the shape of the physical enclosure and in the application of superficial forms, could create a motivating as well as a restful atmosphere. While the viewer should not be conscious of the different walls and ceiling that enclose him, he should by all means be conscious of the effect of the unified surroundings, which should assist rather than compete with the presentation.

Much of the effect desirable in the theatre interior must be obtained by the use and control of light. It is here that the mistake is often made. The walls and ceiling are usually designed as if they were going to be seen in broad daylight, neglecting the fact that the light in the auditorium of a theatre must be kept quite dim during most of a performance. Thus the architectural forms employed are blotted out and have little or no effect on the viewer during the performance. To correct this, most existing theatres light up the various separated architectural motifs, which only become anoying by their incoherent, spotty effect, and detract from the presentation. This same spotty effect is also caused by hanging bracketed lighting fixtures, the use of which would best be discarded. The very forms used to make up the character of the interior must carefully be thought of in terms of light found in a dark space. These forms which should contain bands or areas of light must compose, giving an effect, by varying the intensity of the different parts at different times which could be synchronized with the presentation, as well as the musical and sound accompaniments.

Important as the treatment of the auditorium may be, the sizing and placing of the instrument of presentation, namely, the screen, is even more important, because this should determine the scale of the theatre and the entire seating arrangement.

The size of the motion picture screen now used is approximately fourteen feet in height by twenty feet in width. It is obvious that this size must be increased to achieve effects of scale and diversity of action impossible with the present screen. To properly enlarge the screen, it would have to increase its dimensions both in height and in width; to increase it in width only, as one of the film producers has already attempted, would give an unbalanced picture, which carries the eye from left to right horizontally, thus disconnecting the action portrayed on the screen. The vertical accent is needed to allow for good picture composition, therefore it must be increased in height as well as in width. A screen twenty-two feet in height and thirty-three feet in width would be sufficiently enlarged and yet be in proportion with a theatre, neither too large nor too small.

The enlargening of the screen alone revolutionizes the shape of the theatre; the seating arrangement becomes noticeably affected. The large seating capacity balcony that hangs over more than half of the orchestra floor can no longer be used; it would make the seats on the orchestra floor directly underneath it unusable, due to the fact that these seats would not afford a full view of the complete height of the enlarged screen. Only a shallow balcony could be used. Whether the seating is arranged on a single floor, with the proper gradient pitch, or whether a balcony is introduced, as many seats as possible of the total seating capacity should be placed on a level with a point about one-third of the height of the screen, measured from the bottom upward. This would insure a comfortable view of the screen, thus remedying the necessity of craning one's neck to look up, or of pitching one's body forward to look down at the screen.

The theatre structure could also be so designed as to enable it to serve the different theatre arts. Its very shape, if properly formed to accommodate good sight lines and other requirements heretofore mentioned, would solve itself acoustically. Most theatres have poor acoustics for the simple reason that they are not planned or shaped right otherwise. In many instances the dead pockets, which give most trouble to the acoustics of the auditorium, are caused by the domes or other architectural features employed in their design, or by some whimsical, meaningless shape given the interior as a whole. If a theatre had good acoustics, as well as a space devoted to a stage portion (which is in any case necessary even if the enlarged film is being shown, because the first row of seats must have a minimum distance of at least thirty feet between it and the screen), it could then present a legitimate or musical performance, should the need arise.

How has the legitimate stage been affected by the sound film? Is it destined to go? It may remain stronger than ever as far as its quality of performance is concerned but probably fewer legitimate productions will prosper, for only the very best will be retained. The demand for any but the very best legitimate performance is more than replaced by the talking film. It is also possible that the legitimate stage of the future will be limited to amateur performances, from which might emerge the performers for screen entertainment.

What is to become of the silent film, with its effect of pantomime expression—an art not to be ignored? Whether it combines its effect with sound or not, it is worthy of a comeback, especially with the new impetus the enlarged screen would give it. The silent film still has its devotees; with the addition of sound without dialogue, it could be very effective.

Is there a possibility of television replacing the theatre as such? The competition which the development of television in the individual home may offer the theatre industry should pronounce the need of improving the theatre structure and of creating in it a motivating atmosphere which would cause the patron to be drawn to it in preference to remaining at home to be entertained. Even if as it now appears television will be perfected to a point where one can see and hear in the home all that is being offered at the theatre now, it is a certainty that it would not be as effective to be entertained by it in a living room at home as it would to be in surroundings tuned to that which is being shown. At any rate, a screen large enough to give an illusion of scale of settings and characters in relation to the size of the viewer would not fit in any room of the average home. This suggests that the only possibility of television doing away with the public theatre might lie in the establishing of semi-private television auditoriums as an integral part of residential developments. Therefore it seems that the theatre industry would make an attempt to control television to protect its own interests.

Apparently the theatre industry does not outwardly show any immediate concern to its problem, except by its seeming hesitancy to build new theatres. The normal life of a building should not be much less than twenty years. The plan and design of a theatre, then, should meet the necessities of the next twenty years. A comparative lack of theatre building recently felt has been falsely attributed to the fact that there are too many theatres built to date. It really is an excuse, used for a breathing spell, to allow the basic facts of the problem to assert themselves.

The theatre, both from the production and exhibiting aspects, is facing the greatest opportunity it has had in all its history; it has now within its reach the means to progress aesthetically, in spite of its being a commercial venture.

Architecture, outside of the theatre, in its various types of buildings is freeing itself from the ancestral garb which has for centuries bound it to formulas of form and composition, irrespective of use and function.

That the theatre structure, of all buildings, should persist to clothe itself in architecture inspired by stone columns and arches is most incomprehensible. Wherein lies the fault? Who will lead the way? The minds of many

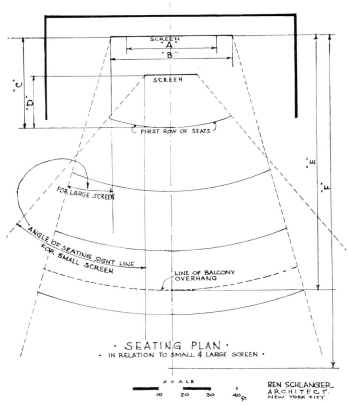

The seating plan diagram suggests how the width and depth of the theatre auditorium, using the large screen, may be determined. "A", is the screen width enlarged for standard use. "B", being wider, allows for a screen whereon can be projected special large scale effects. If possible, most theatres should be able to accommodate this "B" screen size. "C" is the minimum distance between the screen and the first row of seats. "D" is the distance between the smaller screen and the first row of seats (the diagram is not based on this distance nor on the small screen).

Note that the large screen does not allow for as wide an angle of seating sight lines as the smaller screen—thus the fan shape auditorium, giving greater width for seating, becomes obsolete. This doing away with the extreme side seats should be welcomed. "E" is a suggested minimum between the large screen and the beginning of an overhanging balcony. "F" is a suggested maximum from the large screen to the last row of seats. See Longitudinal Section Diagram for further explanation of "E" and 'F".

people may be employed to plan a modern theatre building. We have competent structural, sanitary, air-conditioning and electrical engineers, reliable general building contractors and sufficient experts in other fields— all capable and well advanced in their individual lines of endeavor. It remains for the architect, however, to be imaginative enough to incorporate all this technical assistance at his command with a complete consciousness of the entire problem. The theatre of tomorrow is not very far off; as a matter of fact it is here already—in essence but not in form. To survive as a financial box-office success, the theatre industry must recognize the problem facing it.

The New Fox Wilshire Theatre, Los Angeles, California
S. Charles Lee, architect

AMERICAN THEATRES OF TODAY

CHAPTER X

CHECKING LIST FOR A THEATRE

Prepared by ALBERT D. HILL, *architect*

ENTRANCE
TICKET BOOTH

1—Ticket Vending Machine
2—Change Maker
3—Ceiling Ventilator
4—Electric Heater
5—Money Drawer
6—Hole in Glass and Shutter over same
7—Shutter over Hole above Vending Machine

VESTIBULE

1—Display Frames
2—Photo Frames
3—Photo Frames in Door Panels
4—Ticket Chopper and Electric Outlet for same.
5—Sand Jars for Cigarette Butts
6—Sockets and Standards for Brass Rails
7—Plush Covered Chains and Hooks
8—Cove Lighting
9—Chandeliers
10—Electric Sign for Coming Attractions over Doors
11—Sinkage for Rubber Mats
12—Marble or Terrazzo Floor

STANDING SPACE

1—Capping on Rail
2—Marble Base
3—Marble or Terrazzo Floor
4—Glass Wind Screen
5—Recessed Radiators
6—Drinking Fountain
7—Rubber Mat for same
8—Cup Receptacles
9—Sinkage for Carpet and Carpet Strips
10—Closet for Electrical Panel
11—Telephone Outlets for House Phone
12—Public Telephones

STAIRCASES

1—Mark Materials for same
2—Handrails both sides
3—Center Handrail for Wide Stairs

AUDITORIUM

1—Width of Aisles and Dimensions between Aisles
2—Radius Points
3—Extra Width of 1st and Last Row of Seats
4—Mark all Floor Elevations above or below Stage
5—See that all Doors swing clear of Passages inside and in Courts
6—Fire Doors for all Openings through Proscenium
7—Step Lights
8—Chair Lights
9—Receptacles for Vacuum Cleaner
10—Or Vacuum Cleaner System
11—Exit Lights over all Doors inside
12—Lights over all Doors in Courts
13—Empty Conduits for Organ Wiring
14—Receptacles for Musicians' Outlets
15—Console Elevator
16—Orchestra Elevator
17—Galv. Iron Pipes from Organ to Blower Console and Relay. Size to be given by Organ Contractor. Empty Conduits for Organ Wiring
18—Stud Frame for Organ Shutter in Organ Chamber
19—Blower Room and Air Inlet for same
20—Organ Heater
21—Elevators and Machinery Room for same
22—Method of Relamping all Electric Outlets
23—Angle Iron on edge of all Light Coves for Ladders
24—Suspended Ceilings
25—Plank Walkways over Ceiling
26—Holes through Ceiling behind Coves and Tin Flaps over same for access to Lights
27—See that all Electric Outlets are clear of Fresh Air System and Grilles
28—Hose Reel Recesses, Stand Pipes
29—Manholes to Under Floor Ducts
30—Mark all Kalamein and Tin Clad Doors

COURTS

1—Lighted and Drained, Paving
2—Iron Doors over Transformer Room for Access to same
3—Entrance to Boiler Room and Fresh Air for same
4—Sidewalk Grilles
5—Steamer Connection

BALCONY

1—Mark materials for all Rails Balcony Front
2—Cap on Rail and Bronze Piping
3—Rails on Cross Over
4—Handrails on all Steps
5—Spot Lights and Platforms in front of Balcony
6—Step Lights. Chair Lights
7—Exit Signs over Doors
8—Fountains. Telephones
9—Mark material for all Floors, Walls and Ceilings
10—Show where Carpets will be used
11—Empty Conduits from Sign to Flasher Room for Sign Contractor

TOILET ROOMS

1—Mark all Floors, Walls, Doors, Partitions
2—Electric Hand Dryers
3—Mirrors, Soap Receptacles, Paper Receptacles

MANAGER

1—Manager's Office. Stationary Store
2—Poster Rooms
3—Usher Rooms and Lockers
4—Captain's Room
5—Slop Sink and Janitor's Room
6—Storage Space for Electric Sign Letters

BASEMENT

1—Boiler Room Size of Flues
2—Coal and Oil Storage
3—Refrigerating Plant
4—Transformer Room Drains and
5—Contactor Room under Stage Switchboard
6—Motor Generator Room
7—Meter Room
8—Battery Room for Emergency Lights
9—Musicians' Room
10—Music Room
11—Storage Room
12—Workshop
13—Lavatories
14—Sumps
15—Pumps
16—Incinerator
17—Coal Chute
18—Children's Play Room
19—Sidewalk Lights
20—Paint all Pipe Lines

STAGE

1—Scenery Door
2—Stage Entrance and Vestibule
3—Time Clock
4—Watchman's Clock
5—Wood Floor on Stage
6—Moveable Portion
7—Loose Beams
8—Smoke Pockets for Curtain

9—Footlight Trough
10—Radiation Rear Wall and Skylight
11—Steel for Headblocks
12—Ladders to Grid
13—Access to Roof
14—Skylight and Screen under Skylight
15—Console Elevator and Foundation for Motors
16—Orchestra Elevator
17—Border Lights, Strips, Stage Pockets
18—Exit Lights
19—Elevator or Method of Handling Trunks
20—Drinking Fountain
21—Kalamein Shelves
22—Hose Reels Standpipes
23—Fire Gong System
24—Sprinkler System

ROOF

1—Flagpole
2—Downspouts and Drains
3—Roof Ventilators
4—Fire Escape to Roof
5—Sprinkler Tank
6—Skylights
7—Ventilating Plant

MACHINE ROOM

1—Tin Clad Doors, Angle Iron Frames
2—Gravity Sliding Doors over Openings
3—Air Inlets
4—Ventilators, Fans, Ducts
5—Battery Room
6—Store
7—Music Room
8—Rewind Shelves and Cabinets
9—Rubber Floor
10—Toilet Lockers
11—Flasher Room for Electric Signs
12—Refrigerator System for Drinking Water

Main Lobby, St. George Theatre, Brooklyn, New York
Schlanger & Ehrenrich, architects

Sketch for proposed theatre, Philadelphia, Pa.
W. H. Lee, architect; Armand D. Carroll, associate

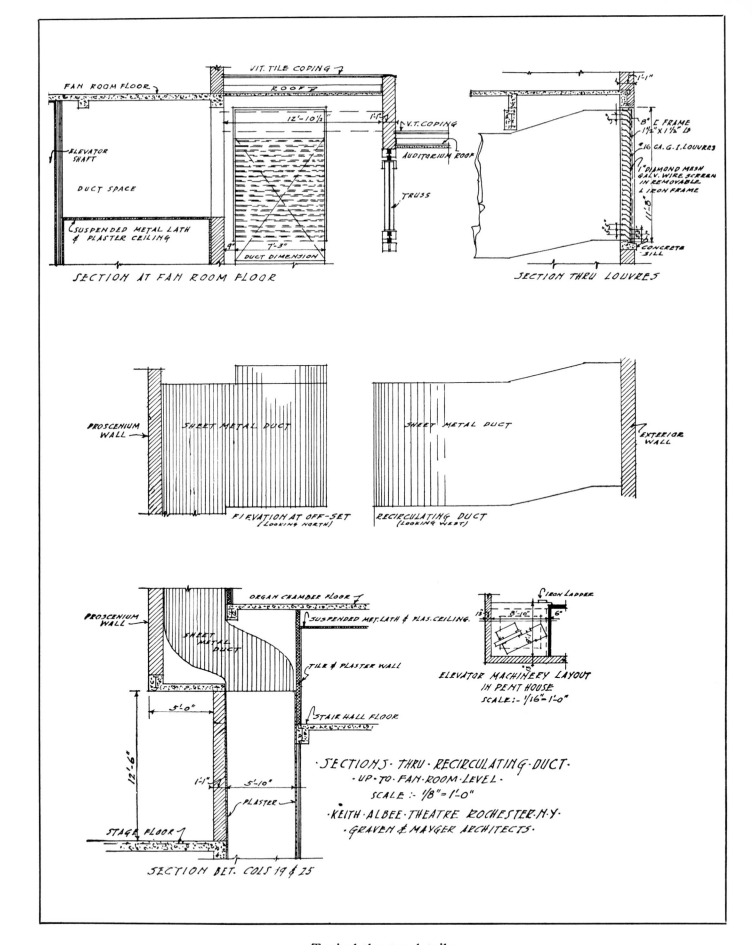

SECTION AT FAN ROOM FLOOR

SECTION THRU LOUVRES

ELEVATION AT OFF-SET
(LOOKING NORTH)

RECIRCULATING DUCT
(LOOKING WEST)

ELEVATOR MACHINERY LAYOUT
IN PENT HOUSE
SCALE:- 1/16"=1'-0"

·SECTIONS·THRU·RECIRCULATING·DUCT·
·UP·TO·FAN·ROOM·LEVEL·
SCALE:- 1/8"=1'-0"
·KEITH·ALBEE·THEATRE·ROCHESTER·N·Y·
·GRAVEN & MAYGER ARCHITECTS·

SECTION BET. COLS 19 & 25

Typical theatre details

60

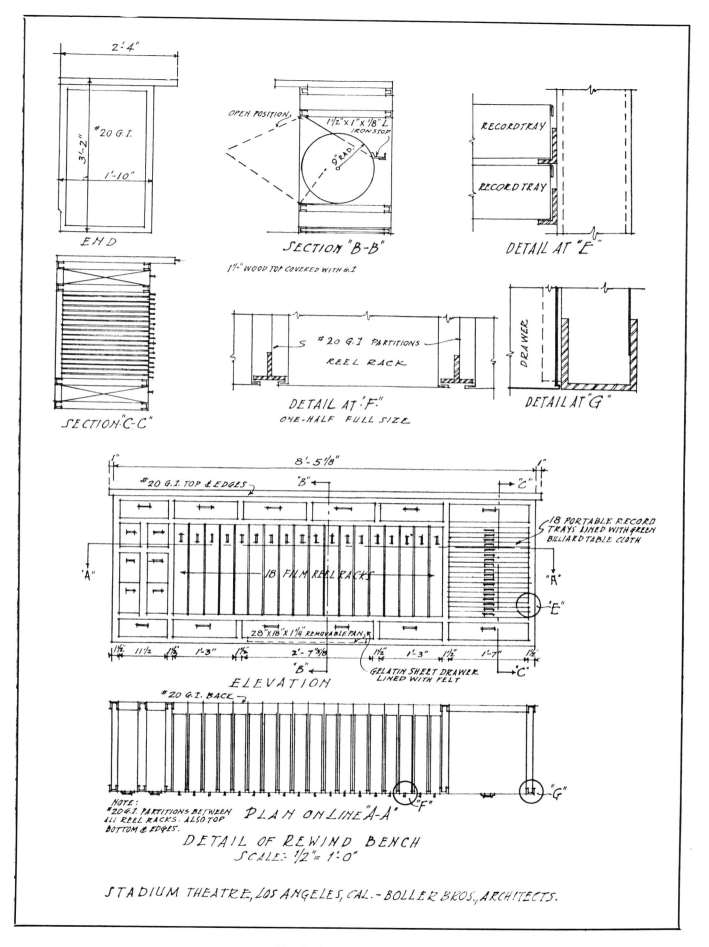

2'-4"

#20 G.I.

3'-2"

1'-10"

END

OPEN POSITION

1½"x1"x⅞"L
IRON STOP

9" RAD.

SECTION "B-B"

1¼" WOOD TOP COVERED WITH G.I.

RECORD TRAY

RECORD TRAY

DETAIL AT "E"

SECTION "C-C"

#20 G.I. PARTITIONS

REEL RACK

DETAIL AT "F"
ONE-HALF FULL SIZE

DRAWER

DETAIL AT "G"

8'-5⅛"

#20 G.I. TOP & EDGES

"B"

"C"

18 PORTABLE RECORD
TRAYS LINED WITH GREEN
BILLIARD TABLE CLOTH

"A"

18 FILM REEL RACKS

"A"

"E"

28"x18"x1¼" REMOVABLE PAN

1½" 11½" 1½" 1'-3" 1½" 2'-7⅝" 1½" 1'-3" 1½" 1'-7" 1½"

"B"

GELATIN SHEET DRAWER
LINED WITH FELT

"C"

ELEVATION

#20 G.I. BACK

"F"

"G"

NOTE:
#20 G.I. PARTITIONS BETWEEN
ALL REEL RACKS. ALSO TOP
BOTTOM & EDGES.

PLAN ON LINE "A-A"

DETAIL OF REWIND BENCH
SCALE: ½" = 1'-0"

STADIUM THEATRE, LOS ANGELES, CAL. - BOLLER BROS., ARCHITECTS.

Typical theatre details

61

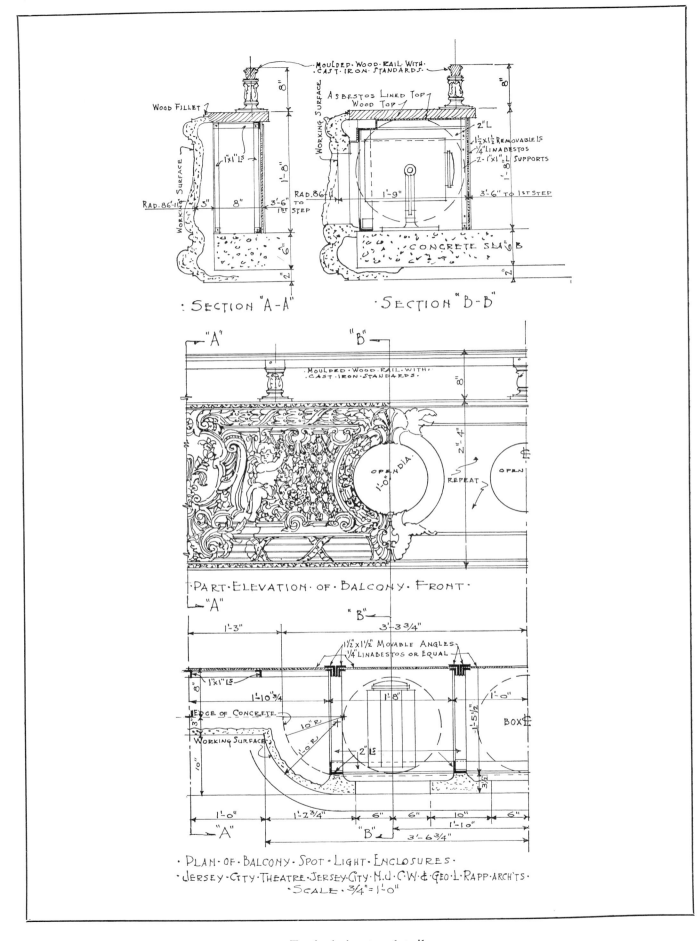

SECTION "A-A" ·SECTION "B-B"

·PART·ELEVATION·OF·BALCONY·FRONT·

·PLAN·OF·BALCONY·SPOT·LIGHT·ENCLOSURES·
·JERSEY·CITY·THEATRE·JERSEY·CITY·N.J·C.W·& GEO·L·RAPP·ARCH'TS·
·SCALE·3/4"=1'-0"

Typical theatre details

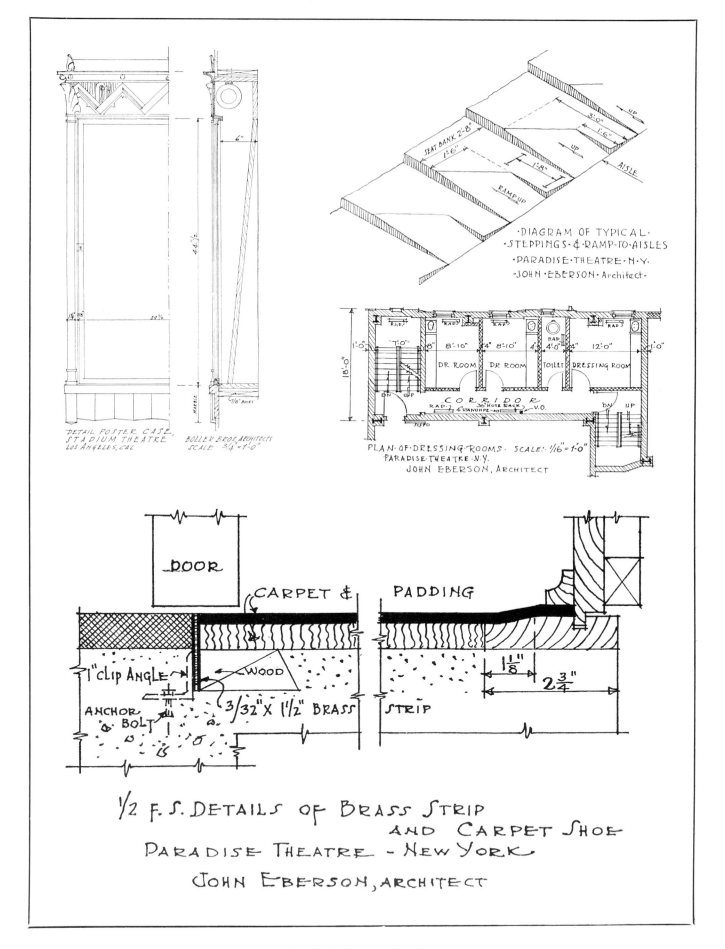

DETAIL POSTER CASE,
STADIUM THEATRE
LOS ANGELES, CAL

BOLLER BROS, ARCHITECTS
SCALE 3/4"=1'-0"

·DIAGRAM OF TYPICAL·
·STEPPINGS·&·RAMP·TO·AISLES
·PARADISE·THEATRE·N·Y·
·JOHN·EBERSON·Architect·

SEAT BANK 2'-8"

PLAN·OF·DRESSING·ROOMS· SCALE· 1/16"=1'-0"
·PARADISE·THEATRE·N·Y·
JOHN EBERSON, ARCHITECT

CORRIDOR

DR. ROOM   DR. ROOM   TOILET   DRESSING ROOM

DOOR

CARPET &   PADDING

1"CLIP ANGLE

ANCHOR
BOLT

WOOD

3/32" X 1 1/2" BRASS   STRIP

1/2 F.S. DETAILS OF BRASS STRIP
AND CARPET SHOE
PARADISE THEATRE - NEW YORK
JOHN EBERSON, ARCHITECT

Typical theatre details

63

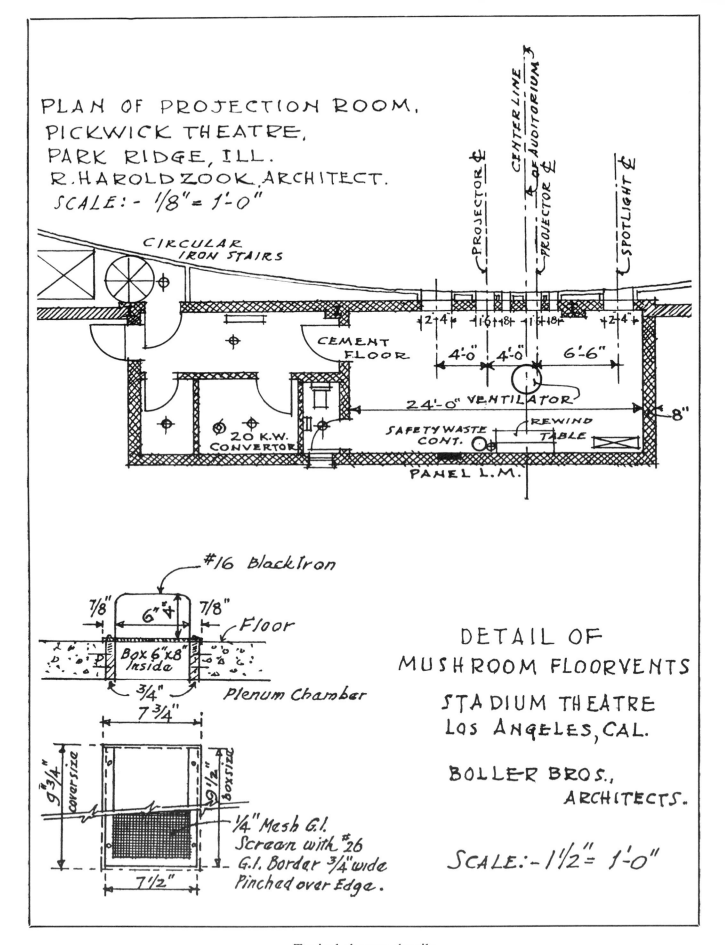

PLAN OF PROJECTION ROOM,
PICKWICK THEATRE,
PARK RIDGE, ILL.
R. HAROLD ZOOK, ARCHITECT.
SCALE:- 1/8" = 1'-0"

CIRCULAR
IRON STAIRS

PROJECTOR ℄
CENTER LINE
℄ OF AUDITORIUM
PROJECTOR ℄
SPOTLIGHT ℄

CEMENT
FLOOR

2" 4" 1'6" 1'8" 1'6" 1'8" 2" 4"

4'-0" 4'-0" 6'-6"

24'-0" VENTILATOR

8"

20 K.W.
CONVERTOR

SAFETY WASTE
CONT.

REWIND
TABLE

PANEL L.M.

#16 BlackIron

7/8"   6" 4"   7/8"

Floor

Box 6"x8"
Inside

3/4"

Plenum Chamber

7 3/4"

9 3/4" oversize

9 1/2" Box size

1/4" Mesh G.I.
Screen with #26
G.I. Border 3/4" wide
Pinched over Edge.

7 1/2"

DETAIL OF
MUSHROOM FLOORVENTS
STADIUM THEATRE
LOS ANGELES, CAL.

BOLLER BROS.,
ARCHITECTS.

SCALE:- 1 1/2" = 1'-0"

Typical theatre details

64

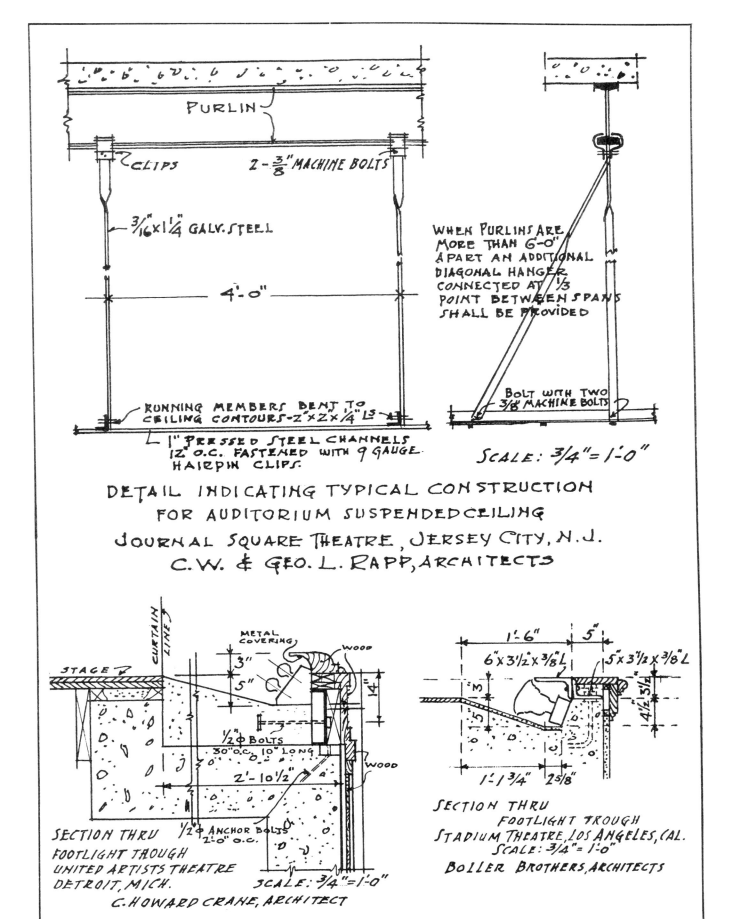

PURLIN

CLIPS

2 - 3/8" MACHINE BOLTS

3/16" X 1 1/4" GALV. STEEL

4'-0"

WHEN PURLINS ARE
MORE THAN 6'-0"
APART AN ADDITIONAL
DIAGONAL HANGER
CONNECTED AT 1/3
POINT BETWEEN SPANS
SHALL BE PROVIDED

RUNNING MEMBERS BENT TO
CEILING CONTOURS-2"X 2"X 1/4" L'S

1" PRESSED STEEL CHANNELS
12" O.C. FASTENED WITH 9 GAUGE
HAIRPIN CLIPS.

BOLT WITH TWO
3/8" MACHINE BOLTS

SCALE: 3/4" = 1'-0"

DETAIL INDICATING TYPICAL CONSTRUCTION
FOR AUDITORIUM SUSPENDED CEILING
JOURNAL SQUARE THEATRE, JERSEY CITY, N.J.
C.W. & GEO. L. RAPP, ARCHITECTS

STAGE

CURTAIN LINE

METAL COVERING

WOOD

3"

5"

14"

1/2"Ø BOLTS
30" O.C. 10" LONG

WOOD

2'-10 1/2"

1/2"Ø Anchor bolts
2'-0" O.C.

SECTION THRU
FOOTLIGHT TROUGH
UNITED ARTISTS THEATRE
DETROIT, MICH.
C. HOWARD CRANE, ARCHITECT

SCALE: 3/4" = 1'-0"

1'-6"   5"
6"X 3 1/2"X 3/8" L   5"X 3 1/2"X 3/8" L

4 1/2"   3 1/2"

1'-1 3/4"   2 5/8"

SECTION THRU
FOOTLIGHT TROUGH
STADIUM THEATRE, LOS ANGELES, CAL.
SCALE: 3/4" = 1'-0"
BOLLER BROTHERS, ARCHITECTS

Typical theatre details

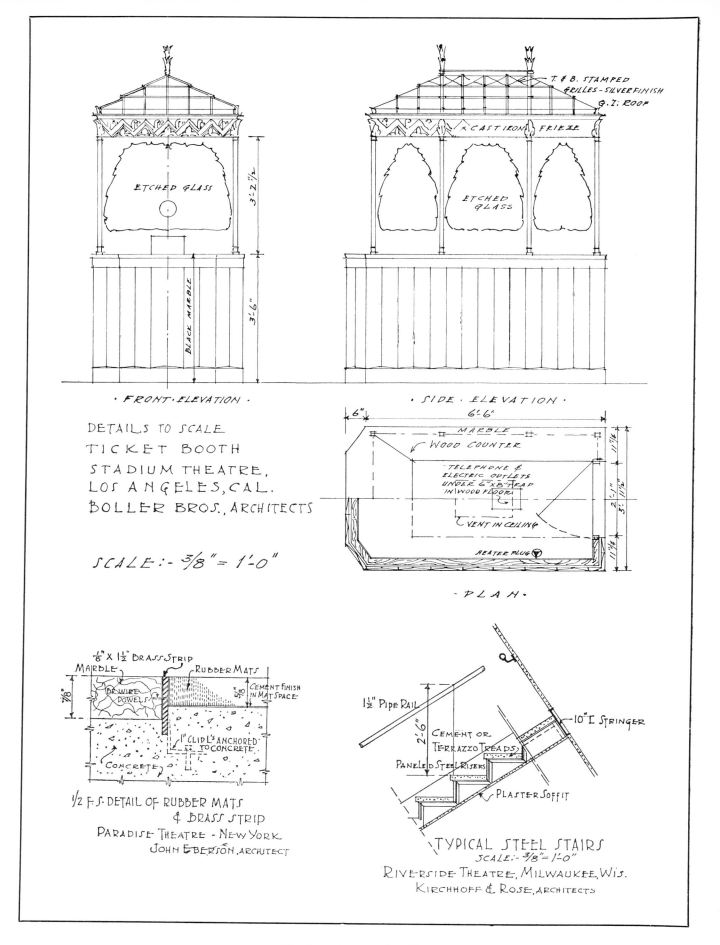

· FRONT · ELEVATION ·

· SIDE · ELEVATION ·

T. & B. STAMPED GRILLES - SILVER FINISH
G.I. ROOF

CAST IRON FRIEZE

ETCHED GLASS

ETCHED GLASS

3'-2½"

3'-6"

BLACK MARBLE

DETAILS TO SCALE
TICKET BOOTH
STADIUM THEATRE,
LOS ANGELES, CAL.
BOLLER BROS., ARCHITECTS

SCALE :- ⅜" = 1'-0"

6"

6'-6"

MARBLE
WOOD COUNTER
TELEPHONE &
ELECTRIC OUTLETS
UNDER 6"X8" TRAP
IN WOOD FLOOR

VENT IN CEILING

HEATER PLUG

· P L A N ·

⅛" X 1½" BRASS STRIP
MARBLE
RUBBER MATS
BK WIRE DOWELS
CEMENT FINISH IN MAT SPACE
⅝"
⅞"
1" CLIP L's ANCHORED TO CONCRETE.
CONCRETE

½ F.S. DETAIL OF RUBBER MATS
& BRASS STRIP
PARADISE THEATRE - NEW YORK
JOHN EBERSON, ARCHITECT

1½" PIPE RAIL
2'-6"
CEMENT OR TERRAZZO TREADS
PANELED STEEL RISERS
10" I STRINGER
PLASTER SOFFIT

TYPICAL STEEL STAIRS
SCALE :- ⅜" = 1'-0"
RIVERSIDE THEATRE, MILWAUKEE, WIS.
KIRCHHOFF & ROSE, ARCHITECTS

Typical theatre details

Majestic Theatre, San Antonio, Texas
John Eberson, architect
Above, Men's Smoking Room; below, Mezzanine Promenade

67

GENERAL VIEW OF BUILDING

DETAIL OF ONE ENTRANCE

Chicago Opera House, Chicago, Illinois—Graham, Anderson, Probst & White, architects

DETAIL OF GRAND FOYER

DETAIL OF LOBBY

Chicago Opera House, Chicago, Illinois—Graham, Anderson, Probst & White, architects

DETAIL OF PROSCENIUM ARCH

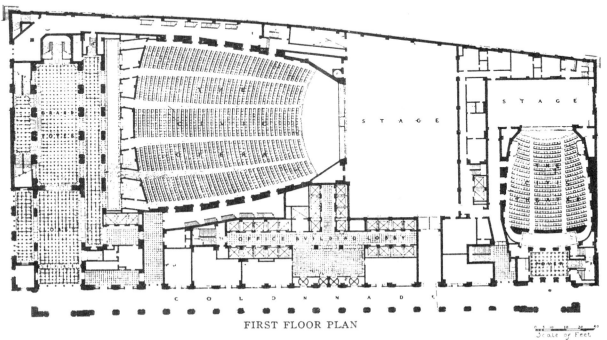

FIRST FLOOR PLAN

THE ORCHESTRA SEATS 1682 PERSONS

Chicago Opera House, Chicago, Illinois
Graham, Anderson, Probst & White, architects
(*Illustrations courtesy The Architectural Forum*)

DETAIL OF SIDE WALL TREATMENT IN AUDITORIUM

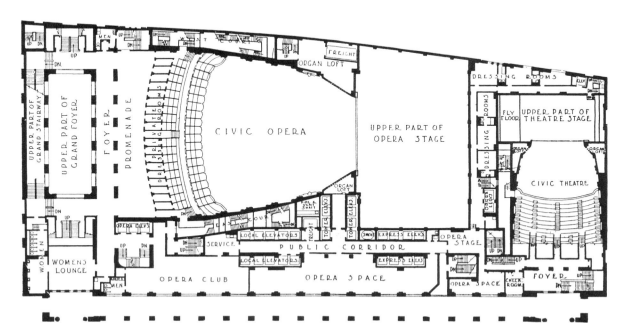

SECOND FLOOR PLAN

ON THE SECOND FLOOR THERE IS A SERIES OF BOXES

Chicago Opera House, Chicago, Illinois
Graham, Anderson, Probst & White, architects
(Illustrations courtesy The Architectural Forum)

DETAIL OF SEATS IN GALLERY

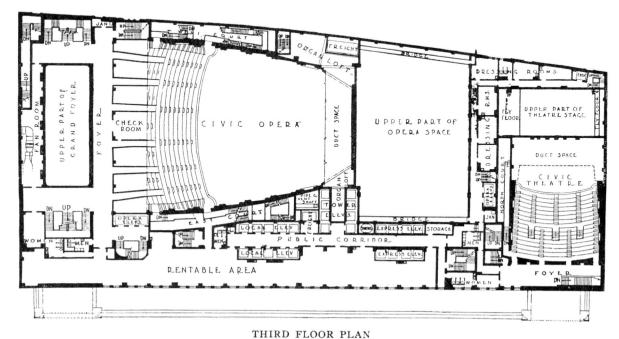

THIRD FLOOR PLAN
ABOVE THE BOXES IS A BALCONY AND A GALLERY

Chicago Opera House, Chicago, Illinois
Graham, Anderson, Probst & White, architects
(Illustrations courtesy The Architectural Forum)

VIEW OF THE AUDITORIUM FROM THE STAGE

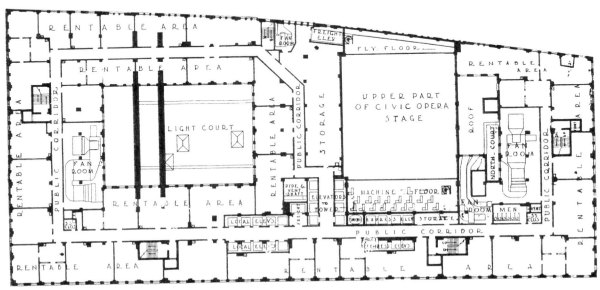

FOURTH FLOOR PLAN

THE TOTAL SEATING CAPACITY OF THE HOUSE IS 3471

Chicago Opera House, Chicago, Illinois
Graham, Anderson, Probst & White, architects
(Illustrations courtesy The Architectural Forum)

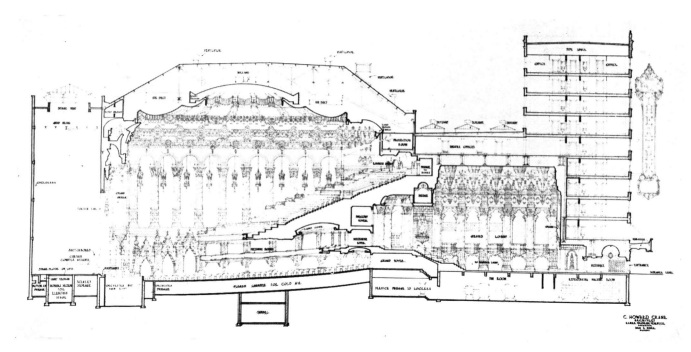

LONGITUDINAL SECTION

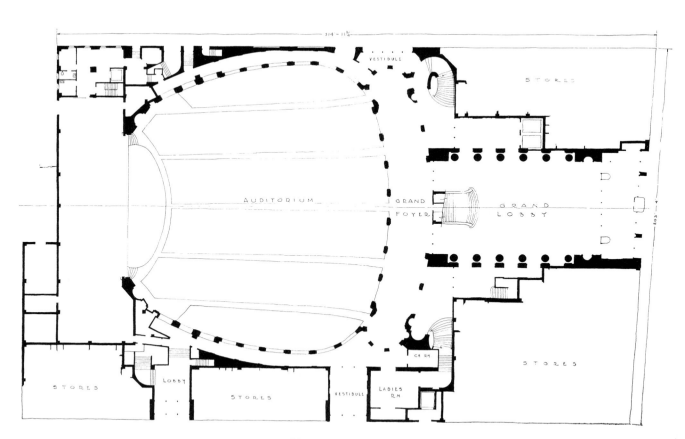

MAIN FLOOR PLAN
ORCHESTRA SEATS 2820 PERSONS

Fox Detroit Theatre, Detroit, Michigan
C. Howard Crane, architect; Elmer George Kiehler, associate
The total seating capacity of the theatre is 5042

Fox Detroit Theatre, Detroit, Michigan
C. Howard Crane, architect; Elmer George Kiehler, associate
Detail of Grand Lobby

75

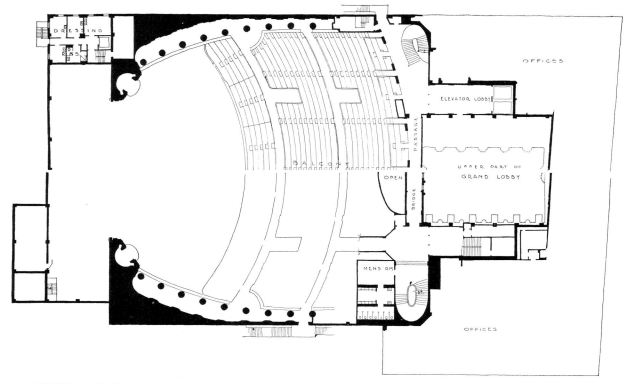

BELOW, ½ PLAN OF 2nd CROSS AISLE AND 4th FLOOR AND ABOVE, ½ PLAN OF BALCONY AND 5th FLOOR
THE SEATING CAPACITY OF THE BALCONY IS 1812

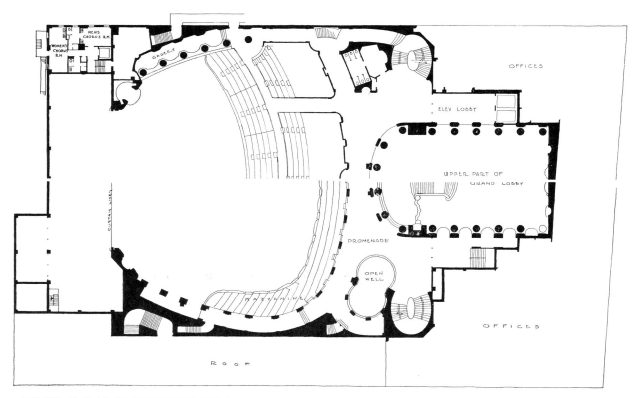

BELOW, ½ PLAN OF MEZZANINE AND 2nd FLOOR, AND ABOVE, ½ PLAN OF FIRST CROSS AISLE AND 3rd FLOOR
THE SEATING CAPACITY OF THE MEZZANINE IS 350

Fox Detroit Theatre, Detroit, Michigan
C. Howard Crane, architect; Elmer George Kiehler, associate
There are 350 seats in the mezzanine and 1812 in the balcony

Fox Detroit Theatre, Detroit, Michigan
C. Howard Crane, architect; Elmer George Kiehler, associate
Views looking from and towards the stage

Fox Detroit Theatre, Detroit, Michigan
C. Howard Crane, architect; Elmer George Kiehler, associate
The grand staircase, above, and the smoking room, below

Fox Detroit Theatre, Detroit, Michigan
C. Howard Crane, architect; Elmer George Kiehler, associate
Showing treatment of side walls in auditorium

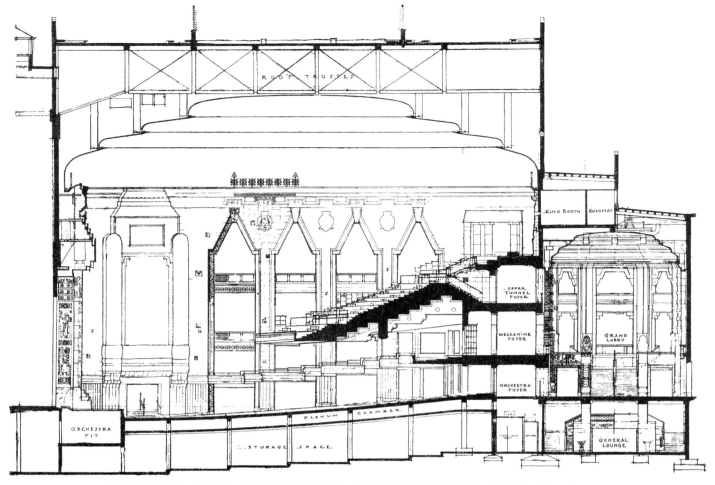

LONGITUDINAL SECTION, REPRODUCED TO A SCALE TWICE THE SIZE OF THAT OF THE PLANS

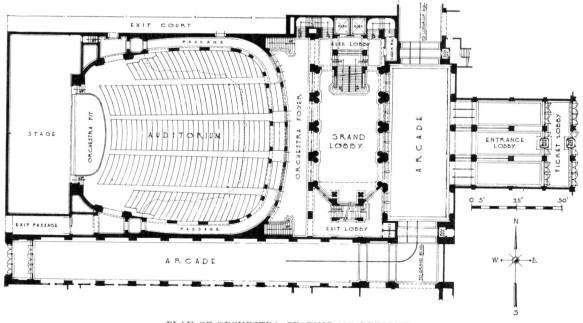

PLAN OF ORCHESTRA, SEATING 1527 PERSONS
21-INCH SEATS

Fisher Theatre, Fisher Building, Detroit, Michigan
Graven & Mayger, architects
The total seating capacity of the theatre is 2711

Fisher Theatre, Detroit, Michigan
Graven & Mayger, architects
Above, details of mezzanine foyer; below, the grand lobby

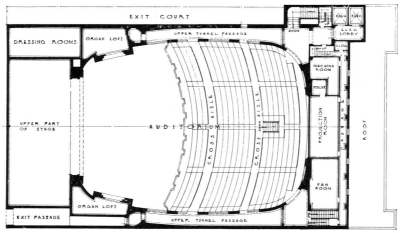

BALCONY PLAN SEATING 852 PERSONS. 20-INCH SEATS

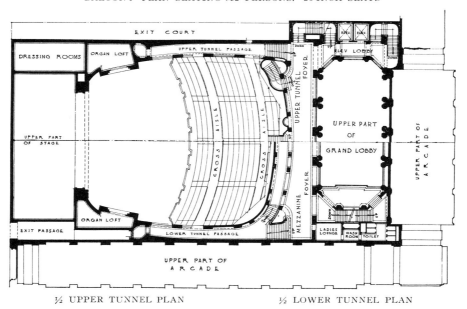

½ UPPER TUNNEL PLAN   ½ LOWER TUNNEL PLAN

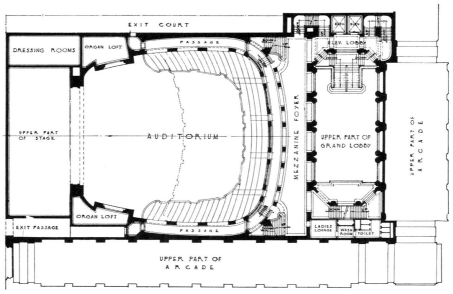

MEZZANINE PLAN SEATING 332 PERSONS. 22-INCH SEATS

Fisher Theatre, Fisher Building, Detroit, Michigan
Graven & Mayger, architects
The auditorium is approximately 115 feet square

Fisher Theatre, Detroit, Michigan
Graven & Mayger, architects
Above, the upper tunnel foyer; below, the auditorium from the balcony

Uptown Theatre, Philadelphia, Pennsylvania
Magaziner, Eberhard and Harris, architects
The modern purpose of the building is reflected in its design

Uptown Theatre, Philadelphia, Pennsylvania
Magaziner, Eberhard and Harris, architects
Detail of treatment of walls in lobby

Uptown Theatre, Philadelphia, Pennsylvania
Magaziner, Eberhard and Harris, architects
Detail of foyer, showing stairs to upper floors

Uptown Theatre, Philadelphia, Pennsylvania
Magaziner, Eberhard and Harris, architects
There are four painted glass panels in the side walls of the auditorium

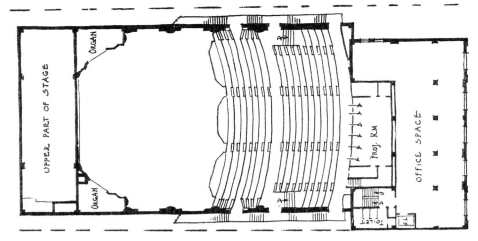

PLAN OF BALCONY

THE BALCONY SEATS 628 AND
THE ORCHESTRA 1494, MAKING
THE TOTAL SEATING CAPACITY
OF THE THEATRE 2122.

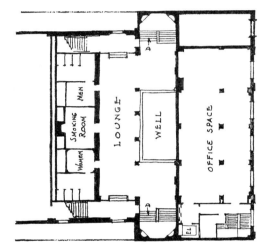

PLAN OF MEZZANINE

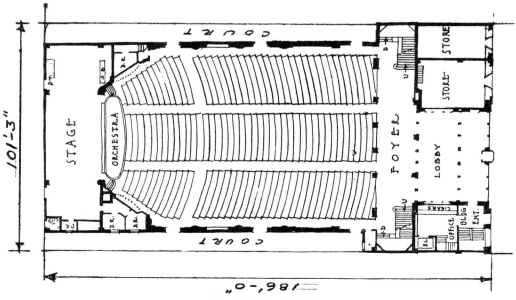

PLAN OF ORCHESTRA

Uptown Theatre, Philadelphia, Pennsylvania
Magaziner, Eberhard and Harris, architects
The size of the lot is 186 feet by 101 feet 3 inches

88

Uptown Theatre, Philadelphia, Pennsylvania
Magaziner, Eberhard and Harris, architects
Two detail views of auditorium

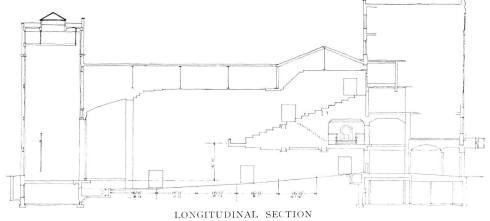

LONGITUDINAL SECTION
SHOWN AT SAME SCALE AS PLANS ON OTHER PAGE.

Uptown Theatre, Philadelphia, Pennsylvania
Magaziner, Eberhard and Harris, architects
These wall panels depict the travels of a human being through the ages of civilization

Uptown Theatre, Philadelphia, Pennsylvania
Magaziner, Eberhard and Harris, architects
Two views of lounge on second or mezzanine floor

91

State Theatre, Philadelphia, Pennsylvania
Ralph B. Bencker, architect
Detail of lobby, showing stairs to balcony

92

State Theatre, Philadelphia, Pennsylvania
Ralph B. Bencker, architect
The modern character of the design is in keeping with its purpose

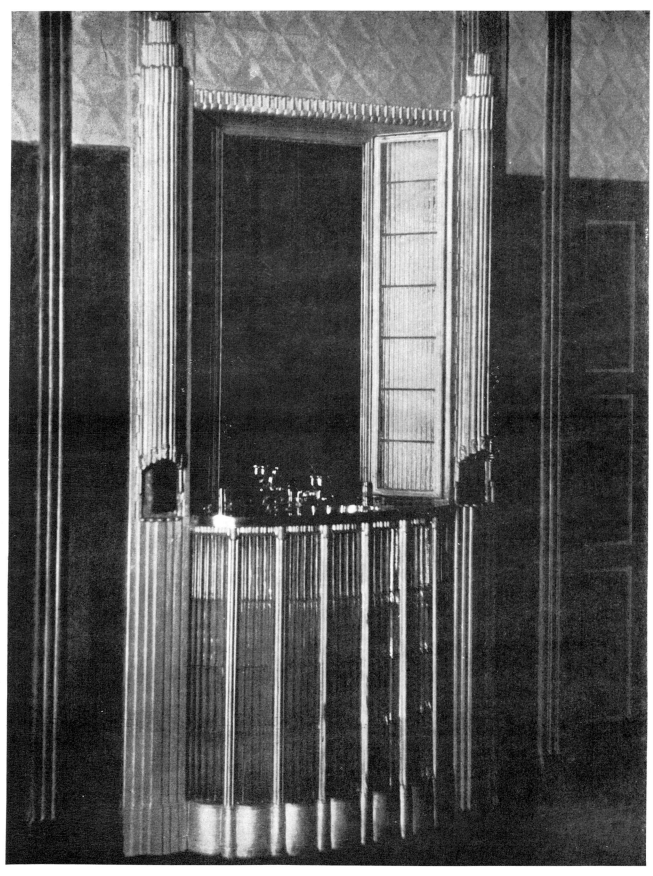

State Theatre, Philadelphia, Pennsylvania
Ralph B. Bencker, architect
Detail of ticket booth in vestibule, built of Keppler relief glass

State Theatre, Philadelphia, Pennsylvania
Ralph B. Bencker, architect
Doors between vestibule and lobby

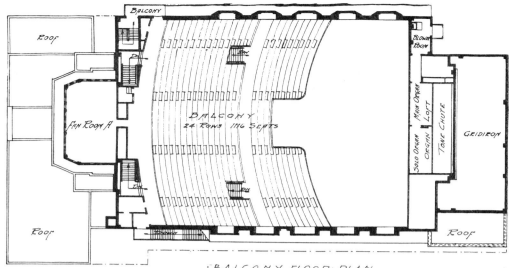

·BALCONY FLOOR·PLAN·

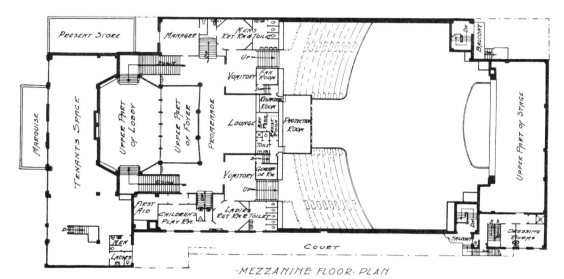

·MEZZANINE FLOOR·PLAN·

FIRST·FLOOR·PLAN·

State Theatre, Philadelphia, Pennsylvania
Ralph B. Bencker, architect
The total seating capacity of the theatre is 3063

State Theatre, Philadelphia, Pennsylvania
Ralph B. Bencker, architect
Views towards and from the stage

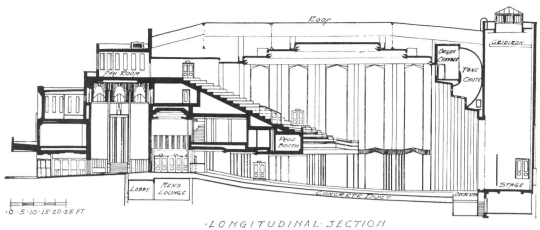

·LONGITUDINAL·SECTION·

State Theatre, Philadelphia, Pennsylvania
Ralph B. Bencker, architect
Detail of wall treatment in auditorium

98

The Carthay Circle Theatre, Los Angeles, California
Dwight Gibbs, architect
A view of the tower when floodlighted

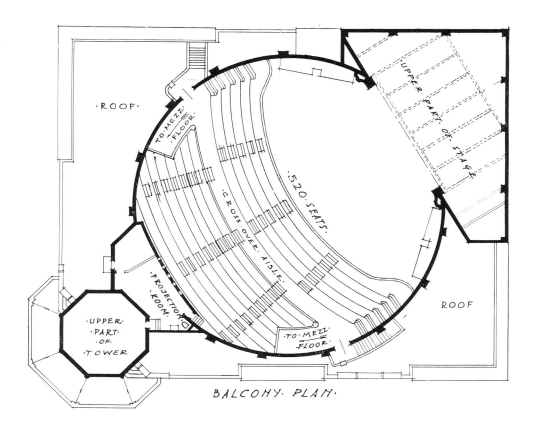

·BALCONY· PLAN·

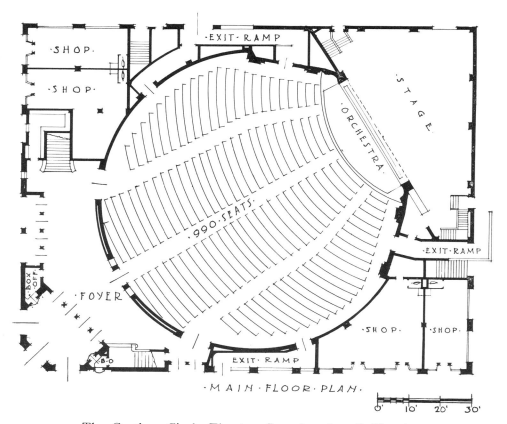

·MAIN· FLOOR· PLAN·

0'   10'   20'   30'

The Carthay Circle Theatre, Los Angeles, California
Dwight Gibbs, architect
The theatre is built on a site approximately 115 feet by 145 feet

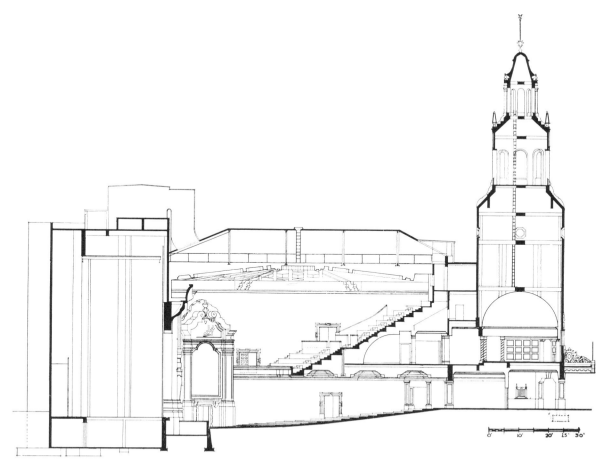

LONGITUDINAL SECTION

The Carthay Circle Theatre, Los Angeles, California
Dwight Gibbs, architect
The seating capacity of this theatre is 1510

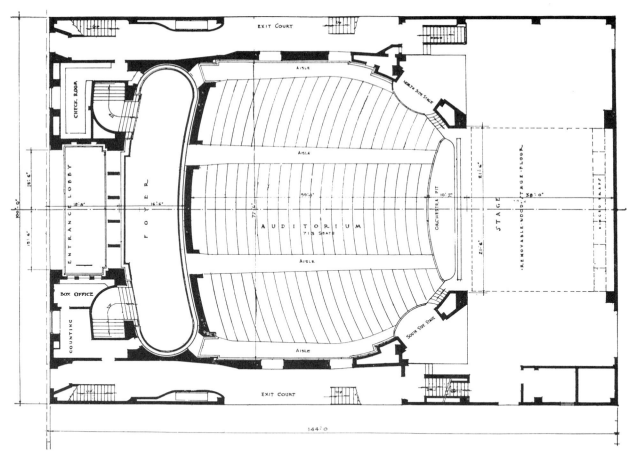

·FIRST FLOOR PLAN·

SCALE IN FEET

Mayan Theatre, Los Angeles, California
Morgan, Walls & Clements, architects
The theatre seats in all 1491 persons

Mayan Theatre, Los Angeles, California
Morgan, Walls & Clements, architects
Two views of the auditorium

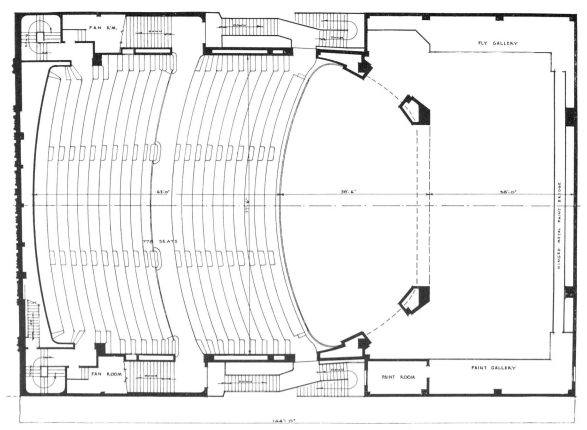

PLAN OF BALCONY, SEATING 778 PERSONS

Mayan Theatre, Los Angeles, California
Morgan, Walls & Clements, architects
Detail of poster cases in lobby

Mayan Theatre, Los Angeles, California
Morgan, Walls & Clements, architects
Above at left, detail of auditorium; at right, staircase balcony foyer, and below, the main foyer

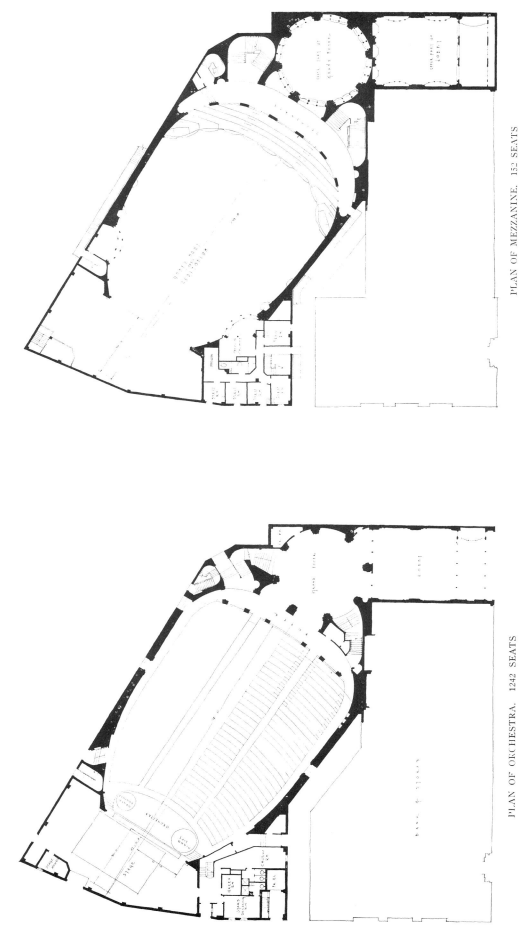

PLAN OF MEZZANINE. 152 SEATS

PLAN OF ORCHESTRA. 1242 SEATS

United Artists Theatre, Detroit, Michigan

C. Howard Crane, architect; Elmer George Kiehler, associate

The full depth of the orchestra is 94 feet

106

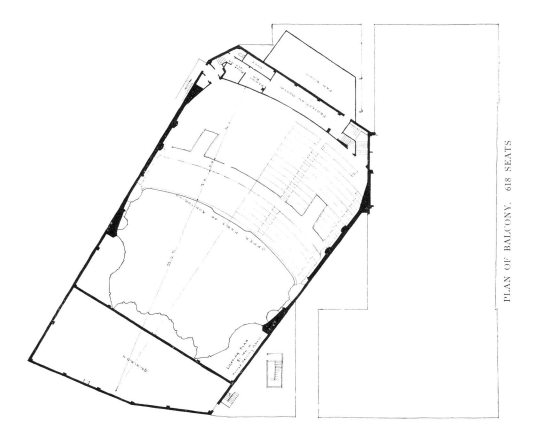

PLAN OF BALCONY. 618 SEATS

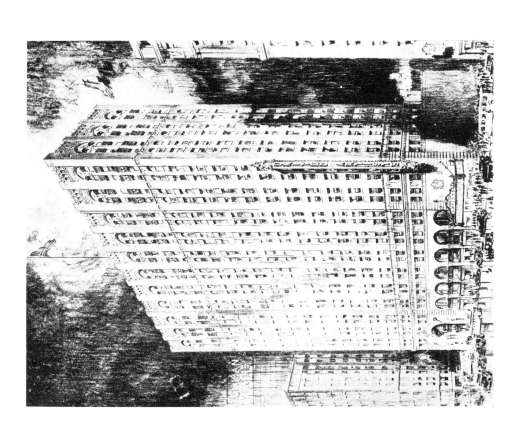

United Artists Theatre, Detroit, Michigan

C. Howard Crane, architect; Elmer George Kiehler, associate

The total seating capacity of this theatre is 2012

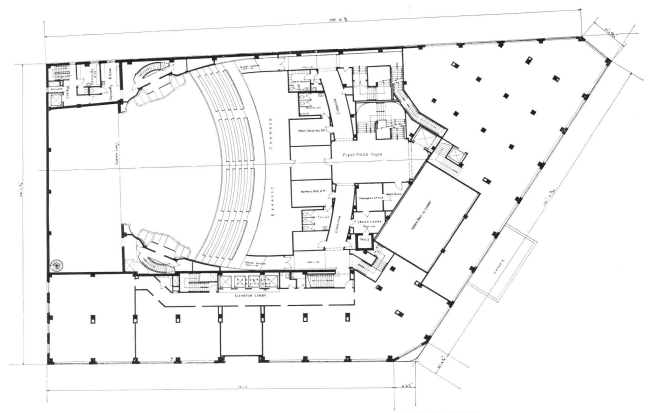

PLAN OF 2nd FLOOR, THROUGH FIRST MEZZANINE FOYER

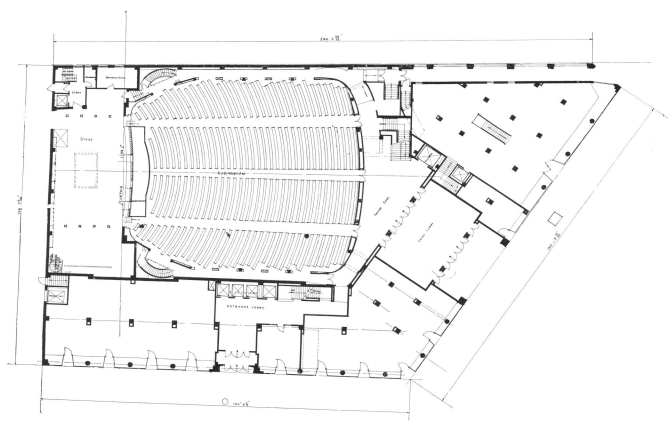

PLAN OF ORCHESTRA

Riverside Theatre, Milwaukee, Wisconsin
Kirchhoff and Rose, architects
The seating capacity of the orchestra is 1412

Riverside Theatre, Milwaukee, Wisconsin
Kirchhoff and Rose, architects
Views looking towards and from the stage

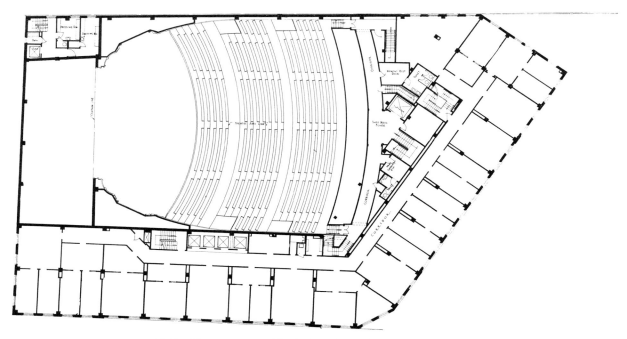

PLAN OF 4th FLOOR, THROUGH THIRD MEZZANINE FOYER

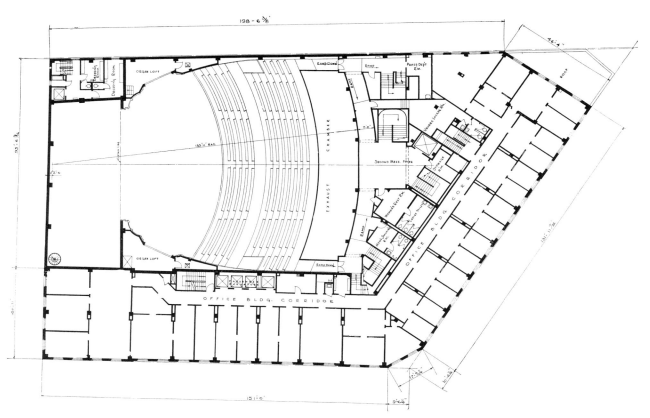

PLAN OF 3rd FLOOR, THROUGH SECOND MEZZANINE FOYER

Riverside Theatre, Milwaukee, Wisconsin
Kirchhoff and Rose, architects
The total capacity of the theatre is 2558

Riverside Theatre, Milwaukee, Wisconsin
Kirchhoff and Rose, architects
Above, sidewall treatment at balcony; below, the foyer

LONGITUDINAL SECTION
THIS DRAWING IS REPRODUCED AT A SCALE LARGER THAN THE PLAN BELOW

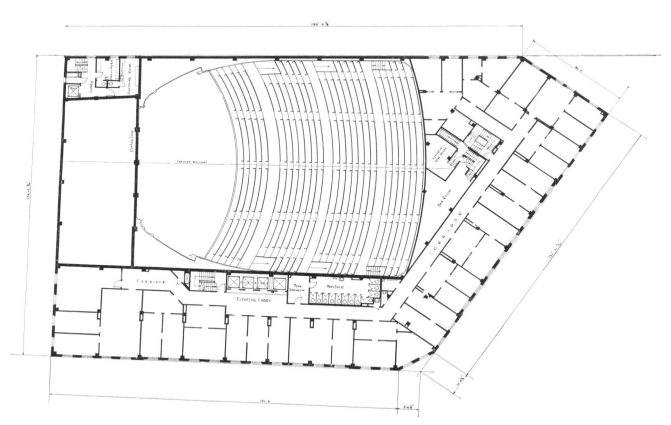

PLAN OF 5th FLOOR, SHOWING COMPLETE BALCONY

Riverside Theatre, Milwaukee, Wisconsin
Kirchhoff and Rose, architects
The seating capacity of the balcony is 1146

Toledo Paramount Theatre, Toledo, Ohio
C. W. & Geo. L. Rapp, architects
General view of the lobby

Toledo Paramount Theatre, Toledo, Ohio
C. W. & Geo. L. Rapp, architects
An example of the so-called atmospheric theatre

Toledo Paramount Theatre, Toledo, Ohio
C. W. & Geo. L. Rapp, architects
View of the grand staircase in lobby

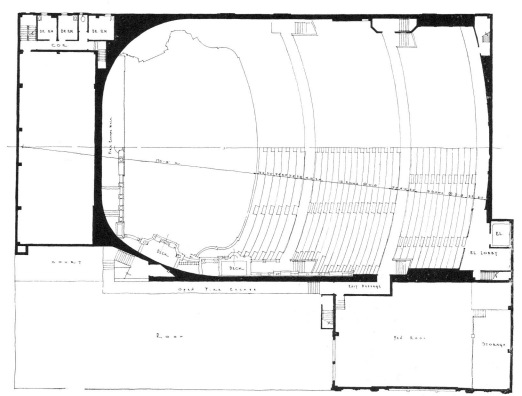

PLAN OF BALCONY WITH 1335 SEATS

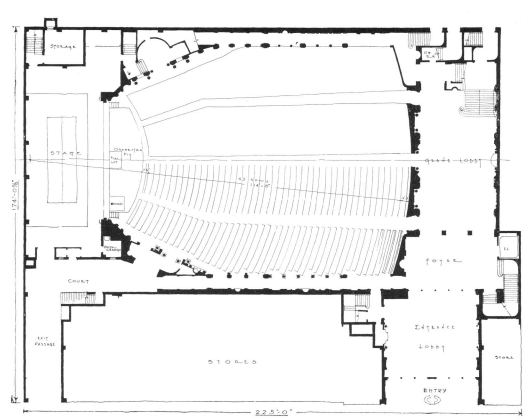

PLAN OF ORCHESTRA WITH 2222 SEATS
THE LOGE SEATS 288 ADDITIONAL

Paradise Theatre, New York, N. Y.
John Eberson, architect
Total seating capacity is 3845

Paradise Theatre, New York
John Eberson, architect
Above, the side wall treatment of the auditorium and below, the foyer

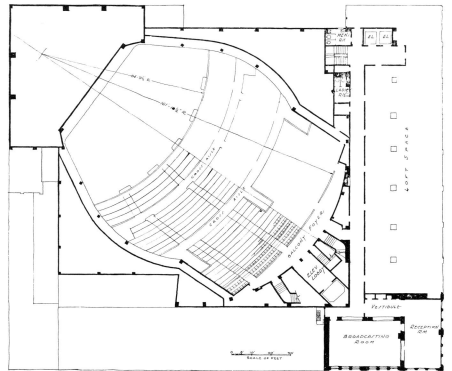

PLAN OF BALCONY
SEATING: SEATS, 902; LOGES, 210

PLAN OF ORCHESTRA
SEATING: SEATS, 1512; LOGES, 118

Warner Brothers Theatre, Hollywood, California—G. Albert Lansburgh, architect

Warner Brothers Theatre, Hollywood, California
G. Albert Lansburgh, architect
View showing treatment of side walls

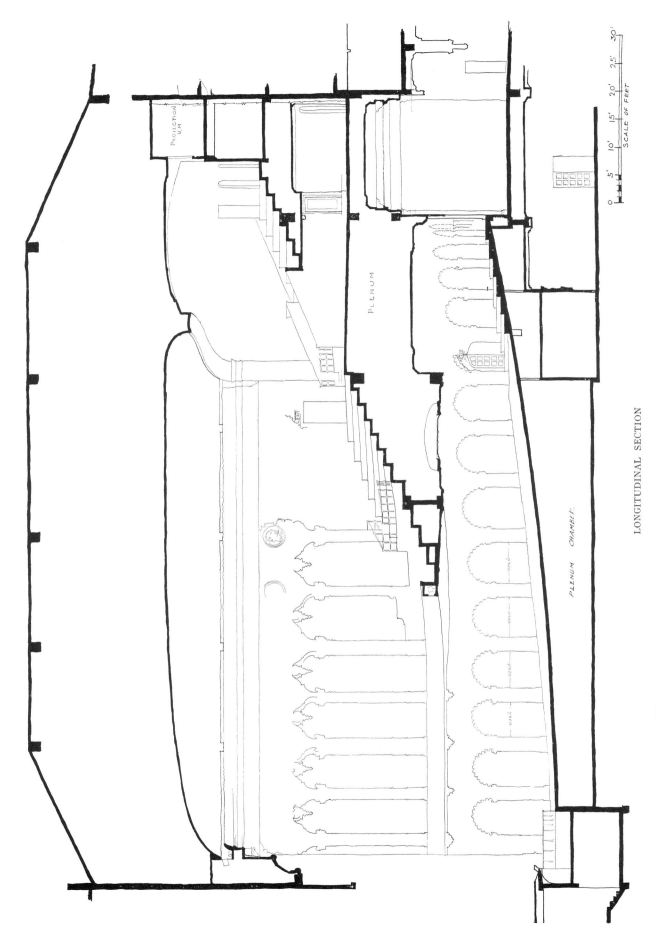

LONGITUDINAL SECTION

Warner Brothers Theatre, Hollywood, California—G. Albert Lansburgh, architect

Warner Brothers Theatre, Hollywood, California
G. Albert Lansburgh, architect
Above, the main floor promenade, and below, the proscenium

Warner Brothers Theatre, Hollywood, California
G. Albert Lansburgh, architect
Promenade to side entrance

Brooklyn Paramount Theatre, Brooklyn, New York
C. W. & Geo. L. Rapp, architects
Views looking from and towards the stage

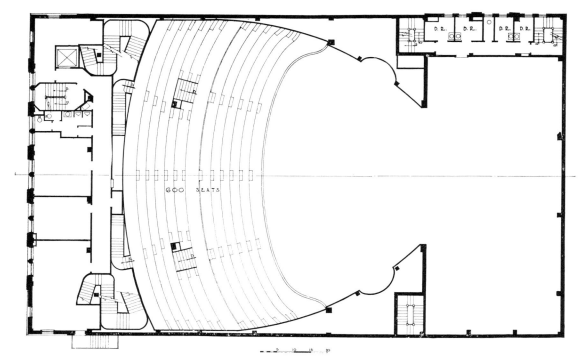

PLAN OF FIRST BALCONY SEATING 588 PERSONS

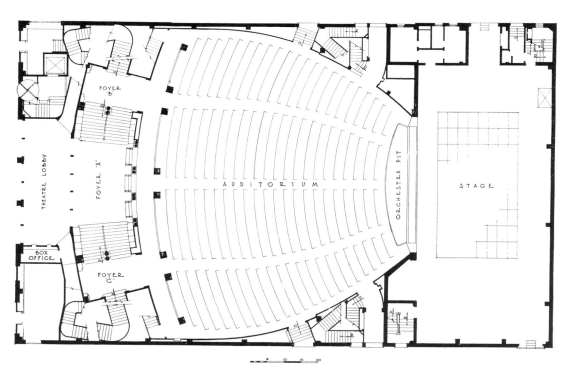

PLAN OF ORCHESTRA SEATING 892 PERSONS

Wilson Theatre, Detroit, Michigan
Smith, Hinchman & Grylls, architects
The total seating capacity of the theatre is 1918

Wilson Theatre, Detroit, Michigan
Smith, Hinchman & Grylls, architects
Detail of wall treatment in auditorium

Now called Music Hall (1969)
(BH)

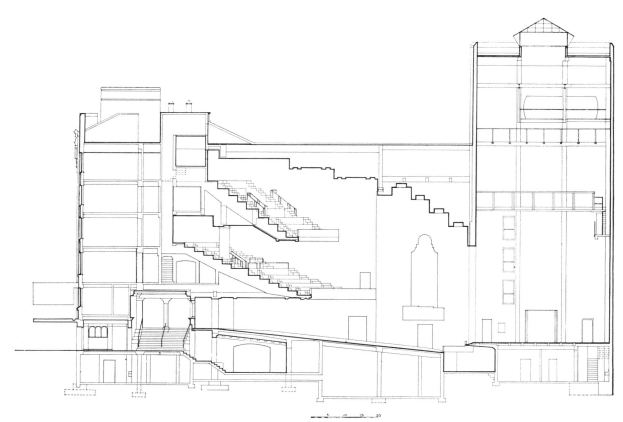

LONGITUDINAL SECTION.   THE SECOND BALCONY SEATS 400

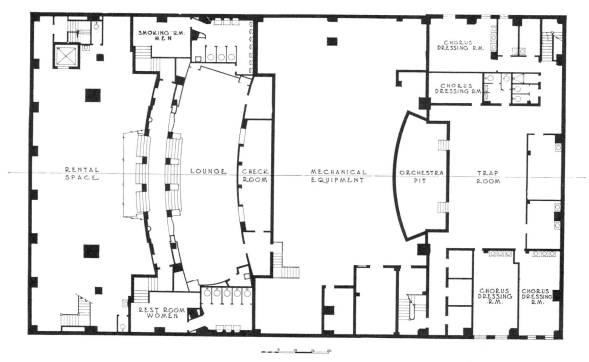

PLAN OF BASEMENT

Wilson Theatre, Detroit, Michigan
Smith, Hinchman & Grylls, architects
The boxes afford seats for 38 additional persons

Wilson Theatre, Detroit, Michigan
Smith, Hinchman & Grylls, architects
Above, the lobby, and below, the foyer, with stairs to balcony

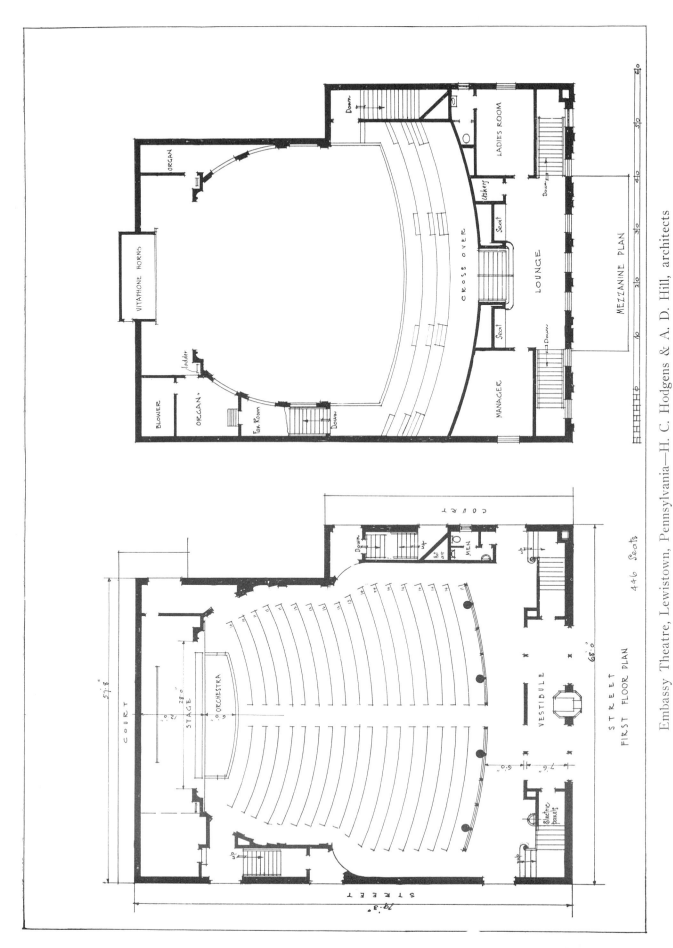

Embassy Theatre, Lewistown, Pennsylvania—H. C. Hodgens & A. D. Hill, architects

128

Embassy Theatre, Lewistown, Pennsylvania
H. C. Hodgens & A. D. Hill, architects
An interesting example of a small theatre arranged for sound pictures

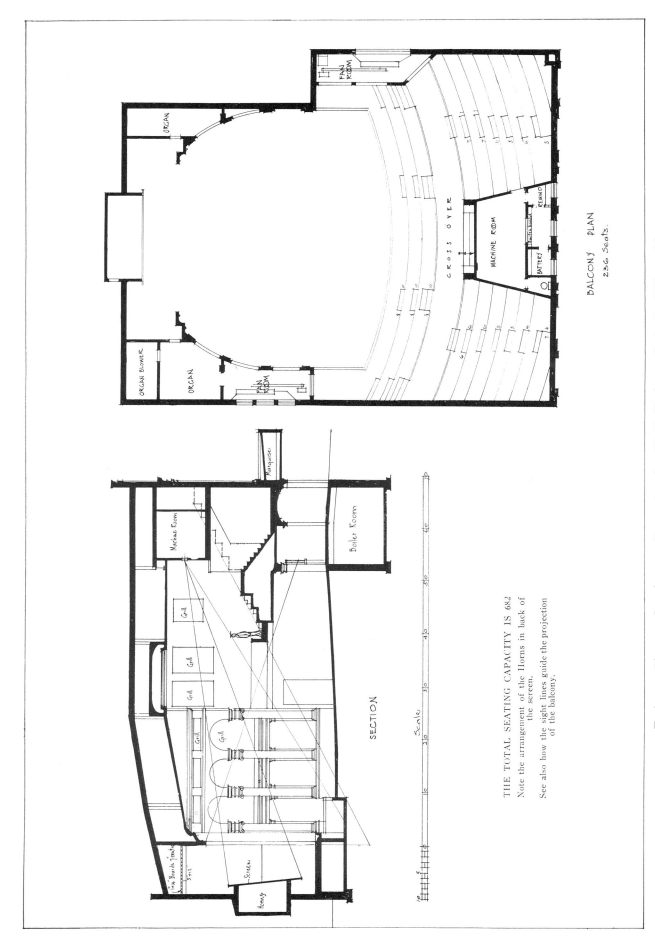

SECTION

Scale

THE TOTAL SEATING CAPACITY IS 682

Note the arrangement of the Horns in back of
the screen.

See also how the sight lines guide the projection
of the balcony.

BALCONY PLAN
236 Seats.

Embassy Theatre, Lewistown, Pennsylvania—H. C. Hodgens & A. D. Hill, architects

Pickwick Theatre, Park Ridge, Illinois
Zook & McCaughey, architects
The design has a character that is in keeping with modern tendencies

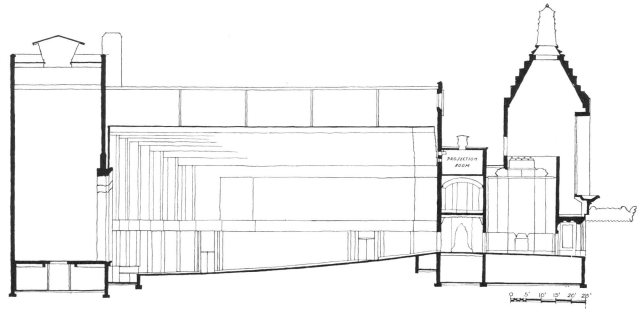

LONGITUDINAL SECTION

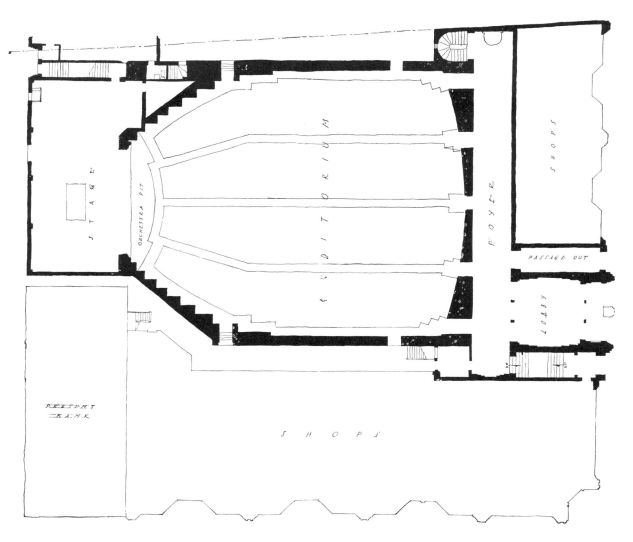

Pickwick Theatre, Park Ridge, Illinois
Zook & McCaughey, architects
The seating capacity is 1500, all on one floor

Pickwick Theatre, Park Ridge, Illinois
Zook & McCaughey, architects
Provisions have been made for the addition of a balcony when necessary

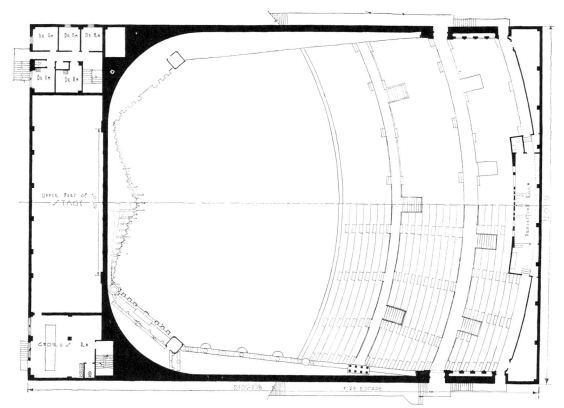

PLAN OF BALCONY SEATING 1338 PERSONS

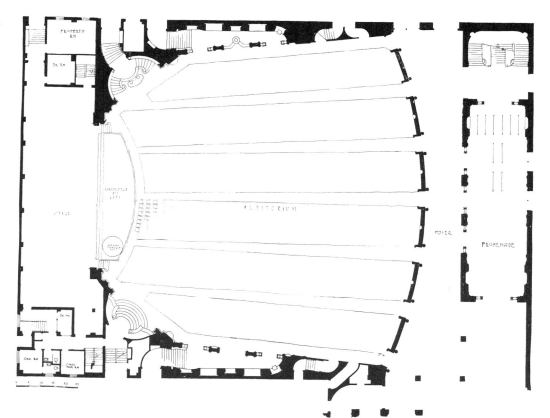

PLAN OF ORCHESTRA SEATING 2268 PERSONS

Paradise Theatre, Chicago, Illinois
John Eberson, architect
The size of the building is approximately 210 feet by 150 feet

Paradise Theatre, Chicago, Illinois
John Eberson, architect
An interesting example of the atmospheric theatre

LONGITUDINAL SECTION

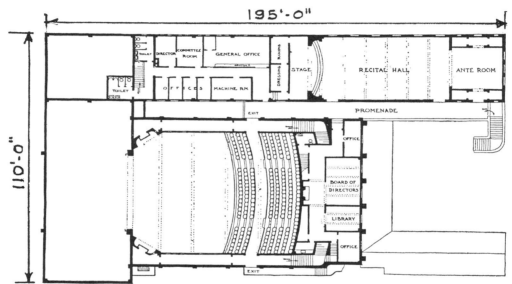

PLAN OF BALCONY, SEATING 214 PERSONS

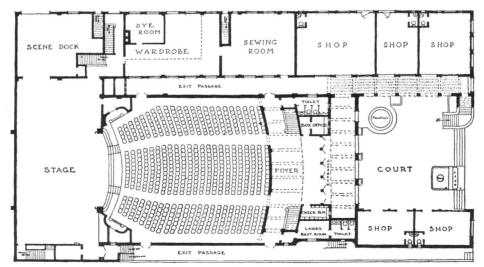

PLAN OF ORCHESTRA, SEATING 608 PERSONS

Pasadena Community Playhouse, Pasadena, California
Elmer Gray, architect; Dwight Gibbs, associate
The theatre has a seating capacity of 822

Pasadena Community Playhouse, Pasadena, California
Elmer Gray, architect; Dwight Gibbs, associate
Exterior and interior views

Kimo Theatre, Albuquerque, New Mexico
Boller Brothers, architects
The design has a character which suggests the theatre

Kimo Theatre, Albuquerque, New Mexico
Boller Brothers, architects
The foyer and mezzanine opening into parlor

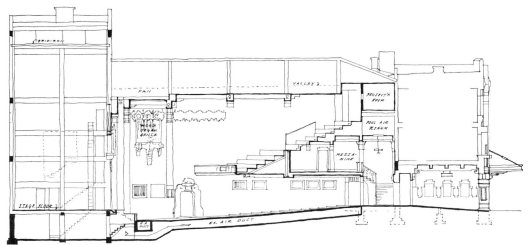

LONGITUDINAL SECTION

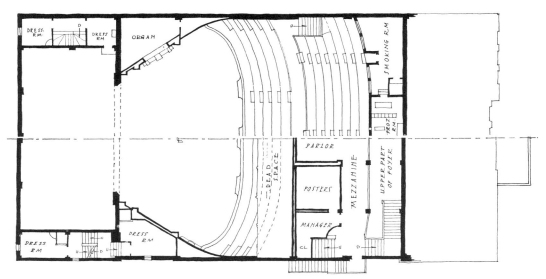

ONE-HALF PLAN OF MEZZANINE, AND ONE-HALF PLAN OF BALCONY

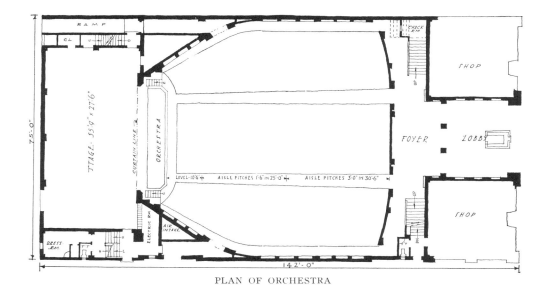

PLAN OF ORCHESTRA

Kimo Theatre, Albuquerque, New Mexico
Boller Brothers, architects
The total seating capacity of this theatre is 1250

Kimo Theatre, Albuquerque, New Mexico
Boller Brothers, architects
Detail of wall treatment in auditorium

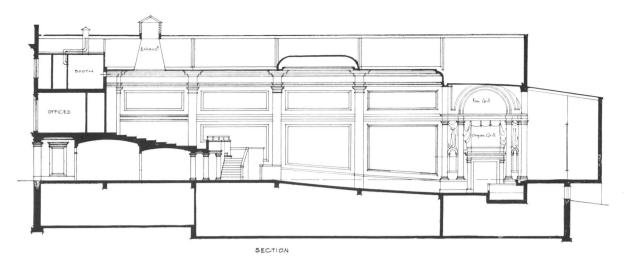

SECTION

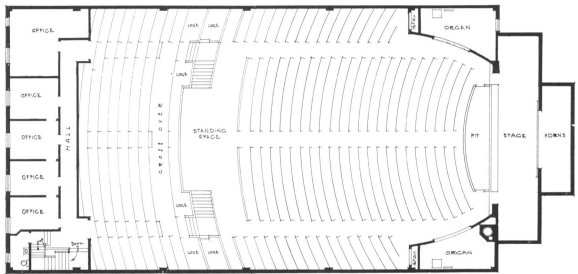

THE SEATING PLAN SHOWS A SEATING CAPACITY OF 1070

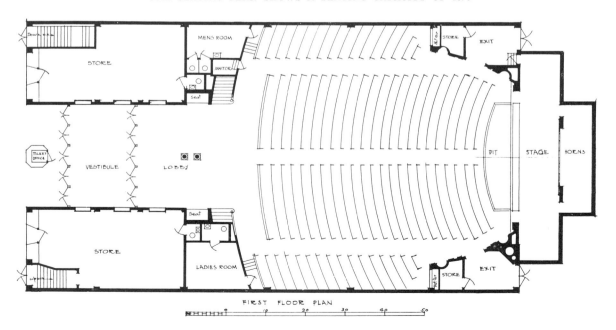

FIRST FLOOR PLAN

Cathaum Theatre, State College, Pennsylvania
H. C. Hodgens & A. D. Hill, architects
This theatre is planned for the showing of sound pictures

142

PLAN OF THIRD FLOOR, SHOWING LOCATION OF PROJECTION ROOM

Cathaum Theatre, State College, Pennsylvania
H. C. Hodgens & A. D. Hill, architects
An example of the stadium type of theatre

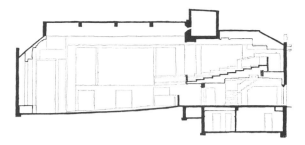

LONGITUDINAL SECTION

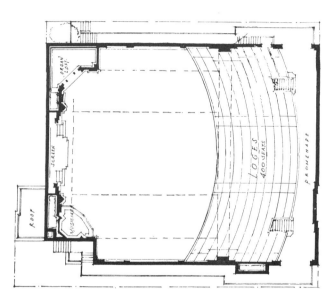

PLAN OF LOGES

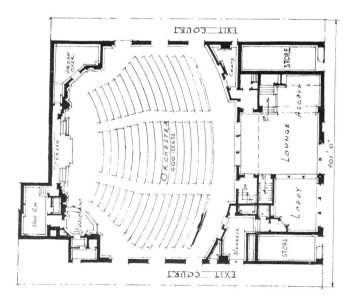

PLAN OF ORCHESTRA

St. George Theatre, Brooklyn, New York
Schlanger & Ehrenrich, architects
The total seating capacity of the house is 1000

St. George Theatre, Brooklyn, New York
Schlanger & Ehrenrich, architects
The walls are decorated in color on plaster

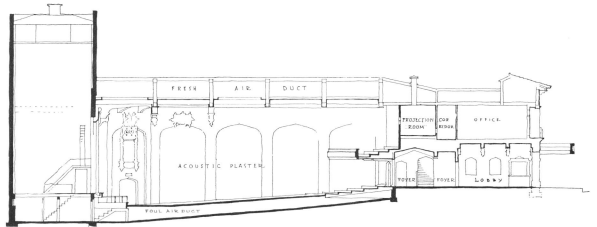

LONGITUDINAL SECTION

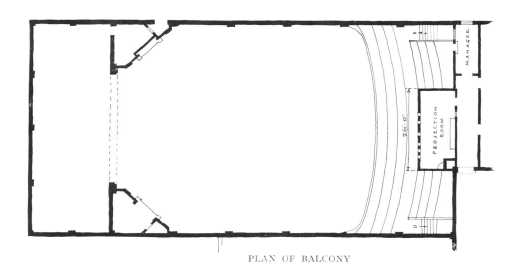

PLAN OF BALCONY

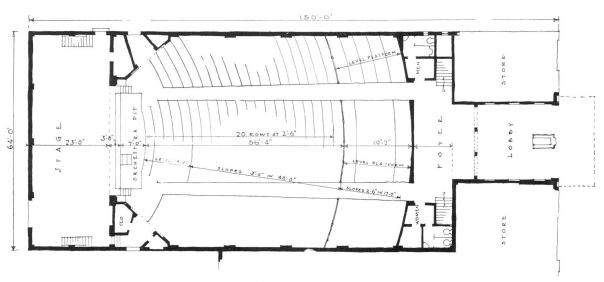

PLAN OF ORCHESTRA

Corona Theatre, Corona, California
Boller Brothers, architects
The total seating capacity of the house is 900

Corona Theatre, Corona, California
Boller Brothers, architects
Views of exterior and interior

Corona Theatre, Corona, California
Boller Brothers, architects
Detail of organ grille and proscenium arch

148

The exterior is of green and purple mottled slate and ochre stucco with orange tile. The decorative panel above the entrance suggests the character of the building.

Maute Theatre, Irwin, Pennsylvania
Douglas D. Ellington, architect
Detail of typical decorative panel used in the auditorium

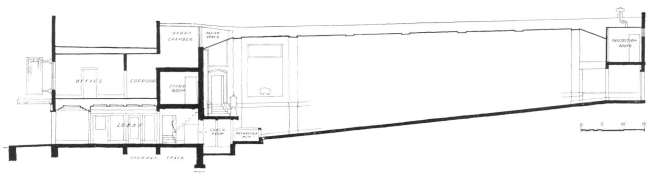

LONGITUDINAL SECTION

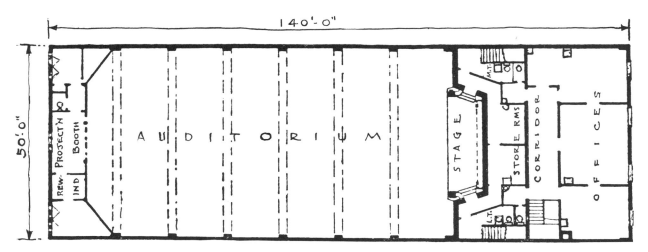

PLAN OF SECOND FLOOR

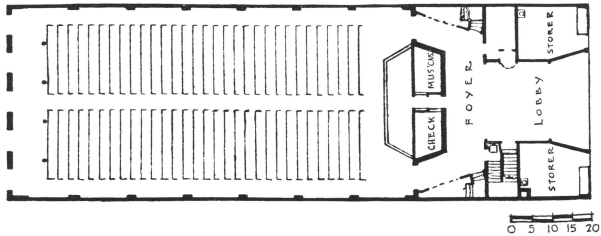

PLAN OF FIRST FLOOR

Maute Theatre, Irwin, Pennsylvania
Douglas D. Ellington, architect
This theatre seats 750 persons on one floor

Maute Theatre, Irwin, Pennsylvania
Douglas D. Ellington, architect
The decorative treatment embodies the masks of comedy and tragedy done in different epochs

FOYER AND LOBBY ELEVATIONS

ELEVATION OF PROSCENIUM

SIDE ELEVATION OF AUDITORIUM

Studies for a theatre for northeast Philadelphia, Penn.
Mr. Magaziner of Magaziner, Eberhard and Harris, the architects, says:
"The motion picture theatre should be the most modern of all buildings"

Sketches for a theatre for northeast Philadelphia, Penn.
Magaziner, Eberhard and Harris, architects
Studies for the exterior and the interior

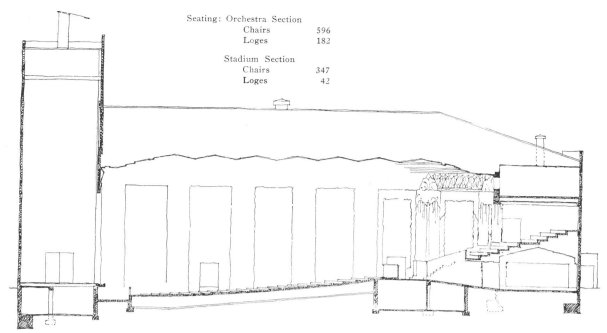

Seating: Orchestra Section
Chairs 596
Loges 182

Stadium Section
Chairs 347
Loges 42

LONGITUDINAL SECTION

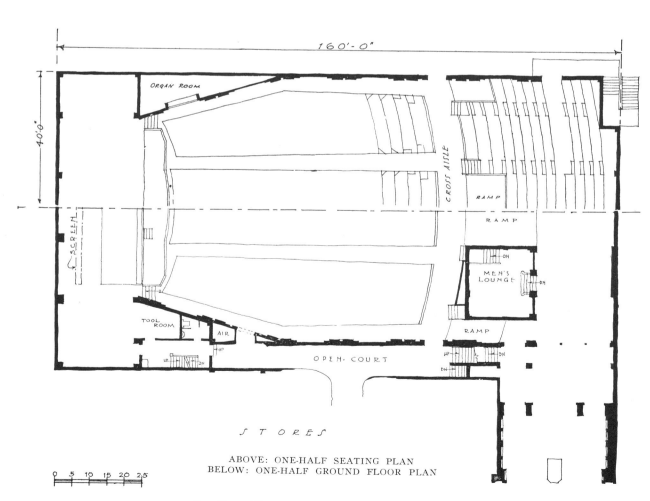

160'-0"

40'-0"

ORGAN ROOM

CROSS AISLE

RAMP

RAMP

SCREEN

MEN'S
LOUNGE

RAMP

TOOL
ROOM

AIR

OPEN·COURT

S T O R E S

0 5 10 15 20 25

ABOVE: ONE-HALF SEATING PLAN
BELOW: ONE-HALF GROUND FLOOR PLAN

Stadium Theatre, Los Angeles, California
Boller Brothers, architects
This theatre, of the stadium type, has a seating capacity of 1167

154

Sketch of Stadium Theatre, Los Angeles, California
Boller Brothers, architects
The design is modern in keeping with present-day tendencies

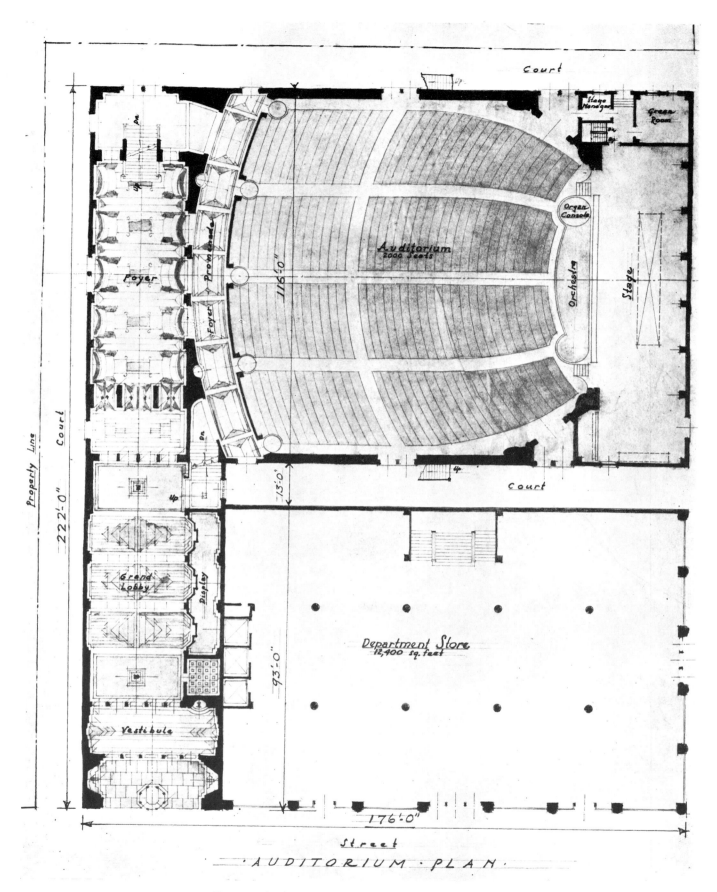

Court

Stage
Manager

Green
Room

Foyer

Promenade

Foyer

116'-0"

Auditorium
2000 Seats

Organ
Console

Orchestra

Stage

Court

73'-0"

Property Line

222'-0"

Court

Grand
Lobby

Display

93'-0"

Department Store
12,400 sq. feet

Vestibule

176'-0"

Street

·AUDITORIUM·PLAN·

Proposed theatre, Philadelphia, Pennsylvania
Magaziner, Eberhard and Harris, architects
The theatre and store cover a piece of property 176 feet by 222 feet

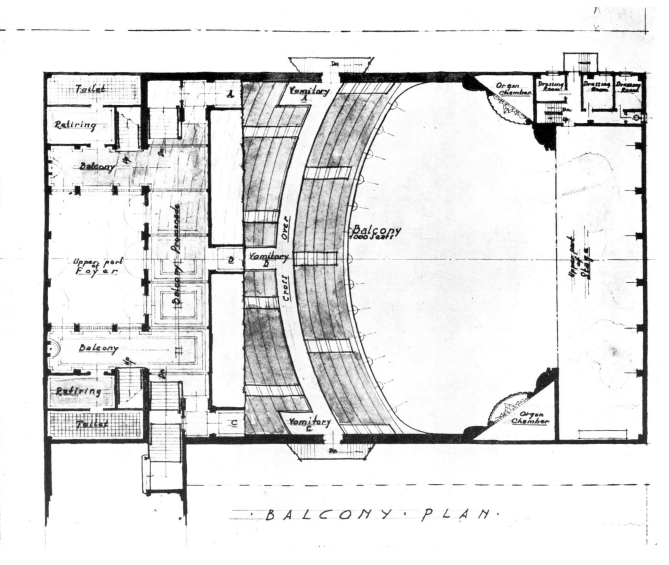

·BALCONY·PLAN·

Sketch for proposed theatre, Philadelphia, Pennsylvania
Magaziner, Eberhard and Harris, architects
At the right of the theatre entrance is a space for a department store

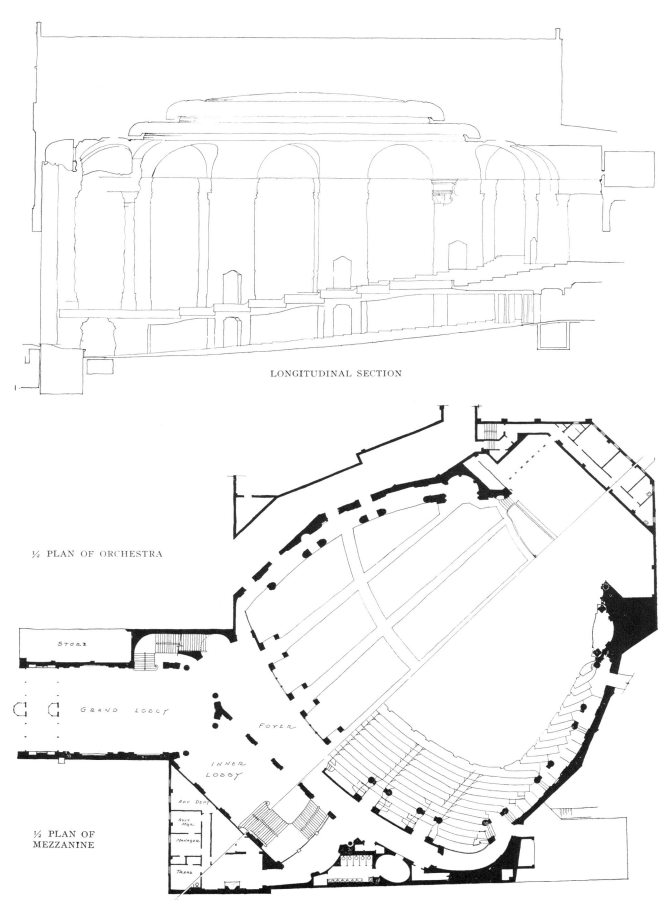

LONGITUDINAL SECTION

½ PLAN OF ORCHESTRA

½ PLAN OF
MEZZANINE

Kings Theatre, Brooklyn, New York
C. W. & Geo. L. Rapp, architects
The orchestra seats 2798 and the mezzanine 878 persons

158

Kings Theatre, Brooklyn, New York
C. W. & Geo. L. Rapp, architects
The total seating capacity is 3676

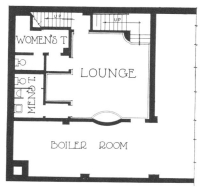

CINEMA
ART THEATRE
CHICAGO ILL
ARMSTRONG FURST TILTON
ARCHITECTS

SECOND FLOOR PLAN

BASEMENT PLAN

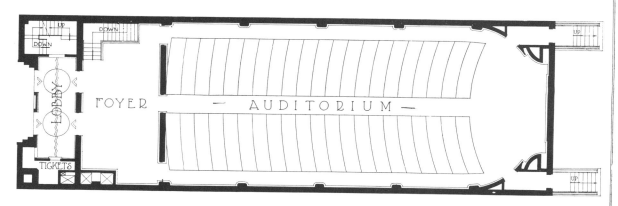

MAIN FLOOR PLAN

Cinema Art Theatre, Chicago, Illinois
Armstrong, Furst & Tilton, architects
Detail of Lounge in basement

Cinema Art Theatre, Chicago, Illinois
Armstrong, Furst & Tilton, architects
Above, the exterior at night; and below, the foyer

Cinema Art Theatre, Chicago, Illinois
Armstrong, Furst & Tilton, architects
Above, the auditorium, and below, the foyer

Cinema Art Theatre, Chicago, Illinois
Armstrong, Furst & Tilton, architects
Detail of proscenium

Cinema Art Theatre, Chicago, Illinois
Armstrong, Furst & Tilton, architects
The modern figure in the foyer between entrance doors

INDEX